MAN, MONEY, AND GOODS

MAN
MONEY
AND GOODS

by John S. Gambs

New York and London
COLUMBIA UNIVERSITY PRESS

To My Father and Mother

PREFACE

A FEW YEARS AGO I met a distinguished teacher of English who, when I was presented, said: "You're an economist? Oh! That subject! I flunked it in college. The fellow who taught me made pemmican out of what I have since learned is one of the most fascinating subjects on earth."

I have often thought of that since. Even as he said it, my desk was littered with manuscript for an introductory book that tried to avoid pemmican like the plague. For a while I wanted to name it "Economics for Those Who Flunked It." That book is now written, but it is not exactly for those who flunked it, I see. It is for them, yes, but it is also for those who never took a course in it, either because they didn't get to college or were scared away from economics or had an inferiority complex about it, as so many of us have about mathematics. And also for those who had tried to fill in the gap by reading books on their own, but had somehow been repelled by introductory textbooks, or completely bewildered by more advanced books. In short I wanted to write a book for mature, earnest, intelligent people who have a sincere interest in economic theory, but have never quite made contact with it: a book that might give readers a few happy hours with the "dismal science"—

for so Carlyle thought of it; a book for inquiring minds.

There are, of course, a few such books on the market. There are a few excellent textbooks. Even the best may, however, seem to be too long and too encyclopedic for the general reader. They are, besides, geared to certain special college needs, like 90 class meetings per academic year and equal-length chapters—needs quite different from those of inquiring citizens from eighteen to eighty. There are also a few extremely simplified books for the general reader, easy to read and sometimes delightful. Their virtues are, however, the source of their defects for they are strongly partisan. The more partisan the more delightful, usually, for the writers have clear and uncomplicated messages; but economics, though perhaps itself not a science, must be approached in the spirit of science, not debate.

Some irreproachable books and many magazine articles for the general reader are purely descriptive of the economic system or of current problems. They have their great claims on the reader, but they are descriptive. This book is about economic theory, not about timely problems. The difference is not always very great, but there is a difference of emphasis. This book specializes in the obfuscations, fogs, booby traps, mazes, brilliant insights, and acrimonious debate which characterize or have characterized economic theory. It selects for discussion precisely that part of economics which ordinarily repels or puzzles, or discourages, or antagonizes the reader—the part that frightens students away, breeds inferiority complexes, deadens interest in the most exciting subject on earth, looks like pemmican, and causes intelligent persons like the gentleman I met at the reception, to flunk.

If this book can make the study of economic theory less

painful to the general reader, one reason is that it is not molded by one type of theory only. Though I was, years ago, deeply influenced by my former teacher, the late Wesley C. Mitchell, and am, in a way, perhaps a little biased in this general direction, I have given competing theorists their full day in court. Thus the reader will not be repelled by the unrelieved doctrinal view of any particular school.

A second and similar virtue is that the book claims for economics only a modest place on the ladder of organized knowledge. Economic theory is often taught or written about as if it fell only a little short of being an exact science and an ultimate truth. The alert reader, with some knowledge of science and of the world, quickly detects the vast difference in scientific texture between a book on economics and one on physics or chemistry. He concludes either that economics is falsely masquerading as a science, or that, somehow, he has lost the thread of scientific process and is unable to pick it up again. He becomes discouraged, for either experience is frustrating. I have made the basic assumption—and it is not a violent one or contrary to the opinion of all—that economics is a kind of philosophizing about how mankind gets its worldly goods, rather than a science. This should be reassuring to the reader. His task changes from that of having to learn one rigid system of alleged truth to that of weighing different viewpoints. He now learns *about* economic theories; he does not learn the one and only economic theory. The broad outlines of the several theories that have been developed to explain how men get their bread by the sweat of their brow are easy to understand and interesting to study. What repels or discourages the general reader is getting lost in the labyrinths of some special theory, and that is what happens to him in most textbooks and treatises. They are for specialists or for students having other than the general needs of the intelligent and inquiring citizen.

Many persons have influenced me, helped me, and given me specific suggestions. Valuable suggestions for improving the manuscript before publication have come from friends and colleagues, particularly: John W. Blyth, Earl W. Count, James Franklin Hunt, George L. Nesbitt, Francis L. Patton, and Gordon Shillinglaw, of Hamilton College; Virgil C. Crisafulli, of Syracuse University; Carter Goodrich, of Columbia University; Henry Clay Smith, of Michigan State College; Wilfrid H. Crook, of Colgate University. The authorities of Hamilton College have relieved me of certain duties in order that I might have more time to write.

The staff of the Columbia University Press has been more than generous in offering aid. My wife has helped me in so many ways, large and small, that I would hardly know where to begin acknowledging my debt; like the public debt (see Chapter 15), it will, I fear, never be paid off.

Obviously, none of the people named above has the least responsibility for whatever may be found in this book. I alone am to blame.

JOHN S. GAMBS

Clinton, New York
October, 1951

CONTENTS

Part One

INTRODUCTORY

When Fan Che asked Confucius,
"What is Humanity?"
the master answered,
"To love men."
When he asked
"What is knowledge?"
the answer was,
"To know men."

Inscription in courtyard of a Chinese temple, as
translated by Nora Waln in *The House of Exile*
(Penguin Books, Limited, 1938), p. 163

1. DEFINITIONS FIRST

WHAT IS ECONOMICS about, and how do we study it? It is often defined as the science of wealth or as the study of how mankind gets its living. Statements of this kind are certainly useful, but they are also too general. When we try to take the next step we meet difficulties. We meet difficulties in pinning economics down because its practitioners are in disagreement about the scope and nature of their science, and attempts to particularize lead to protests from opposing schools of thought. The only definitions on which agreement is possible are broad ones like those given above, or facetious ones like: "Economics is whatever an economist wants to talk about."

The reader may have misgivings about studying a science in which disagreements arise at the very start. His doubts are indeed well founded but should not too quickly turn him away. After all, there are still differences of opinion even in astronomy and physics, chemistry and biology. Psychology remains a free-for-all. No considerable field of knowledge is so completely understood that all of its scholars speak with the same voice. The process of reaching a balanced conclusion often requires a sifting of the testimony of contradictory witnesses. In any event, stress on differences should not obscure the fact that all sciences, including even economics, agree on many things. There is, besides, an enormous store of historical and descriptive matter—economic facts—that is well worth knowing and concerning which there is little dispute. I shall hope that the burden placed on the reader of suspending judgment and viewing the same thing in different lights will not be too heavy.

One of the dominant schools of the day looks upon economics as a study of what happens when we try to reconcile the scarcity of things with the insatiable wants of human beings. Most things worth having, except the air we breathe, are scarce—scarce enough, at least, to command a price and not to be available to all in generous quantity. Even such common things as sand and gravel are scarce, since building contractors have to pay for them. On the other hand, apples with exactly three large and four small worms in them are probably quite rare; but since men have not yet found much use for such fruit, they are not scarce in the economist's interpretation of the word.

These disposal-of-scarce-goods economists are great fellows for studying how prices are formed because, in a capitalist society at least, prices determine how goods are used and how they are apportioned. If lumps of coal really were black diamonds, and priced accordingly, we would not burn them in our furnaces; if gold were as cheap as wood, we might possibly use its alloys for roofing, screening and guttering. Prices also determine who gets what. They are, in a capitalist society, the basic method of rationing. The price system has been referred to as a method of "rationing by the pocketbook." Those who "have the price" may consume abundantly; and those who do not must get along with less.

Among the less dominant and dissenting schools is one that considers the study of the disposal of scarce goods too restrictive. Some members of this class focus their interest on the moral codes, business practices, social institutions, legal framework, and the like, under which we get our food, clothing, and shelter. They study an economic system—capitalism, for example—in much the same objective and judicious way that an anthropologist studies the Klamath Indians or some primitive tribe of a South Sea Island. They ask and try to answer questions that have little to do with the disposal of scarce goods. One, for example, is whether business cycles are inevitable in a laissez-faire system like ours. This question cuts deeper than appears on the surface. The issue probes psychological depths. It asks whether men who are taught from the cradle to "make" money and seek profits can also be taught to do the things that are needed to stabilize the economy.

Many of these same economists are concerned with a problem involving the concept of evolution, or cosmogony, or self-generating change. This resembles history, but the history of how the solar system was formed rather than how Elizabeth treated Essex. These economists wonder how and why we change from subsistence to commercial economies, how feudalism develops into mercantilism, mercantilism into capitalism, capitalism into . . . what? A leading idea here is that men, by minding their own business and taking the easy and seemingly logical next steps, soon find themselves in a terrible mess; they are then compelled to do something that is not easy. The new something may be migration, or a painful change in occupation, or revolution—in any case, something unpleasant, and unpleasant because in great transitional periods the tempo of social change is stepped up faster than man can comfortably adjust to it. A simple example is that of farming areas that farm themselves into a dust bowl. Inhabitants are then confronted with a Hobson's choice, like joining the Okies or submitting to the agricultural policies of an energetic Secretary of Agriculture. Vladimir Simkhovitch has traced the fall of Rome to soil exhaustion. Harriet Bradley explains the English enclosure movement in the same way; the farmers farmed so well (if not too wisely), Miss Bradley says, that they had to stop farming and raise sheep.

These are but the simpler examples. In a later chapter we shall see how Wesley Mitchell uses somewhat the same idea to explain the business cycle. What he says—to oversimplify outrageously here—is that men, by doing what comes naturally in prosperity, inevitably bring on depression, and vice versa. The concept leads to the conclusion that we are rather pushed around by our economic system. It entices us into doing the next and easiest thing, which, in the long run, may be a very bad thing. This in turn suggests that perhaps we should be more hospitable toward the application of controls—toward the aim of pushing rather than being pushed. And then, when we realize how bad some of the controls are that have already been applied, we begin to think that controls only make things worse and invite being pushed around even more. But I am going ahead too fast, and there is danger of confusing the reader, prematurely.

There are also, of course, economists of a special type who follow the doctrines of Karl Marx, others who are more interested in practical day-to-day welfare than in the more rigorous exercises of theory, still others who differ from their colleagues primarily in the realm of method. Among the latter is a group that seeks to mold the major principles of economics into the form of equations and mathematical symbols as in physics.

Thus, economics is something like the field of art, with its classicists, neoclassicists, impressionists, and surrealists. Although there are really deep cleavages among the schools, their methods, their definitions, it cannot be said that there are equally great disagreements on the practical problems they should try to handle. All economists agree that inflation and widespread unemployment are uneconomic, and that economists should study how to avoid both. There are sound and unsound monetary systems, and economists should, it is generally agreed, seek to establish criteria for sound money. Economists of quite different faiths might easily reach a consensus on the type of development program needed to raise the levels of living in backward countries like Libya or Bolivia. In all such practical matters there is a large measure of agreement about what economists should study and do. The great cleavages—as in religion, philosophy and art—are doctrinal.

By way of summary of this section, we give below a handful of representative definitions of economics taken from the works of the masters. In these definitions, the older phrase "political economy" is more or less equal to the newer word "economics."

Oeconomy, in general, is the art of providing for all the wants of a family, with prudence and frugality. . . . What oeconomy is in a family, political oeconomy is in a state (Sir James Steuart, 1712–1780).

Writers on Political Economy profess to teach, or to investigate, the nature of Wealth, and the laws of its production and distribution: including, directly or remotely, the operation of all the causes by which the condition of mankind, or of any society of human beings, in respect to this universal object of human desire, is made prosperous or the reverse (John Stuart Mill, 1806–1873).

Political Economy treats chiefly of the material interests of nations. It inquires how the various wants of the people of a country, especially those of food, clothing, fuel, shelter, of the sexual instinct etc., may be satisfied; how the satisfaction of these wants influences the aggregate national life, and how in turn, they are influenced by the national life (Wilhelm Roscher, 1817–1894).

Economics is a study of the "community's methods of turning material things to account" (Thorstein Veblen, 1857–1929).

Economics . . . is concerned with that aspect of behavior which arises from the scarcity of means to achieve given ends (Lionel Robbins, 1898–).

. . . Economics is . . . a social science; that is, it deals with the behavior of men in organized communities. Its special province is the behavior of social groups in providing the means for attaining their various ends (Wesley Mitchell, 1874–1948).

Since, in many minds, there is misunderstanding about the relationship between business and economics, some clarification is called for here. Except in the most metaphorical sense, a businessman is not a practical economist, and an economist is not a business theorist. To be sure, some businessmen are excellent economists—some of the greatest, like Ricardo and Keynes. And some economists are smart businessmen. But the realms are quite different. It is true, they work with similar materials: prices, costs, demand, supply, the results of competition, banking practice, taxes, and so on. Even so, some of these things mean different things in the two domains. The businessman is interested in making his firm prosper. The economist is interested in why a nation or region, or why the whole world, prospers or languishes.

Perhaps I can put the idea best by saying that the economist has no interest in any particular firm or industry, but in the balanced whole. The businessman is interested in making money. In his personal capacity an economist likes to make money, too, and prefers a good job to a poor job; he aspires to write books that sell widely; and when he buys United TV, common, he prayerfully hopes it will go up fifty points in fifty days, like any other American citizen. As an economist, however, he may deplore any rapid stock-market rise. He sees that it may lead to a severer break than might otherwise occur, or he may believe that the greatest good to the greatest number is not served by the mushroom-ing growth of a new industry. As an economist he surveys the whole and may deplore the very developments that enrich him personally. Businessmen, too, may similarly deplore. To the degree that they can see the difference between their own interest and the general interest, they, too, are economists. Indeed, all of us, whether ditchdiggers or priests, are partly businessmen and partly economists. As businessmen we seek our individual prosperity; as economists we study the factors making for the general prosperity. Sometimes both kinds of prosperity can be pursued together; sometimes not. The business of the businessman is profits; how to make a profit is not an important part of economics.

This is as good a place as any to return to something I wrote a moment ago about the definitions of common words in economics, as compared with the businessman's definition. Perhaps one of the most striking cases is that of the word "competition." Here is the definition of a businessman, speaking under the highest authority. David F. Austin, writing on competition in steel in a brochure put out by the United States Steel Corporation, states: "Businessmen use the term 'competition' to describe the action of two or more sellers in attempting to secure the same piece of available business." [1]

Now, when there are *only* two sellers, economists assert that competition falls short of pure competition—so far short that such a situation is described by them as duopoly, which means roughly a monopoly shared by two. When there are more than two, but still only a few sellers, competition is still considered to be imperfect, and the situation is described as oligopoly—a monopoly shared by a few. Only when there are so many sellers and so many buyers that no individual on either side can act in such a way as to influence the market is true competition said to exist—at least, so says the economist.

The issue to which I call attention is not whether the economist is right or the businessman wrong. That has nothing to do with it. I am only trying to show that business and economics use the same word in vastly different meanings. Certainly the businessman, right or wrong, deserves our sympathy; he is often engaged in bitter struggle for survival, which brings on stomach ulcers, only to have the ugly word "oligopolist" hurled at him.

The fact is that two rather different ideas are involved. The businessman, whether small and highly competitive (in the economist's sense), or large and monopoloid, is the victim of many pressures and anxieties: the possibility of being left at the post by substitutes or inventions, by sudden shifts

[1] United States Steel Corporation, *Business . . . Big and Small . . . Built America* (New York, 1950), p. 70.

of demand, by the accidents of unfavorable publicity for himself or his product, or by a hundred other unhappy circumstances. No monopolist—not even one who is a monopolist by any man's definition—was ever handed his monopoly on a silver platter, or has been allowed to keep it without threats from every quarter. Indeed, merely to hold his monopoly intact, he is engaged in a bitter struggle for self-preservation which *feels* like competition. In short, the fight to hold one's own, to survive in the face of sniping from every direction, gives the businessman the sense of tough competition.

The economist, watching from the outside, is looking at different things and for different things. However sympathetic and understanding he may be as an individual toward the harassed life and milk-fed ulcers of an individual businessman, he must ignore these personal facts. As an economist he must recognize that there is a difference between the structure of a market on which there are very few sellers and one on which there are hundreds or thousands, as on the stock exchanges. He is also bound to take note of the fact that markets based exclusively on the lowest price differ in texture from markets based on such other elements of competition as prestige of product (Rolls-Royce), a widely known firm or brand name, greater formality of service (as in the swank shops), nonfunctional attributes (as of the breakfast cereal that is alleged to "talk" when you pour on the milk).

Thus, in using the word "competition," businessmen and economists often speak of different things; they bring different experiences, feelings, observations to bear on their interpretation of the word. What is confusing is that both may use the word, partly, to describe things that *are* identi-

cal; and it is with surprise that they later sense divergencies
of meaning. This is not the only deceptive word. Cost is
another. Rent, interest, land, capital—these and still others
often refer to different things in the two spheres.

So much for trying to find out what economics is about
and noting its differences from the deceptively similar field
of business. A preliminary chapter like this also needs—as
its opening sentence implied—an answer to a second question, namely, How do we study economics? Obviously not
in a laboratory. Do we have to make field trips, as in botany?
Since test tubes, telescopes, and Bunsen burners are not used,
what are the appropriate tools and methods?

The classic, but not necessarily the best, method of study
—the reader will have to form his own conclusion in due
course—is the so-called abstract method. It is a method
which, basically, assumes that we live in a perfectly functioning, highly competitive economic society into which
some new event (like a higher income tax) is introduced.
The repercussions of this disturbance in the perfect system
are then deduced. Often a mathematical diagram is used,
like Figure 1. Here supply and demand curves are made to
tell a story about price changes. Two of the curves in the
diagram are really straight lines. In the eyes of a mathematician, a straight line is a special case of a curve. It is therefore
quite proper in diagrams of this kind to speak of all the lines
as "curves."

At this point not all readers will understand the diagram
completely or have a very clear idea of what is meant by
the "abstract" method. The question of method in general
and of diagrams in particular, will bob up again and again.

Throughout the history of the development of economic

theory there has been opposition to the abstract method. The method found great favor among the British, but between 1860 and 1900 was challenged by a German historical school. The Germans held that a study of past economic phenomena would pile up a mountain of facts; that, through

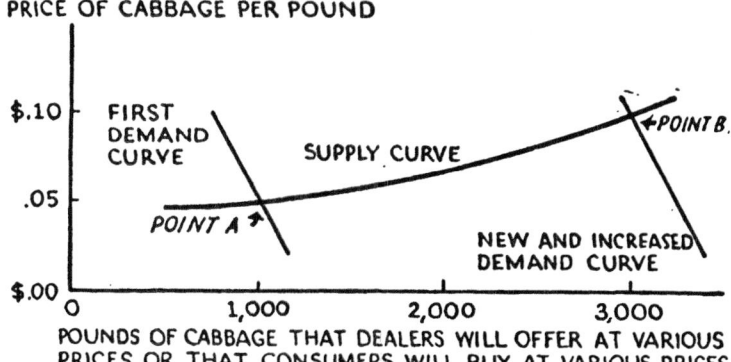

PRICE OF CABBAGE PER POUND

POUNDS OF CABBAGE THAT DEALERS WILL OFFER AT VARIOUS PRICES, OR THAT CONSUMERS WILL BUY AT VARIOUS PRICES

FIGURE 1

Point A: When supply and demand curves meet here, the price of cabbage is 5 cents per pound, and dealers are willing to offer for sale 1,000 pounds. The item 5 cents is found by reading the figure at the left of the intersection; the item 1,000 pounds is found by reading the figure just under the intersection.

Point B: If demand is increased we draw a new demand curve, higher and to the right of the original curve. The new curve crosses the old curve at a point which indicates that the new price is 10 cents and that at this more favorable price dealers are willing to offer 3,000 pounds for sale.

scientific induction, the mountain would yield important generalizations, principles, and laws. Instead, it yielded a mouse. Other schools have taken roughly similar positions —though their chief similarity has been revolt against the abstract method.

Perhaps the most successful challenge to the abstract method has been the coming into existence of a large number of eclectic economists, who, using a variety of methods, lean heavily on description and statistics. Thus, statistical methods are used to make up tables like the following, which contain information of considerable significance to economic science:

In 1929
32 percent of all income receivers had incomes of $1,500 or less;

30 percent of all income receivers had incomes between $1,500 and $3,000;

8 percent of all income receivers had incomes between $3,000 and $4,500;

30 percent of all income receivers had incomes above $4,500.[2]

As to field trips, one would think that these would be a most fruitful source of economic theory. One cannot help thinking how much of theoretical value to biology came out of Charles Darwin's historic field trip through many seas on the *Beagle*—though one must perhaps give greater recognition to Darwin's genius than to his field trip. Yet field trips are not much used by general theorists in economics.

Many of the specialists do, of course, maintain contact with the objects of their specialty through something like field trips. Economists who specialize in labor problems have personal acquaintances among trade-union leaders and employers; they mediate or conciliate in disputes; they attend trade-union meetings and conventions. Experts in the economics of transportation, taxation, agriculture, international trade, social insurance, and so on, all have their appropriate connections with the governmental officials or private persons who do the world's work in the fields of their interest.

The preceding remarks on methods of studying economics relate to the more obvious matters; in its profounder

[2] Adapted from M. Leven, H. G. Moulton, and C. Warburton, *America's Capacity to Consume* (Washington, D.C., 1934).

aspects, method in any of the social sciences is an elusive and intricate business. Much remains to be written about it, for what now goes under this heading is often emptily argumentative or elementary. Man does not study well what is too close to him. And students of economic method, in its profounder aspects, are confronted by the difficulty of studying what is so close a part of every man's life and so intimately tied up with food, clothing, shelter, the welfare of his children, the security of his declining years. If John Smith has provided reasonably well for his old age, then to him and to others like him, any economic proposal that threatens the worth of his annuities is socialistic, confiscatory, economically unsound, and a blot on the fair face of virtue—even if, in its longer-term and wider aspects, the proposal contributes to a program of generally increasing prosperity.

In this respect economic method is still not much advanced beyond the point that the physical sciences were at the time of Francis Bacon, about 1620. We still should pay heed to Bacon's four classes of false idols, or preconceptions that prejudice the mind at the earliest stages of scientific thinking. Many misconceptions in economics may arise out of our prejudices concerning the nature of man (*Idola tribus*); those induced by our individual status or surroundings (*Idola specus*); those absorbed through common speech (*Idola fori*); those coming from fables or tradition (*Idola theatri*).

Many students also bring to the study of economics the idol or bias of Utopia. These believe that the function of economics is to mark out a clear road to a four-hour day, five-day week, full employment, womb-to-tomb security, international peace, full social equality between races and sexes, and, in other ways, an unqualified brotherhood of

man on earth. Such students have damaged the science of
economics considerably and sometimes helped to discredit it.
On the other hand, they have helped economists to remember that no science—not even the precise science of physics,
astronomy, or chemistry—is studied without an ultimate
view toward ultimate human ends.

Other students bring to economics the idol or bias of conservatism. It is not quite so easy to define the aims of the
conservative as it is those of the Utopian. Certainly they do
not want merely to conserve what is, since most of them
would be quite willing to give up John Lewis, high income
taxes, and Federal peacetime budgets of 50 billion dollars.
Yet if they were taken back to the days when those things
did not exist, they would still find many things unendurable
—we know that conservatives of that day had their own
little list of things that never would be missed. Perhaps the
essence of conservatism is that it, too, is Utopian, but finds
its Utopia in an idealized past. Or perhaps it is a sort of
patriarchal attitude which assumes that the best interests of
the commonality are closely and harmoniously related to
the personal interests of political and economic leaders. Neither view is pressed on the reader; the point is that a strong
conservative bias, however defined, has not particularly
spurred progress in the study of economics. On the other
hand conservatism has thankfully restrained the free use of
extreme remedies which, often harsh and violent, are as
likely to kill as to cure.

Many students bring as handicaps to the study of economics a few half-learned truths, often passed on by word of
mouth, from father to son. Some of these obstruct the learning process painfully and may even remain with the student
long after the more precise view of the economist on the

same subject has been presented. For example, many believe that the good, old-fashioned, immutable law of supply and demand determines price, and that you can't fool around with this law or you will upset the applecart. To an economist the preceding sentence is almost devoid of sense. It is true that the forces of supply and demand exert themselves on the process of price formation, but economists are pretty careful to avoid talking about a "law." Moreover, successful tampering with both supply and demand has worked from time immemorial. Monopolists restrict supply; advertisers increase demand. A combination of the two processes works fine for the beneficiary and upsets no applecarts of theirs. Even under more highly competitive conditions, understanding of how the forces of supply operate is not always easy and invites no simple, one-shot generalization. As the reader will learn, supply and demand move in mysterious ways their wonders to perform. Other and similar half truths abound. Some of them, it should be honestly confessed, have been circulated by economists themselves. All of these differ from bias in that they are fallacy rather than prejudice.

Another of the rather more subtle hindrances to economic study is the human desire to find a scapegoat. Pick up the paper any time and you will find somebody blaming the Republicans or the Democrats for high meat prices or low farm prices. "The villains of inflation are the Treasury and the Federal Reserve Board," says a speaker quoted in the New York *Herald Tribune* (October 3, 1948). On some other day it was labor's "third-round" wage increase that has ruined the nation. And the day before that it was the greedy monopolists. Tomorrow some other unique cause will be sought as the single explanation of an economic evil.

Economics at its best, in common with all the other sciences, must see events as the outcome of processes, and often interacting processes, rather than of specific causes. If we have inflation it is because a thousand factors have combined to produce it, not because the National Association of Manufacturers is dominated by inhuman profit seekers, or because the AF of L and CIO are officered by heedless demagogues, or because the Board of Governors of the Federal Reserve banks are puppets of Treasury officials or Wall Street. The economic system is rather like a growing plant than a machine. Changes are the result of development, not of pushing a lever.

It is often annoying to ordinary men that economists can give but little aid in the search for culprits. It is always reassuring to find specific causes, and emotionally satisfying to discover and denounce scoundrels who blight our economic world. And, of course, there sometimes are specific causes and real villains. Particularly when the causes come from outside our economic system. Drought causes famine in China. The Black Death caused wages to rise. Wars cause prosperous nations to go off the gold standard overnight, though the general and slow abandonment of the old-time gold standard has been caused by many things other than war. But most of the time the event on which we focus our attention is not only caused by a thousand contemporary forces, but also has roots in a long past. Thus, even an apparently simple economic event is often hard to explain, for economists are very lucky if they can discover only a few of the many determining causes and can unscramble a few of the relations among them.

The plan of this book is intended to take account of some of the difficulties mentioned above. "Conservative" and

"Utopian" economic theories will be discussed and given their labels. It will sometimes be pointed out that this or that theory cannot be fully comprehended unless the reader is willing to put aside a possible prejudice—and I can only hope that no reader will take offense at this. The aim is not to suggest a fault but to warn that there are intellectual booby traps ahead.

In this chapter we have reached toward a definition of economics, and reaching without grasping is perhaps as much as we need to do, since no short definition is likely to satisfy anybody. We have talked about methods of studying the subject, and the obstacles that confront us. Now, before we take up economic theory proper, let us look at some of the principal features of the actual economic world.

2. RICH WORLD, POOR WORLD

THE PURPOSE OF THIS chapter is to look at some of the principal features of our economic world. Here we are, two and a quarter billion people on this spinning globe, all of us trying to get at least food enough to keep body and soul together, to find places to sleep, to get some sort of protection from heat or cold or rain, and to secure the material things needed to achieve a few intangible goals, like giving and getting love or worshiping a god or insuring a decent burial.

How do we do it? The first thing to say in reply is that we do it through some kind of social organization. The number of Robinson Crusoe's still in existence can safely be disregarded. We live through our fellows and they live through us. This association of human beings is not an unmixed blessing, for economic disturbance in one part of the world may bring disaster to other parts, sometimes directly and sometimes through a chain of cause and effect so long that few can see all the links. What happens in a few sparsely settled silver states of the United States may bring increased poverty to inland Chinese communities. Our economic destinies are tied together for weal or woe—but mostly for weal, or less woe, at any rate—since few of us would venture to wrest our living directly and alone from stern nature. Even the savage does not carve out his economic destiny unaided; he has the help and protection of his tribe.

The second thing to say is that we do it through a code, or through institutions, taboos, prejudices. The code is unbelievably complex. Some groups are permitted to allay their hunger by consuming hog meat; others are not. Human flesh or cooked snails are prized here but abhorred elsewhere. It is not proper to demand ten dollars from a drowning man as the price of his rescue, but quite proper to demand money for bread from a hungry and penniless man. This code, part custom, part law, has been developing for a long time. Great rulers, religious leaders, philosophers, and others have had a hand in shaping it. Like morality, it differs with time and place.

A third great principle underlying our economic life is the so-called division of labor. The upshot of this principle is that few if any of us do an all-round job of making things to gratify our wants. We do not make our own golf clubs or mine our own coal. Indeed, very few of us, except farmers, carry anything through from seed to fruit, literally or figuratively. Even on small farms there is a husband-and-wife division of labor, while the children specialize in doing light chores. In factories, as is well known, nobody makes a complete thing; each worker spends the whole day grinding off a rough edge or punching holes. The division of labor is intrafirm and interfirm, intrastate and interstate, intranational and international.

The division of labor is necessarily accompanied by some method of recompense or conversion or exchange. No worker would devote the best years of his life to screwing nuts if he did not have the guarantee that this labor—so unfruitful if considered in isolation—could easily be turned into food, clothing, and shelter. In our society but not in all societies, the system of recompense requires money, markets, and, as always, a code governing transfers.

The above paragraphs on human association, codes of economic action, division of labor, and transfer of goods, by no means exhaust the list of basic requirements of any developed economic system (including ours), but they do suggest some of the indispensable conditions underlying economic life. We can sum them up by saying: to make a living we give our time freely to more or less specialized activities engaged in mostly on behalf of others, confident that the others within our human association will turn over to us, in accordance with existing codes some, at least, of the things we want but do not ourselves produce.

The basic pattern is incomplete without one further element. Few if any economic systems have had the fraternal structure which might, from the preceding sentence, be inferred to exist. Highly developed and enduring economic systems reflect the propensity to aggression that comes so easily to human beings and that carries within it elements of coercion and restraint. Nomadic tribes have tended to overrun settled agricultural communities, to rule over them, and to enjoy not only the immediate product of their labor, but also the fruit of many generations of past labor. An African tribe, the Kipsings, are a pastoral people who use the same word for going to work as for going to war; in both cases the object is to get cattle.[1] Our forefathers took

[1] Paul Einzig, *Primitive Money* (London, Eyre & Spottiswoode, 1949), p. 128.

the United States away from the Indians. Excursions to capture slaves are a long-established human institution, by no means abolished today if we may believe stories we read of Russian concentration camps, not to mention Hitlerian slavery. The first voyage of the English East India Company had one cannon for every 13 tons of freight, and took its return load of pepper away from a Portuguese ship instead of getting it in India. The human habit of taking rather than making is firmly entrenched, and no economic system has been or is free of it.

Now, taking demands labor, in a sense, and often arduous and dangerous labor, for it involves anxiety, timely use of threats, ability to outwait the other fellow, legalistic chicanery, and even violence. Yet taking is not a labor to be included under the concept of "division of labor," which suggests a constructive and even fraternal association of persons. How to treat these aggressive labors has always been something of a problem in economic theory, more often dodged than handled firmly; and when handled firmly, often handled badly. One reason is that, curiously enough, aggression is often not clearly perceived. Man has a blindspot about his aggressive tendencies, seldom recognizing their existence. But enough of this for the present; questions relating to the labors of coercion will come up again in later chapters.

We carry on our economic activities in human association and under certain codes. There have been many kinds of association and many codes. Some have been based on slavery, some on feudal ties, some on agrarian democracy, some like ours, on free pecuniary transactions. Most associations have been mixed; the economy of the United States before

1860, for example, was partly an economy of free monetary transactions, partly an agrarian democracy, and partly a slave economy.

The contemporary world is divided into three types of economic association: capitalism, communism, and a mixture of the two, like British socialism. We could probably fit most of the nations of the world into one of these three classes, but it is doubtful whether this arbitrary approach to economic classification is very useful. There are other and perhaps more fundamentally important categories. Important economically, that is, rather than politically.

Two thirds of the world's population live in sprawling, unintegrated economies. They depend on primitive agricultural methods for their inadequate food. The soil on which this chronically hungering majority lives includes most of Latin America, excepting a narrow coastal fringe in Chile, Argentina, Uruguay, and Brazil; non-Siberian Asia; and all of Africa except the southern tip. In these areas, general introduction of wheel cultivators (like those used by amateur gardeners in the United States) would be a technological revolution. These people consume on the average only 2,150 calories a day; many consume less, for "average" means that some are below and some are above; and, in breaking down economic statistics of this sort, it is usual to find that more than half are below, while relatively few are above; these few are often comfortably above—indeed far above—the average. How badly off that large majority really is may be gauged by the fact that the minimum number of daily calories required to sustain life is 1,800; the average figure is only 350 calories above the danger line.

In this large, starving part of the world, nearly four fifths of the population is illiterate. There is only one physician for about 6,000 persons, compared with six for the more advanced parts of the world. (Of course in the wealthiest localities of the advanced regions there are even more doctors.) Inhabitants of the backward areas can count on living only 30 years; in the more advanced economies life expectancy is 63 years. From waterfalls, donkeys, elephants, and an occasional motor with sinus trouble no doubt, the backward countries get a fraction more than one horsepower-hour per day per capita of non-human energy; the comparable figure for the highly integrated economies is 26.6.[2]

Economically it is not very important whether the members of this impoverished fraternity of nations are, like China, communistic; or like Bolivia, capitalistic; or, like India, headed by a socialist premier. For them there is a symbol of union that transcends the hammer and sickle, or the French nightcap of capitalist republicanism. This symbol—if they were to adopt one—should be the crude stick they use to stir the ground with, a pointed stick sometimes tipped with metal.

An interesting and incidental fact to note about all this is that many of the issues of economic theory as developed by Europeans and Americans are almost nonexistent among two thirds of the world's inhabitants. Economic theory, as we shall see presently, is much concerned with the value of money and the behavior of markets. Money and markets are almost as scarce in this vast agricultural poorhouse as they were in medieval days. The happy few in the North Atlantic community, or in Australia and New Zealand, are concerned with international investment, full employment, booms and busts, contracyclical public works, deficit spending, and the like. These are among the grand themes of Western economics. For hundreds of millions who have no

[2] The statistical material used here is taken or derived from *The Point Four Program*, U.S. Department of State, Publication 3347 (Washington, 1949).

surpluses to send abroad there is no problem of foreign investment. For hundreds of millions who are trying to grow a little rice for their families and to find a little fishtail to flavor it with occasionally, the problem of deficit spending to maintain full employment scarcely arises. There are no business cycles in Cathay—because there is no business, only subsistence farming.

I do not really mean to imply that economic problems in the Western sense do not exist at all in the underdeveloped areas, or that China or India or Nigeria have never engaged in any foreign trade. I only mean that many of the categories of Western economic thought are not very significant in noncommercial, nonindustrial areas, and that many Western "economic laws" have only an attenuated force in Africa, Asia, and the Andes—where the starveling two thirds live.

What about the other third? Well, one half of these, mostly in the Soviet Union, stand intermediate between the pointed-stick-using agriculturalists and the Western industrialized nations of the North Atlantic community (plus Australia and New Zealand). We can summarize their level of living as follows, at the same time comparing it with the still higher European and North American nations:

Criteria for Level of Living	Intermediate Areas (Soviet Union, Eastern Europe, Italy, Spain, Union of South Africa, coastal areas of part of South America)	Developed Areas (United States, Canada, Scandinavia, Western Europe, Australia, New Zealand)
Calories	2,760	3,040
Nonhuman energy in horsepower hours	6.4	26.6
Life expectancy	52 years	63 years
Physicians per 100,000	78	106

Both areas, intermediate and developed, are much more highly integrated and interdependent than the other two thirds. Even the intermediate area uses 5 times the horse-power employed in the backward countries. And five times anything in economic life is something! How would you like five times your present income, or a five-times-heavier income tax!

The richest countries in this wealthier third are capitalist countries and the poorer ones are principally the member republics and satellites of the Soviet Union. Yet a few capitalist countries are, like the Soviets, in the lower half of this more prosperous third: Italy, Spain, Argentina, Greece, Chile, Uruguay, and the wealthier parts of Brazil. It should also be noticed that in several of the better-to-do nations, capitalism has been much diluted by socialistic experiment: Scandinavia, Australia, New Zealand, and last but not least, the United Kingdom.

Since the end of the Second World War, which devastated Europe and destroyed morale, the United States, unscathed, has achieved a phenomenal economic position. There is no parallel in history. Blessed with almost every economic gift and resource except compactness—fewer mountains and deserts would spare us a lot of hauling back and forth—blessed with almost everything, we now outmanufacture the rest of the world put together. In agriculture we are not so formidable, but even here we are great and can show surpluses in many products. The degree of our self-sufficiency is the despair of the remainder of the world, which can find very little to send us in exchange for what they want from us. We are like the exasperatingly rich member of a family whose relatives can find nothing to give him at Christmas; like him, we already have (almost) everything we want. We ourselves have met the problem by simply giving away part of our great production—not only in the Second World War and in postwar reconstruction but for many years before that: the story really begins back in 1917, and the end is not in sight.

Just a word about poverty even in the wealthier countries. It should not be assumed that everybody is comfortable in the rich nations. One fourth of all American families had incomes of $2,000 and less in 1949. This is considerable poverty for the United States in an era of high prosperity and very high prices. In the wealthy countries of Europe a similarly unequal distribution of income prevails. Everywhere there is a genuinely poor third or fourth, underfed, underclothed, and underhoused. If then, we add the relatively few but still considerable number of poor people in the wealthy nations to the poor of the Soviet Union and then add to that the very poor of Asia and Africa and Latin America, we have a great deal of poverty in the world. From this we can only conclude that the economic endeavors of the world seen as a whole, are not admirably efficient.

Why are there so many poor? Why, in view of all the productive wonders of modern science? One answer might be a battery of new and surprising questions that turn the tables on the questioner. How can we know whether we are poor? What standards of comparison have we? Are earthly creatures poorer than the inhabitants of Mars? Do we make similar statements about natural phenomena, complaining that the boiling point of water is too high, or that iron is too heavy?

Here we run into one of the great difficulties of the social sciences. Strictly we have no right to speak of this world as being poor since we cannot compare its level of living with that of other worlds or of the bourne from which no traveler

returns. Moreover, poverty is a subjective rather than objective thing. A happily married but underfed couple may,
in one sense, be richer than a well-fed couple filled with
reciprocal hate. This, and similar observations about enriching one's soul with the beauty of sunsets or the song of birds
or the wealth of friendship, are part of the ancient wisdom
of man. It is also part of the creed of many economists who
refuse to measure wealth in terms of income—since wealth
in a final analysis, is satisfaction, and satisfaction is not a
public fact, therefore, not a scientific datum.

On the other hand, the physical sciences do not present
us with similarly exasperating problems. A cubic inch of
lead does not, in China, weigh one pound and in the United
States ten; the boiling point is not 212° at sea level in South
Africa, and 150° in New York City. If we did have such
variations in natural phenomena, and if we noted that people in the low-weight and low-boiling-point areas seemed
to be getting along better than the rest of us, we might be
tempted to complain that, for the world as a whole, gravity
pulled too hard and the boiling point rose too high. But
levels of living do vary widely. In some countries levels are
high and people obviously prosper; in others, the people
languish in poverty. In the face of these observations we
find some justification for asking why so many are poor.
There is even greater justification in the fact that we assume—perhaps too lightly, however—poverty to be within
human control, whereas gravity and boiling point are
not.

Cutting through the knot of philosophy we ask again:
Why is the world as poor as it is? This is one of the great
problems of applied economics, and the present book as a
whole will incidentally suggest answers to the question. Pro-

visionally and dogmatically a few introductory statements
can be made:

1. Nature, if she is not to be niggardly, demands both
energy and understanding before she yields abundantly.

2. Bad or weak governments, of which there are many,
do not adequately provide certain requirements, like roads,
canals, schools, that are basic to healthy economic activity.
Underdeveloped countries often have underdeveloped governments. Nora Waln, in her book about China during the
1920's, gives us a striking example of how a Chinese governor
insured the continued economic effectiveness of a waterway.
"Then this morning the Civil Governor's second Green
Skirt called. She came to ask me to send Uncle Shao-Chun
a message from her husband. The Governor regrets that
there is no money in the provincial treasury to hire engineers to man the waterways. All he can do is to lead an
official procession to worship the Rain God and petition
that there be no flood rain this year." [3]

3. Man's efficient working years are short by comparison
with the total span of life. A representative, hard-working
American college graduate spends only 15 percent of his
total living hours in gainful occupation.

4. Man competes for his goods against the destruction of
bacteria, rats, lice, earthquakes, fire, erosion.

5. Superstition and tradition often inhibit the more work-
manlike propensities. Though there is perhaps less primitive
superstition in the great industrial countries than in the backward countries, it must not be thought that animism, vague
fears, belief in luck, and so on, exert no restraining influence
on the production of industrial goods.

6. There is a sort of cycle of increasing want that seems

[3] Nora Waln, *The House of Exile* (New York, Penguin, 1938), p. 151.

to operate in economic affairs. Poverty precludes the raising of capital and lack of capital perpetuates poverty. John King Fairbank, in his brilliant book on China, has cited a "minor example" of this sort of vicious circle: "Lack of forest or other fuel [in many parts of China] compels the farmer to burn plant stalks, which impoverishes the soil; he enriches the earth by his own excrement . . . , but this spreads disease germs, particularly intestinal parasites, far and wide over the farm land; to preserve his health he must heat all food and water, which requires fuel." [4]

7. Despite the magnetism of factories during the past two hundred years, about four out of five of the world's inhabitants still live and work down on the farm; and a vast fraction of these work with medieval tools and science.

8. Without being too Nietzschean about it, one must observe that men do easily resort to violence. Wars, exploitation, domestic violence (as in bitter strikes)—these are, in the long run, impoverishers. Mankind's toleration of the predatory employments and quick recourse to bloodshed when negotiation begins to be difficult have reduced his supply of worldly goods. Perhaps by selective breeding, higher civilization, or sounder education, man may yet become a patient, negotiating biped. For the present, however, conflicts of interest are often settled by coercion, threats of coercion, and recourse to violence.

9. Huge and increasing populations, particularly in Asia, appear to eat up the fruit of each economic gain as it is made. Thus, very little can be wrung by them out of currently increased production and saved over to provide for better machines, better plows, and the other durables required to

[4] *The United States and China* (Cambridge, Harvard University Press, 1948), p. 215.

make visible progress away from direct poverty. In the overpopulated regions—which account for half the human beings of the earth—a mighty effort must be made to bring the level of living to the point at which it even begins to compare favorably with Western standards.

10. In capitalist nations the business cycle, with its often uneconomical production during booms and its stifled production in depression, robs the world of the full benefits made possible by the superb technological leadership of capitalism.

11. There is a strong and generous urge in man to share the little he has with supernal entities. Thus, totem poles, statues to heroes, tombstones, ancestral shrines, and the like, abound even in the poorest parts of the earth.

The last statement on supernal entities, brings up another difficult point in economic valuation. We must look at its implications before we go on to list certain other reasons for human poverty that resemble it. To make the point I have in mind, I would ask the reader to consider the economics of an Indonesian village I once heard about from an anthropologist. The members of this village, at the harvest, divided their communal rice into two equal parts. One part was fermented into wine, which they forthwith drank in a long-drawn-out festival. When they came to, they parceled out what was left of the rice, used it as food, and tried to live on it until the next harvest. But after ten months or so, the food ran out. Until the new harvest, they lived in extremest penury, often leaving the village to lead a purely animal existence of survival in the jungle. During this time some of the weaker ones died of privation. Question: how *really* poor was this village?

Now, if an individual in our culture spends half of his

modest but adequate income on narcotics and is consequently forced to deprive himself of needed food, we never think of him as poor. We think he is unwise or mentally ill. But the same evaluation cannot be made of entire communities living under their institutions, or to entire nations. You cannot indict a whole culture, to paraphrase Burke. Each Indonesian in this tribe comes close to starvation because the society he lives in demands that he consume wine instead of food; and the society as a whole has adopted the institution of drink-wine-rather-than-eat for reasons at which we can only guess. Perhaps they believe that if the gods of the harvest are not honored by large fermentations, they will withhold all rice the next year; thus, to them, it is very *economic* to waste half their food in strong drink. But from the viewpoint of an outsider, not sharing the aspirations, theology, or superstitions of such a community, these Indonesians are poorer than they need to be. From the viewpoint of some rebel in the Indonesian community, the poverty is imposed; similarly, his demand for rice wine is imposed. If he had a greater measure of control over his own life he would take more rice and less wine. Since, however, he prefers membership in the community to more food, he puts up and shuts up. He may, of course, try the precarious life of social reform.

Human want comes out of two things: lack of goods and unwise use of what goods there are. Or, a combination of the two. When we speak of unwise consumption we do not have precise standards of wisdom in mind, but we do have some notions of the prudent man's use of wealth. We think of abundant and wholesome food as coming first; of clothing, warm in winter and cool in summer as having high priority; of shelter and fuel for a warming fire as more

essential than luxuries. But that, as a matter of fact, is not
how any human group consumes. Waste, display, generos-
ity, vanity, superstition, custom, ritual—all step in before
the primary physiological needs have been met. And many
of the wants that arise through custom, ritual, and the like
are imposed on the individual by the society. Rice wine is
made to displace rice-as-a-food. Totem poles come before
calories; families go into debt to provide expensive funerals.
The questions raised by this discussion are questions of ultimate human values and cannot better be answered by economists than others—indeed, not so well as others. No answer is attempted here, but the reader is invited to consider
other examples of how basic biological wants may be neglected because other kinds of needs override.

Economic unities are not always matched by political
unities. Three nations may share what is, economically, one
coal area; two rival cities may dominate one harbor; the same
river may go through several states or nations, often with
unfavorable effects on transportation, land conservation,
flood control, forestation, electric-power development, and
so forth. In other words, we prefer local and national self-
determination to the greater economic wealth that surrender
of this right would yield.

Much of our clothing is ceremonial and without biological
function. There are many situations in which a man could,
during the summer and with perfect modesty, wear four-
dollar pyjamas rather than a $17.50 seersucker suit which
soon looks slept-in anyhow. What goes for men's clothes
goes for women's—plus an infinitude of things we consume
or too soon discard only to keep up with the Joneses.

Many readers will be surprised to note that in the list of
reasons for human poverty I made no mention of the unequal

distribution of wealth and income. The notion that many
are poor because a few are rich is widespread, but it suggests rather than proclaims a truth. The cold fact is that,
if everything actually produced were distributed by the
rule of equality, there would be poverty for all. Mankind
has never made enough things to maintain every human being
on the level of frugal comfort. On the other hand this fact
may distort a possible and important truth. There is cause
to believe that a more nearly equal distribution of wealth
would be a powerful stimulus to increased production—
perhaps greater than any other we might apply. But until
this belief is better supported by fact or theory than it now
is, it cannot safely be listed as a reason, certainly not the
great reason, for the world's poverty.

Our survey has suggested that we live in a curious, crazy-
quilt, inefficient economic world. Man appears to yearn for
great material wealth, yet does little about it, seeming to
prefer wars, reckless consumption, numerous progeny. He
sometimes seems to be pushed around by his economic system rather than to be in control of it. We have also seen that
economic activity, despite our quite proper use of such
words as "individual initiative," is in fact a social activity;
in other words, human beings must depend on their fellows
if they expect to secure the material things required to satisfy
wants.

Now let us go on to look at this same economic world
through the lenses of standard economic theory.

Part Two

STANDARD ECONOMIC THEORY

3. INTRODUCTION TO STANDARD ECONOMIC THEORY

THIS CHAPTER INTRO-
duces Part Two, which is
devoted to a rapid survey
of standard economic theory—often referred to also as orthodox or neoclassical theory. This kind is widely taught in
the upper schools of the Anglo-American community, traces
its heritage to David Ricardo (1772–1823), John Stuart
Mill (1806–1873), and Alfred Marshall (1842–1924), dominates the editorial policy of learned journals, and commands
the respect of many of our leading economic savants. This
standard or neoclassical theory is, however, only one approach to the problems of economic life. Later we shall
study other approaches and all will be evaluated as we go
along.

To smooth the way I have selected a group of apparently
miscellaneous items for inclusion in this introductory chapter. They are selected less on the basis of their relationship
to each other than on the basis of their relevance to the larger
problems of Part Two. There are a few unrelated but preliminary things that must be put behind us if we are to go
forward rapidly.

A basic thing to know about standard economic theory is its explanation of how the economic universe holds together. What is the cement, spit, or gravitational force that keeps it from flying apart? If one thinks hard about economic life—the hard kind of thinking Newton did when he wondered why the apple went down instead of up—one begins to wonder why there is any order at all in economic life. How amazing our economic organization really is can be fully appreciated if one stops to ponder earnestly the logistics of a Sunday School picnic. That requires a general chairman with almost dictatorial power; careful planning; various sub-chairmen in charge of food, recreation, transportation, also vested with authority; plus endless telephone conversations about watercress sandwiches with mayonnaise. All this central direction for just a few hours' picnicking! And yet there is no central direction for our vast American economic system which feeds 150 million people more or less adequately three times a day more or less; transports them billions of miles from sun to sun; and finds a bed for nearly all nearly every night. To be sure, economic life is not unplanned in detail. Each businessman plans for the welfare of his firm. But there is no over-all planning. Government, particularly in wartime, is increasingly organizing economic life. But, again, government in the past century and even today, has been and is responsible for relatively little.

There are other evidences of unenforced order in our economic life. There is proportion and economy. It is rare that two men are sent to do the job of ten. Bulldozers are not used to shove away a few pecks of dirt, and steam shovels are not used to dig post holes. There are—except for one or two featured by the *New Yorker*—no farms on Manhattan Island. Materials like wood or gold, bricks or sapphires, are always dedicated to their special and "proper" uses. Prices are roughly the same, for the same things, over wide areas; it is clear that there is a system of interrelated prices. And except for price-fixing by some manufacturers and other bodies, it is equally clear that there is no central price-fixing commission (like OPA during the war).

All of these evidences of order are impressive—as impressive in their way as the order of the solar system, which prevents planets from colliding and keeps the stars in their courses.

Adam Smith is to be credited with explaining how the economic system organizes itself automatically, and his theories have not been much improved upon by later standard theorists. His explanation has undergone clarification, amendment, expansion, but the basic principles have not been superseded.

First, according to Adam Smith, we must consider that man seeks his own interest and is naturally adapted to "trucking and barter." Having, besides, a propensity to specialize in production, he creates surpluses—the shoemaker more shoes than he can wear, the farmer more food than he can eat, the weaver more cloth than he can use. What is more natural, then, than that each should seek to exchange his surplus for the other man's surplus? Thus the first and basic organizing force is that men naturally take to the kind of economic life we now have; making different things, and exchanging what they do not need.

The second organizing force is price on a free market. On this Smith is less clear; what follows includes the ideas of others. If too many shoes are being made, considering demand, their price will fall in the presence of a free market and the absence of government controls. It may fall below the cost of production of the less efficient shoemakers and if so, some men, at least, will stop making shoes. The supply will go down and prices will go up. If too many have dropped out of shoemaking, the prices will go back up again; they may go so high that some of the shoemakers will reenter their trade. This process of trial and error will continue back and forth until a balance or equilibrium is reached. And so for all other commodities.

Price has the further function of ordering scarce goods to their "highest" uses. Here is a huge tract of land. It can be used for anything from a farm or golf course to an oil refinery or base for skyscrapers. What decides how it shall be used? Price. The owner will, of course, sell to the highest bidder; the highest bidder is the one who can make the best (most productive and hence most profitable) use of the land. Thus, all of us are insured against frivolous or trivial uses not only of land, but also of labor and capital and natural resources, for they are similarly used to best account. Those who would use any kind of good to perform trivial functions are outbid by those who are able to use it most productively. To be sure, a very wealthy man may buy rich farm land precisely because he wishes to keep it unproductive socially, and wishes to insure privacy, elegance, and quiet for himself. But exceptions are not important in the aggregate.

Several considerations help to make the process of price adjustment smoother than might seem at first glance. One is the almost unlimited possibility of substitution; the protein in cheese for the protein in eggs; flying machines for orchard-spraying machines. Another is the eternal exchange of market information. Men and women love to talk about prices. Unintentional eavesdropping in subways, hotel lobbies, restaurants almost anywhere in the world is rewarded by such sounds as "five dollars," "only one dollar," "seventy-five thousand francs," "thirty bob." Through all means of communication from the telephone to the grapevine, news quickly gets around about shortages, oversupply, faltering or unshrinking demand. Men act in response to this knowledge because proper and timely action yields a profit. But proper and timely action also rectifies a shortage, or an oversupply, or appeases vigorous demand. Nature abhors an economic vacuum—that is, an unexploited opportunity for profit. Somebody always steps in to fill the vacuum and make the profit—hence meets a human need.

A third organizing principle was formerly found in Say's law. Jean-Baptiste Say (1767–1832), a French economist, held that overproduction was impossible. Demand and supply are virtually the same thing—or, at least, they are to each other as a hole in the ground is to the dirt taken out of it. People are always willing to accustom themselves to a higher standard of living; if, therefore, more is produced, more will be bought, precisely because more is produced. There can be no real disparity between supply and demand. Literal faith in Say's law would induce one to deny the possibility of sustained periods of mass unemployment, and for a long time standard economics did not seriously search out the causes of persistent unemployment. But it was so hard during the 1930's to ignore unemployment that many economists apostatized in respect of this doctrinal point—a matter to which we return in Chapter 12, on business cycles. Yet, for a century, Say's law was held to be an organizing force.

Many standard economists pondering the explanations given above, have tended to see something deeper, something more than mere economic organization. They would say that the desire of each purchaser to buy cheap, of each seller to sell dear, of each man to work at the most highly paid occupation or invest in the most profitable business— that all these forms of individual selfishness result in the greatest good to the greatest number. Bernard Mandeville, as early as 1714 saw, at least dimly, this paradox, which he wrote about under the title, *The Fable of the Bees; or, Private Vices, Public Benefits.* Going perhaps a little further than the economists later went, he wrote:

> All Trades and Places knew some Cheat
> No Calling was without Deceit
>
> Thus every Part was full of Vice
> Yet the whole Mass a Paradise

Scandalized complaints were lodged against the book; it was condemned and publicly burned; but Adam Smith and other economists—not to mention the average citizen of today— accept the idea that the vice of self-interest is transformed into a public benefit by the magic of economic process. Alexander Pope came closer than Mandeville to striking the right note with his couplet:

> Thus God and Nature formed the general frame
> And bade self-love and social be the same.

Whether or not one agrees with the theories of economic organization here put forward—and they are open to question as we shall see later—they are admirable in that they seek to do certain very important things. They are an ingeniously devised bridge between the individual and society, between freedom and order, between anarchy and organization, between atomism and pattern, between egoism and altruism. They are, if equally valid, as important in the realm of economics as the law of gravity is in astronomy. Both account for the forces that hold things together in worlds that have no central direction by deliberate human act.

Another pediment of standard economic theory is its ikon, as I shall name it, of a free, competitive society. The word "ikon" is used here without emphasis or color, but in its simple sense of a picture or image: the simplified abstraction of the economic system. The idea of representation only is implied, not worship. This ikon is intended to bear to the economic processes the same relationship as a terrestrial globe in a classroom bears to the complex and diversified world of reality.

Standard theory explores economic life by first assuming the existence of a perfectly functioning economic universe governed by pure competition—mostly competition based on price or quality. The universe is the basic plan, blueprint, diagram, or ikon. In it there are no monopolies—at least not in a "first approximation," and governmental intervention except as a neutral umpire is negligible. "Normality" is also assumed: there are no great wars, no great depressions, no great booms, no reconstruction after a great war. Changes of any sort, if admitted at all, are gradual and orderly. There is, however, fluidity. People are not tied down; workmen can go wherever wages are highest without regard to family ties or homeowning; capitalists can, without much friction or delay, convert from processing peanuts to making steel if the latter becomes a more profitable activity. Needless to

add, in such a system, people will always know where to
buy cheapest and sell dearest; they always seek the greatest
economic gain of the firm, or the least economic loss.

Everybody knows that the counterpart of such an ikon
does not exist, but standard economists are not perturbed by
this knowledge. They say that mathematics and the physical
sciences assume unreal and "perfect" entities, or ikons; why
should not economics? There is no such thing as a true
sphere or plane or completely efficient machine or perfect
vacuum, except in the mind; why should not economists
have their heroic unrealities or abstractions? The issue, they
would say, is not whether the ikon selected conforms to anything, but whether the ikon helps man to understand reality.
On this latter point they are completely reassured. Standard
economists are thoroughly convinced that the economic universe of their fantasy helps them to comprehend the real
world of economics.

We should, in this introductory chapter, also consider
the major divisions of standard theory. It is broken down
for convenience into four major subdivisions: the production, exchange, consumption, and distribution of goods. The
pattern of textbook organization suggested by these four
themes is the norm, which, however, has often been breached
and is changing gradually to conform to some of the newer
trends discussed in Chapter 6. These four terms have meanings in economic theory rather different from those attached to them by the ordinary man, especially the business man.

Under production the economist studies the economic
and general rather than the purely technical causes of higher

or lower production. He therefore assigns to technology or business the problem of finding out whether this particular machine does the same work as another with less fuel, or, whether that machine "pays for itself" in three or seven years. His study is on another plane but, in truth, it is sometimes hard to tell where technology leaves off and economics begins. For example, under production, standard economic theory makes much of the law of diminishing return. This law, applied to land, teaches us that if you putter and fuss with a crop, adding much water or Vigoro, you will soon come to a point at which additional results decline while effort and expense rise; ultimately, the increased benefits attributable to increased labor or fertilizer or water or other productive factor will cease to be rewarding—indeed, it is possible to kill plants with excessive care. Is this biology or economics? Whatever it is, economics claims the field.

The taproot of economics is not, however, its theory of production. It is the theory of value, which is equivalent to the theory of exchange. It is, in effect, the theory of how prices are arrived at: the prices of goods, of workers (wages), of capital (rate of interest), and so forth. Precisely why the theory of value should have played so important a part in economic theory is not too easy to explain on reasonable grounds, particularly in view of the fact that Adam Smith, the father of economics, took as his theme not value but rather the problem of how to increase the wealth of nations. As I shall explain more fully in a moment, Ricardo, the next great writer, took one aspect of value and made it the central problem of economics and his influence on academic theorists was perhaps greater than Smith's. In a sense, then, the answer is partly historical. It would be hard to refute the statement that study of the business cycle could just as well have been made the heart of economic theory. Indeed, that is precisely what is happening; and some of the newer and more venturesome writers of the day are focusing their textbooks on industrial fluctuations. We, however, shall follow the more conventional arrangement, but shall give business cycles full treatment in a later chapter.

Distribution is the third category of standard economic theory. Here is one of the many cases in which businessmen and economists use the same word to mean different things. To the former, distribution may mean finding outlets for their wares, relations with retailers, packaging, shipping, surcharges for broken lots, and the like. To the economist, distribution means the getting of income and study of differences in income. The kinds of questions he asks under this heading are: why do lenders get interest; why do landlords get rent; what causes high rents here and low rents there? It is really a special kind of study of prices or value. But instead of relating to the prices of consumer's goods like bananas or theatre tickets, distribution studies the prices of such things as factory labor; of land used for production; of commercial loans, the price of which is measured by the rate of interest.

It was this part of value theory that particularly interested Ricardo. He lived in a period when an economic conflict—indeed a class struggle—was going on between the landed aristocracy and the rising factory owners. The landowners wanted a high price for wheat and a tariff against importation, since their rents would be greater if wheat were dear. Factory owners wanted a low price for wheat because cheap grain meant cheap bread; and, in those days, when bread was an even greater item in the working-class budget than it is today, cheap bread meant low wages. Lower wages meant higher profits to industry—at least, so they thought. Now all of this is the raw material for a theory of distribution: determinants and relationships of wages, rents, profits. Ricardo's intense interest in such questions set the style in economic writing for over a century. But since, as will be shown in later chapters, distribution is really only a special case under a theory of value, successor economists have faithfully followed Ricardo by stressing value instead of distribution. Even such a great variant as Karl Marx follows Ricardo slavishly in this.

Until recently consumption has not been given much attention by economists. Except for a few conjectures used in formulating their theory of value, economists have tended to see little in consumption theories that would advance their work. There have been exceptions, like Thorstein Veblen, John A. Hobson and John M. Clark—but these three despite their genius are not in the direct line of orthodox succession.

Before we open the door to the inner sanctum of standard theory we must pause for a mathematical briefing, which is required reading only for those who do not know how to use a two-dimensional system of coordinates to locate a point—a much simpler matter than it sounds. Those who are violently allergic to simple mathematics will lose something by skipping these pages, but not too much.

If you are staying at the Mystic Hotel, corner of Fifth Street and Third Avenue in a city laid out on a gridiron pattern, you can explain to the folks back home just where you are in words, or by a diagram which says the same thing (Figure 2).

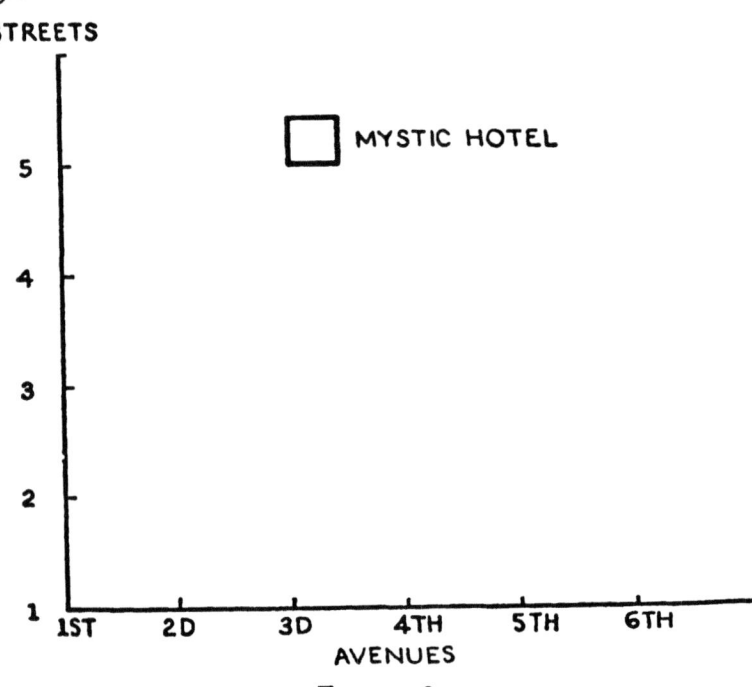

FIGURE 2

Now, we can use an almost identical method to say things about economics. If we want to say that Mr. Jones bought six neckties at two and a half dollars apiece, we can say it the hard way, with a diagram (Figure 3).

We can say something even more complicated. If neckties had been dearer, Mr. Jones might have bought fewer of them: only two at $10 each, or four at $5 each. If much cheaper, many more: ten at a dollar apiece. These three hypothetical transactions, plus the actual one of the paragraph above, may be represented on one diagram (Figure 4).

This has all been honest and straightforward. But now we

∶ NECKTIES

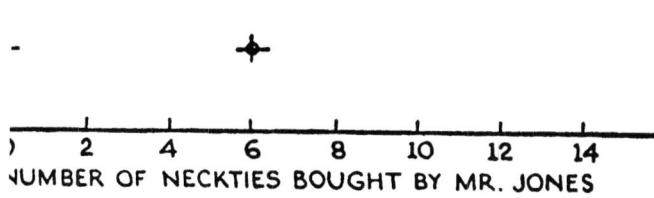

NUMBER OF NECKTIES BOUGHT BY MR. JONES

FIGURE 3

ƆF NECKTIES

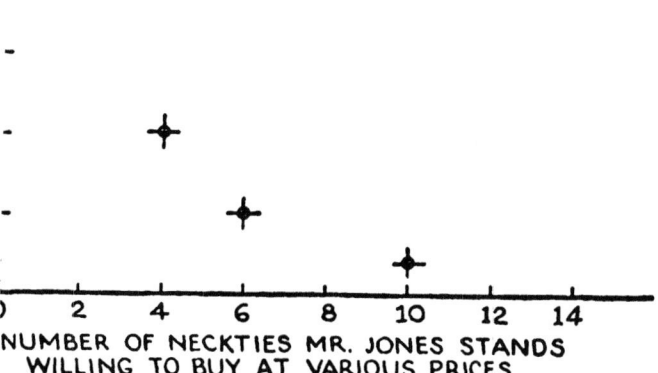

NUMBER OF NECKTIES MR. JONES STANDS
WILLING TO BUY AT VARIOUS PRICES

FIGURE 4

make our first inference. We connect the points by a smooth and continuous line (Figure 5).

Economists and mathematicians make the assumption, when such a smoothed line has been drawn, that it is reasonable procedure to take any point on that line and read off, from the horizontal and vertical scales, how many ties Mr.

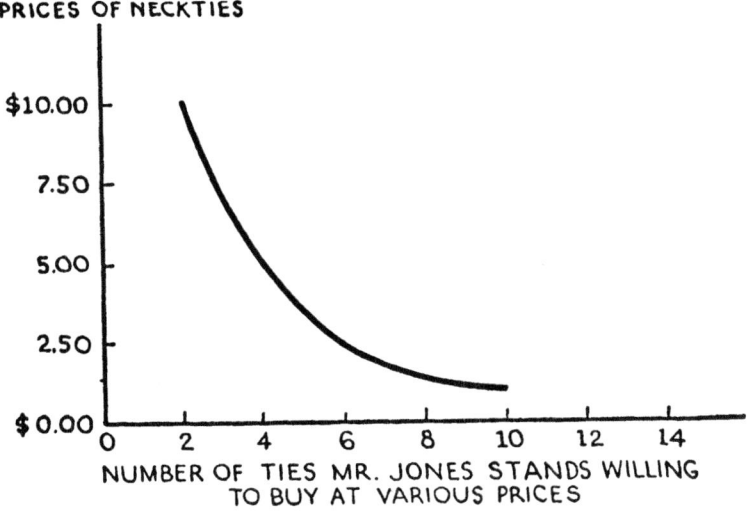

PRICES OF NECKTIES

NUMBER OF TIES MR. JONES STANDS WILLING
TO BUY AT VARIOUS PRICES

FIGURE 5

Jones would have bought at whatever price within the range of our data. Thus, in Figure 5, Mr. Jones is willing to buy five ties at $3.75, or eight ties at $1.25 (both approximately), as well as the combinations previously spoken of.

If the reader understands this system of saying things with points and lines located in a frame, there should be no difficulty with the diagrams of the next chapter.

The present chapter has cleared the way for the study of one brand of economic theory. It has called attention to the main categories of the science of wealth as seen by standard (or neoclassical) economists, set forth some of its assumptions, described its central ikon of a completely competitive system. Finally, we reviewed the principles underlying diagrams used in simple problems. With this out of the way, we should be able to make rapid progress toward the understanding of standard economic theory.

4. VALUES AND PRICES

THIS CHAPTER INQUIRES into what standard theory has to say about the value of things we use up as consumers. The prices of things we buy to resell or the cost of labor or raw materials fall into a different class and will be discussed in the next chapter. The word "value" in economics is very close in meaning to the word "price." There are some differences: "price" must always be stated in terms of a national currency, but value is a general concept; money itself is subject to the forces of valuation, therefore cannot be used as the ultimate yardstick. For many purposes, however, economists tend to use the words interchangeably, and we shall distinguish between them only when the problem in hand demands the making of a difference.

Why does a fountain pen cost 50 times more than a plain penholder? Why do radios and beds cost about the same? The first modern answer given to such questions was that the value of things depended on the average amount of labor congealed in them. On this theory, beds and radios must require about the same number of days or hours to manufacture. Adam Smith, David Ricardo, and Karl Marx are among the great names associated with this doctrine.

The labor-theory of value, even in its most naive form, has a certain usefulness, for many things that require lavish human effort are normally dear and many things that require very little labor are normally cheap. But it is only a rough guide. In a farmer's market, the same bunch of carrots may sell at 15 cents in the morning and at 10 cents in the evening of the same day; obviously the fifteen-cent carrots contain as much congealed labor as the ten-cent carrots.

Later economists, and even Adam Smith in his moments of inconsistency, expanded the labor theory to include all the costs of production. "Costs of production," incidentally, does not mean exactly the same thing to the economist as to the businessman. The economist includes a reasonable benefit to the businessman as a cost of production; the businessman, however, thinks of this same benefit as his profit: the difference between cost and selling price. The economist, viewing the entire process from the outside, recognizes the fact that businessmen would not produce or resell at retail if they did not receive a return; and this return is a cost, like any of the other costs of production.

The total-costs-of-production theory does, indeed, provide a fuller explanation of value than labor costs alone, but even this has flaws—indeed, the same flaws as the labor theory of value, for things often sell at more or less than their average cost. On the other hand, costs of production are a useful and often reliable guide to price or value.

The next major step in value thinking was to go to the other extreme. In the last quarter of the nineteenth century economists rose to say that nothing had any inherent value—no permanent value congealed *in it*. Human beings were the evaluators; nothing is cheap or dear but thinking makes it so. Stanley Jevons (1835–1882) and the Austrian, Karl Menger (1840–1921), are usually credited with having made this dialectical contribution to economic thought, though the same idea had come to the minds of others before them. But Jevons and Menger added a little twist to this idea which made the difference between a merely interesting statement and an analytical tool that economists could manipulate to get certain useful results.

Here is the little twist. Seeking the value of things-as-a-class is the wrong approach to value theory. What is important is to think of the usefulness of separate units in a class. Thus, as a consumer of butter, I want very little of it: just an occasional pat. Indeed, several hundred pounds of butter delivered at the same moment—remember I cannot resell under the ground rules of this chapter—would be quite a nuisance to me. On the other hand, there are times when I am willing to pay a dollar a pound; and for a small square served in a restaurant, I pay at the rate of two or three dollars a pound. A young man will be willing to pay a thousand dollars for his fiancée's engagement ring; but he cannot be induced to buy her a second or third diamond ring unless the price is appreciably lowered. He prefers to use the money to furnish the prospective home. Thus, value depends on units already available. That was the Jevonian-Menger twist: as consumers we evaluate one unit dearly; successive units are evaluated at less; and additional units may have no value at all.

This type of economic thinking, which goes forward by steps or units or dosages, is known as marginal analysis, for the last unit under consideration is the marginal unit. It is the unit which, though still desirable, has the least utility to the individual concerned, and therefore the one which marks the marginal utility of the product. It is, incidentally, not necessarily the last unit in a chronological sense—just as it is not really the seventh highball that makes the reveler sing *Sweet Adeline*. The seventh is exactly like the first highball, or any other in the series. It has no special virtue; it apparently produces a special effect only because it was preceded by six others like itself. Seven drinks cause singing; seventh drinks, in themselves, do nothing; they are inherently like the other drinks.

Jevons, Menger, and later, the American, John Bates Clark (1847–1938), and their disciples, worked on the marginal-utility concept of value, exploring every path suggested, including a few blind alleys. Many economists felt that these marginal savants had discovered something important and realized that the old labor and costs-of-production theories were deficient. Others felt that the new unit-valuation procedure alone could not explain much. It was subjective; it involved, they said, circular reasoning and the creation of an indefensible standard of social value. In this situation, Alfred Marshall (1842–1924), an English economist, appeared. He fused the marginal theories and the older theories in a way that composed outstanding differences between most of the pro- and anti-marginalists.

To understand what Marshall did we must go back a little. Men had long observed that supply and demand were related to price: reduce supply, up goes price; reduce demand, down goes price. This being true, why did Adam Smith, Ricardo, Jevons, Menger, and the others go out of their way to explain price by inventing the labor and other theories of value? Our answer must be a guess, but we have the right to assume that supply and demand seemed too obviously simple to them. Everybody knows that supply and demand exert a strong influence on price. But was there not something beyond this truism? Something deeper, more

permanent, more profoundly woven into the very fiber of
each commodity or perhaps in human beings themselves?
In posing this question they were partly right. To explain
value or price by glibly saying "supply and demand" is to
explain very little. Something more profound is needed.
But the something-more-profound is to be found neither in
the commodity to be valued nor in the soul searching of a
buyer, but in the words "supply" and "demand" themselves.
This is what Marshall discovered. His method, therefore,
was to scrutinize the full meaning of the phrase "supply and
demand." In doing this, he found that both the objective and
subjective theories of value had important contributions to
make, as we shall see.

What Marshall and his followers said, in effect, was something like this:

1. Adam Smith, Ricardo, Mill, and others, by embracing the
labor or cost-of-production theories of value placed emphasis
on supply, on the niggardliness of nature, on the obstacles to
supply. Jevons and Menger emphasize human valuation—that
is, demand. By studying supply *and* demand *and* their interaction a synthesis of the two viewpoints is made.

2. Problems of value would be clarified if we introduced the
dimension of time. What happens in the short run is quite different from what happens in the long run. By making proper
allowance for time we shall be able to break up a hard question
into several easier ones.

Here we have the guideposts of the standard economic
theory of value during much of the past half century. Its
task has largely been to study supply, demand, their action
and interaction over short and long periods, and of the
effect of price itself on the quantities bought or produced.

We now proceed to the main headings under the Marshallian outline and begin by scrutinizing in turn the words
"demand" and "supply."

Demand for consumers goods is governed by Jevons's principle of diminishing utility: the principle that the more we have of anything, the less we want any more of it, and, therefore, the less we are willing to pay for increased quantities of it. This principle is embodied in tables known as "demand schedules"—much used by the practitioners of standard theory. Here is an example of such a schedule, with comments.

MRS. SMITH'S WEEKLY DEMAND SCHEDULE FOR BUTTER

At $2.00 a pound, Mrs. Smith will not buy butter regularly; she will buy only for holidays, normally using margarine, goose fat, and other substitutes.

At $1.50, Mrs. Smith will buy one pound of butter weekly. This is only enough to use sparingly at the table. Her other butter needs are met by substitutes. She makes no cookies, cakes, or the like.

At $1.10, Mrs. Smith will buy 2 pounds of butter. She still uses substitutes for many of her needs, but the real thing can be used more freely at table and on a few cooked vegetables.

At $ .85, Mrs. Smith will buy 3 pounds of butter. No close substitutes are required, but butter is still too expensive for cookies and cakes.

At $ .70, Mrs. Smith will buy 4 pounds of butter. Cookies, cakes, are beginning to appear.

At $ .55, Mrs. Smith will buy 5 pounds of butter. Cookies, cakes, candies, hard sauce.

At $ .40, Mrs. Smith will buy 6 pounds of butter. Now there will be hollandaise sauce on broccoli. She will more freely bestow cookies on the neighbor's children.

End of Mrs. Smith's demand schedule for, even at $.30 or $.20 a pound, she has no uses for more butter, and will not buy more than 6 pounds weekly.

One thing to keep straight about such a schedule is that it expresses the whole range of demand at some given period of time only. It tells us nothing about how much butter Mrs. Smith will buy if she unexpectedly inherits a large fortune, or if her husband's salary is doubled—or reduced. Each price-quantity combination in the schedule equally well expresses her judgment on how best to balance a sacrifice of money with a benefit in the form of butter, but only under unchanged circumstances. It follows, then, that her demand is not greater when she buys 6 pounds at 40 cents than when she buys 2 pounds at $1.10. Both combinations express with equal accuracy her demand for butter and her reluctance to part with money. But if Mrs. Smith should suddenly become very wealthy, her demand might become greater. In that case, her entire schedule would have to be revised upward before it could express her willingness to buy more butter at every price now given in the schedule. Indeed, our revision might have to carry the price up to $50 or even $100 per pound for, if Mrs. Smith should really come into money, there would be no ordinary limit to the price she would be willing to pay.

Since geometric diagrams of demand will later be used to study price, let us at once convert Mrs. Smith's demand schedule into a geometric figure (Figure 6).

The reader may also wish to see how increased demand

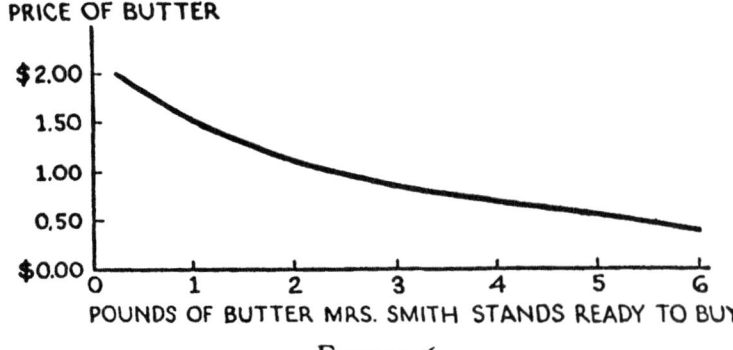

FIGURE 6

is represented on a diagram. The dotted line in Figure 7 represents the hypothetically increased demand of Mrs. Smith, after a modest inheritance. This is contrasted with the line representing the demand schedule already diagrammed (Figure 6).

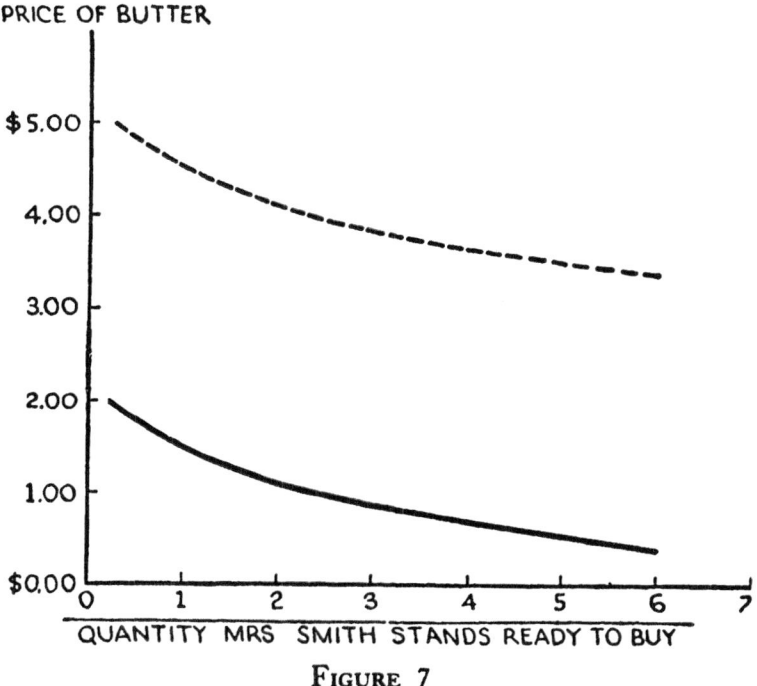

FIGURE 7

In the United States there are perhaps 35 million Mrs. Smith's. Each has a weekly butter schedule more or less like *the* Mrs. Smith. Some are much better off, and are willing to buy 7 or 8 pounds at $10 a pound. Some are poorer and will not buy freely even at 30 cents a pound. Some poor people are passionately fond of butter and will give up other things for it; some rich people do not like it and will buy very little of it, even if cheap. But, for all that, the majority of the schedules will follow the general pattern: more is bought at low prices than at high prices.

We can add up all the demand schedules of all housewives and get a collective demand schedule, like this:

AMERICAN HOUSEWIVES' COLLECTIVE DEMAND SCHEDULE
FOR BUTTER FOR ONE WEEK

Price per lb.	Approximate Purchase (in lbs.)
$10.00	1,000,000
5.00	4,000,000
2.00	11,000,000
1.50	15,000,000
1.00	23,000,000
.50	39,000,000

Demand schedules have the fatal defect of being unreal and unverifiable. They are useful tools, but not statements of fact. Attempts have been made to get real demand schedules. They do not yet amount to much. On the other hand the curve does meet at least some of the criteria of common sense and daily observation. If we should happen to know—and this we can know approximately—that housewives will buy x pounds a week at an average price of y cents per pound, then we are safe in saying that they will buy less if the price goes up and more if the price goes down (assuming no other significant change in the supply-demand picture, such as the discovery that eating no butter at all relieves hay fever). And that is the principal thing economists expect a demand curve or schedule to say.

There are a few more things to consider before we go on to study supply. Some things have what is known as elastic demand and some have inelastic demand. Table salt is a good example to illustrate inelastic demand. Cutting the price in half would not send the housewife rushing downtown to buy and feed her children more of this delicacy—that is, a substantial drop in price would have little effect on her purchases. On the other hand, a substantial rise in price would not vastly curtail the amount used. Many common objects of small value and infrequent use are characterized by inelastic demand: carpet tacks, Mother's Day cards, medicines, and the like. Elastic demand is the exact opposite; small increases or decreases in price have a powerful effect on demand. The best cuts of meat, good wines, fur coats, and the like are normally objects of elastic demand. On the whole there are few good substitutes for goods of inelastic demand and many for goods of elastic demand.

It should also be noticed that theory makes no distinction among certain biological qualities of demand. The poor family that cannot afford enough food is considered to have a low demand for food—not because they do not *want* food, but because their wants are ineffective in the market. They cannot bid up prices. Demand is not demand unless there is money behind it. In this sense of the word we must rule that most American women have no demand for mink coats, star sapphires, or Florida vacations. The proof is that the majority of women do not buy these things. And very poor people have but the feeblest demand for food, clothing, and shelter.

Supply is the converse of demand. The higher the price, the greater the amount that will be offered for sale. Some of the reasons for this are obvious; in the very short run many owners of things locked up in storage or of animals on the hoof will, if prices suddenly rise, quickly and gleefully unstore or slaughter their possessions for the favorable market; in the longer run, manufacturers are stirred to greater pro-

ductive efforts if prices, and therefore profits, promise to
remain high.

There are, however, less obvious and countervailing
forces at work. On the whole, there is a tendency for substantial increases in output to send up the costs per unit of
output. Farmers who seeing prices rise want to grow more
cotton must bring worse or dearer land under cultivation.
Manufacturers who want to produce much more will have
to pay penalty overtime rates to their workers; new and
inexperienced men will be employed; breakage and rejects
multiply. Both farmers and manufacturers will be competing for raw materials with others who are likewise induced
to increase production by rising prices. In brisk times, when
prices and demand are high, exasperating freight-car delays
may halt production entirely while overhead costs continue
to cost and cost and cost. There is, then, a limit, or at least
a brake, on the amount that is called forth by a rise in price
(or demand); that limit is the increasing cost of production.

Some manufacturers will, of course, for a while, be in
the pleasant position of shrinking their costs per unit as they
expand production. Some factories are so organized that
each new piece turned out costs less than the piece before it.
But this agreeable situation has its limits. Manufacturers
even in these circumstances, if they expand production far
enough, will eventually come to the point where each new
piece produced begins to cost a little more than the last, for
nobody can long escape the penalties of using inexperienced
workers, buying raw materials at higher prices, and, in general, producing more than his factory was "geared" to produce when it was first planned. It is also true that some costs
do not change much, regardless of the volume produced.
Many handmade articles requiring only simple tools and a
room of one's own belong to this class. Lace, peasants' wood

carvings, certain pampered crops like orchids are standard examples. Their costs conform to the principle of constant cost. Since the importance of constant-cost goods is probably small in the total of goods produced, economists nod pleasantly at this principle, but save their warmest smiles for goods produced at increasing costs.

In view of these facts it should not be surprising to learn that when economists draw cost-of-production curves ("average total unit costs," in economese), the usual curve first goes down and then up (Figure 8).

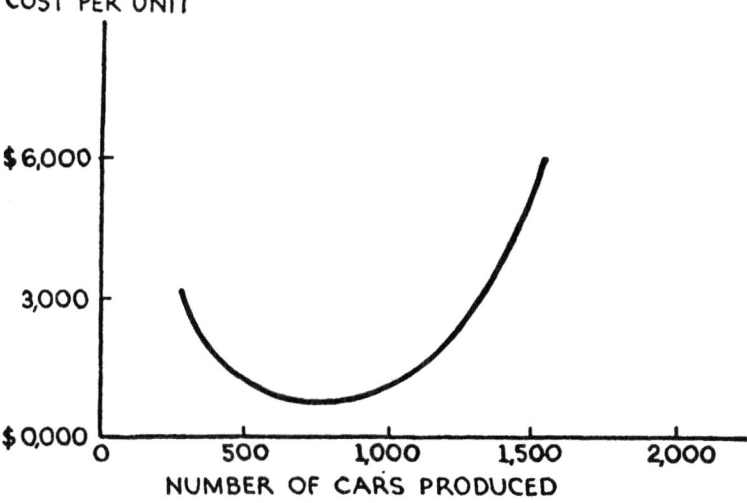

FIGURE 8

The part of the curve that goes downward gives recognition to the fact that the first few outputs of manufacture or farming may be expensive. If Ford were to cut down production to ten or twenty cars daily, each car would cost perhaps a hundred thousand dollars. A whole network of enormous plants would be eating up thousands of dollars hourly regardless of how few cars were coming off the assembly line. The bottom part of the curve, nearly flat on our diagram, indicates the more efficient area of production; presumably the Ford apparatus (as we are here imagining it) is "geared" to produce from 500 to 1,000 cars daily. Any production greater than a thousand a day becomes expensive again; therefore, the right-hand end of the curve rises.

Our brief analysis of cost-of-production leads us directly into a basic law of supply, a law as basic to supply as the law of diminishing utility is to demand. Here it is: a price increase calls forth a larger volume of production, which, in turn, may go so far as to increase the cost of production. This fundamental concept can, like demand, be shown on a schedule, and such a document is named a "supply schedule" —quite as significant in standard theory as is the demand schedule. Below is an example of a supply schedule and its appropriate diagram:

At the anticipated price per bu.	*Farmer Brown is willing to cultivate enough land and plant enough seed to produce*	*Remarks*
$ .50	100 bu. of corn	At this price there is so little money in corn that he would rather go fishing than devote himself seriously to corn growing; he will not use fertilizer and will do little cultivating; it will be almost a volunteer crop. But he does produce 100 bushels because he needs the cash proceeds for tax money.
$ .90	500 bu. of corn	At one dollar, corn is a fairly good crop; it warrants some fertilizing and cultivation. On the other hand, the price is not good enough to warrant renting additional land or taking on another hired man or neglecting cows, chickens, painting of barn, spraying apple trees.

At the anticipated price per bu.	Farmer Brown is willing to cultivate enough land and plant enough seed to produce	Remarks
$1.50	1,000 bu. of corn	At $1.50 corn is really worth a considerable effort and an appreciable outlay. Premium seed is worth buying; fertilizer may be used freely (even though its price may have gone up, since all farmers are expanding their production of corn). The barn and the apple trees may be neglected, and a hired man is worth taking on.
$2.00	1,300 bu. of corn	Two dollars a bushel is almost an unprecedented figure. At this price a 6 percent loan might be made to permit renting additional land. Not only the barn and the apple trees may be neglected, but also the cows and the chickens. An additional horse or hired man could be used, or perhaps, instead, the old tractor could be traded in for a new and more reliable one.
$2.50	1,500 bu. of corn	$2.50 is a fine price, but it has its drawbacks, because now everybody is corn-crazy. Fertilizer costs have risen. New tractors cannot be delivered until autumn. All nearby land has been taken up. Hired men are not available. But every effort should be exerted to grow and harvest a large crop.

At this point we reach—for all practical purposes—the end of Farmer Brown's supply schedule. Even at an anticipated $3.00 per bushel, he could scarcely try to produce more than 1,500 bushels. Costs have risen too much; wages have gone up; fertilizer has gone up, and, not only that, it is doubtful whether the plants can use extra food advantageously. There is some doubt as to whether he could make appreciably greater gains by producing more.

The supply curve is drawn below (Figure 9).

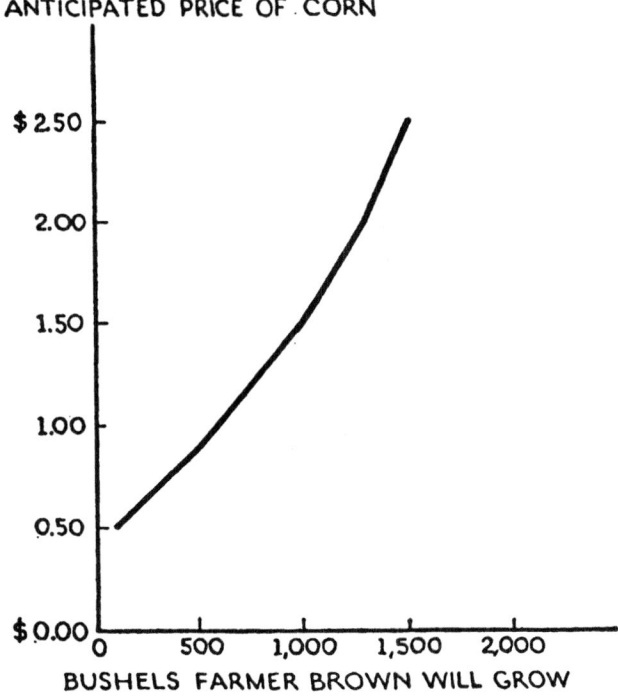

ANTICIPATED PRICE OF CORN

BUSHELS FARMER BROWN WILL GROW

FIGURE 9

The usual supply curve resembles (but is not identical with) the up-going, right-hand half of the average unit cost curve drawn in Figure 8. The down-going part at the left has been amputated, for we assume that farmers will never grow less corn at a high price when they can grow more at the same or lower price. Although the full length of the average total unit cost curve given in Figure 8 is useful to the economist for many purposes, the down-going part is omitted in many problems and what is left is like the supply curve. Stated otherwise, a supply curve may also be viewed as a cost curve.

Like demand curves, supply curves are creatures of the imagination. They are merely a way of saying two things:

1. As prices (price expectations) rise, producers are willing to put more goods on the market.

2. Omitting special cases, costs of production rise if the amount produced is appreciably increased (assuming that the economy is not in a deep depression or otherwise producing far below capacity).

And these are the principal things to be remembered about the simpler, more usual curves. They, too, may be elastic or inelastic: elastic ones refer to commodities whose production is greatly stimulated by small price increases; inelastic ones to commodities that respond less to price increases. In January, after Thanksgiving and Christmas feasting is over, most available turkeys have been consumed. A large price increase for turkeys in the dead of winter would not do much to bring forth appreciable quantities of the birds. On the other hand, the willingness of the public to pay only a little more for knitting needles, would probably bring forth enormous quantities.

So now we have demand schedules and curves and supply schedules and curves. What do we do with them? We bring together the schedule makers. In the theatre of our imagination we make demanders and suppliers confront each other in a market, and watch to see what happens. The demanders are potential buyers, with their schedules; the suppliers are potential sellers, with their schedules. The combined schedules below are a sort of box score of the economic game as it stands in a free and competitive wheat market just before sales are made.

COMBINED SUPPLY AND DEMAND SCHEDULES FOR A
SMALL WHEAT MARKET

If the price per bu. is:	Buyers are willing to buy:	And sellers are willing to sell:
$1.40	5,000 bu.	2,000 bu.
1.50	4,500	2,500
1.60	4,000	3,000
1.70	3,500	3,500
1.80	3,000	4,000
1.90	2,500	4,500
2.00	2,000	5,000

In a market to which buyers and sellers have come with the intentions summarized in the table above, the price will have to be $1.70, and the amount bought and sold will be 3,500 bushels. This is the only point at which there is a meeting of minds, and since a characteristic of a true market is that there is only one price, those who do not buy or sell at $1.70 withdraw. Some potential buyers and some potential sellers are disappointed. The disappointed buyers will presumably find substitutes, do without, or wait for the price to go down. The disappointed sellers will presumably hold their grain in storage, hoping for a better day; some may decide to use the grain directly to feed their chickens or other livestock. Figure 10 represents what is contained in the table and explanations above. The diagram shows the point at which the two sloping lines meet and cross. Price and quantity are found on the vertical and horizontal lines, respectively.

We still have to take into account the concept of Marshallian *time*, and its effect on price. *Time* in economics is really not time at all, but rather an attempt to distinguish between the shorter run and the longer run of events. We must make the assumption that the relations of supply and demand for a commodity call forth very different kinds of calculation and behavior on the part of a manufacturer or other supplier, depending on whether the kind of action he takes is rare, occasional, or customary. In many ways, the idea is not too much unlike our own behavior as consumers. On rare

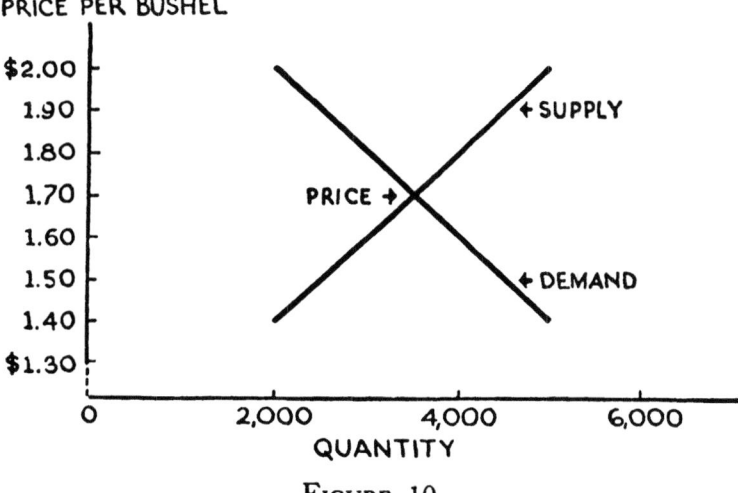

FIGURE 10

occasions, like honeymoons, we spend money at a rate that would be ruinous if persisted in for long. This would be our short-run rate of spending. Our long-run rate of spending is such that income and outgo must balance.

In similar fashion manufacturers, retailers, and other kinds of suppliers have short-term and long-term responses to the pricing process. The long-run response is easy to suggest; no producer will continue indefinitely in business unless prices received meet all costs of production incurred (including a reasonable return composed of profits or wages of superintendence or reward for risk, or whatever one may wish to name that something extra). Briefly, in the long run, prices must cover costs. Or, to put it differently, in the long run prices and costs tend towards equality in a competitive society.

The process involved in bringing about this equality in a completely competitive industry is fairly obvious. Let us assume the industry is that of plastic raincoats, a relatively new product. At first, the demand for these new coats is great, and the price is high. High prices invite a swarm of manufacturers to enter this business and swell production. The volume of garments now becomes so great that prices decline. Low prices will weed out the least efficient producers—that is, producers whose costs are above the prices offered. But weeding out these inefficient producers reduces the number of coats produced and tends to raise prices again, though not to so high a point as before. After seesawing for a while, the price-demand-supply relations of the industry will reach an equilibrium and cost of production will approximately equal price.

The easy statement, "cost of production will approximately equal price," conceals a very real difficulty. Whose costs? If the price of the raincoat (paid to all manufacturers) is $3.00, we may rightfully assume that the most efficient among them can turn the garment out for $2.50, others can do it for $2.75 or $2.85. Only the least efficient manufacturers among those remaining in the business (after the weeding-out process described just above) run costs up to $3.00. Thus, we must change our simple "price equals cost" formula to: "price equals the cost of the marginal producers." Or, we can move in the direction of even greater abstraction and assume that, in the very long run, in a truly competitive economic system, other things remaining unchanged, all manufacturers will become equally efficient and will incur approximately equal costs in making the same plastic raincoats.

In any event the thing really worth noting is that under the Marshallian analysis, a rough equality prevails between prices and costs of production in the long run. Some readers, disappointed in this seemingly obvious conclusion, may say that Adam Smith, more than a hundred years before had said substantially the same thing, and so had Ricardo and Mill and others. Well, the answer to that is that Smith, Ricardo, and Mill were really pretty fuzzy about cost of production and did not see the point at which cost of production is limited by demand. Marshall found subtleties that others had not seen, saw the interplay of supply and demand through cost of production, and gave us a more sophisticated theory. And, of course, he emphasized the difference between short run and long run. Only in the long run, he says, is there a tendency to equality between price and cost. In the short run the story is different.

In the short run costs play a minor role in price determination. If too many farmers bring too many raspberries to market on Saturday morning they will have to sell them for what they can get, regardless of cost. And yet there is a kind of cost to be taken into account even so; it is a psychological cost, no less real because it is not taken out of the pocketbook and counted out in dollars and quarters. It is an "opportunity cost." Here is how that works: if the farmers are offered too little for their raspberries many will withdraw them from the market because they would rather take the berries back home and use them within the family— deep-freeze them, make jellies, marmalade, or give them away to appreciative neighbors. They might, besides, be able to salvage the quart boxes and crates in which the berries are packed and use them some other time. Thus we find that even when producers are in a ruinous and temporary squeeze between heavy supply and light demand, they still must be offered a price high enough to cover the cost of an alternative use for the berries (and the crates). This principle was implicit in the supply schedule given on page 66, which noted that a farmer might rather go fishing than grow much corn at 50 cents a bushel, or keep fences in repair rather than strain himself unduly to grow several thousand bushels at a dollar.

If, on the other hand, few farmers bring berries to market and if the demand is strong, then berries will, on that market, sell very high—quite possibly at a price two or three times higher than the cost of production of the least efficient grower. This observation further confirms the general principle of short-run price, namely, that cost of production plays only a small role in determining price. The principle works both ways: towards excessively low and excessively high prices.

At this point, a bewildered reader may justly complain to the author as follows:

"At the beginning of the chapter you talked about Ricardo and how he thought that value was something inherent in an object—and it looked as if we were going to find out what it really is that gives things their value if congealed labor does not. Instead, you end up with a lot of diagrams of imaginary situations and play a kind of educated tick-tack-toe and assume that where curves intersect you can read off price and quantity—which are imaginary, anyway. Who cares about quantity, anyhow? I thought we were talking about the true value of a thing. Look, I own an Empire table, genuine antique. I want to sell it. I want to know what its true worth is. I don't care about marginal costs, or any other kind of costs. I want to know what its true economic value is so that I can sell it at the right figure. I ask you, and you wave little lines at me. Doodlers, that's what you are! If I want to know what the value of my table is, I'll call up a dealer I know in Dedham. He's got more economics in his little finger than Jevons and Marshall had in their whole bodies! I wouldn't let them appraise the pants of the postillion of my grandmother's paternal aunt."

We have called this a just complaint. But, actually, economists cannot appraise the exactly proper or fair price of any given commodity. They do not profess that they can. This makes them, at best, only sage counselors in such practical affairs as determining the value of a public utility which is expected to make a "fair" profit on a "just" valuation. Economists have only a little light to shed, and that little is on a process rather than on the fixing of absolute prices.

The diagrams function at their best when a change is introduced into a given situation, like a tariff. By using them and the principles discussed above we can discover that tariffs will normally raise the price of things imported, and, if produced at increasing cost, by an amount smaller than the amount of the tariff duty. Or that, if decreasing-cost goods (television sets, say) are taxed, the consumer pays more than the amount of the tax, assuming, of course, full and free competition.

Monopoly prices are a special case and are rather easier to get at. Suppose a man really invents a better mousetrap, after all, and patents it—one that does not snap at your fingers, is permanently baited, and automatically reduces the carcass to a small heap of sterile ashes. He makes his traps in small quantity at first and finds they cost him three dollars apiece. Since his product is unique he has no guide in the form of a going price for a similar gadget already on the market. At first, his marketing policy is a complete blank, except for one fact: price must cover his costs and yield a profit. In these circumstances it would not be completely absurd to charge as much as $25.00, for surely several hundred Americans every year would wish to buy so efficient a trap. Neither would it be absurd to charge $4 or $5, for then tens of thousands of customers, annually, would be able to buy. The inventor would, if wise, balance the advantage of small sales at a high profit against mass sales at a low profit.

After puzzling out the price-quantity enigma, he may reach the conclusion that the best chance for greatest total profit is to pursue a medium course; medium price—perhaps $7.50—and medium sales.

But one more thing must be taken into account. Our inventor had figured that his costs would be $3.00 per trap. This figure is meaningless, except as a sort of anchor to his calculations. Costs of producing vary with quantity. Perhaps the cost will go down to $2.50 if a thousand are produced monthly. And if ten times that many, costs may go down even lower. Now our mouse-catching man has to juggle a third variable, cost. Selling price, quantity sold, cost, these three sliding figures have to be adjusted in such a way as to yield a maximum gain. He may discover that he should cut his selling price far below $7.50, hereby picking up several new layers of customers; and, because of the reduced cost per unit as well as great volume, he may realize an even

greater over-all profit than his earlier calculation had indicated.

There are other ways of maximizing gains. For the drawing room, a de luxe, chromium-plated mousatorium might be
devised to sell at $10.00; while a less elegant utility model
for use in kitchen, attic, and lakeside cabin, might sell for
$5.00. Or, a $15.00 market might be cultivated in the United
States and a $3.00 market developed in Latin America.

The key question is, of course, the aggregate demand
schedule—that is, how many mousatoria will be bought at
what prices. At first, our inventor will be fumbling in the
dark. It is only after he has had some preliminary marketing
experience that he can make useful predictions concerning
the number of potential customers he shuts out or picks up,
respectively, by a 20 percent increase or decrease of price.

In any event, we learn from this that even a monopolist
is not completely free to set prices at any arbitrary figure
—granted, of course, that he wishes to reap the greatest
possible profit from his monopoly. A very high price reduces sales and may cause him to produce at high cost. A
more modest price may add to profits through heavier sales
and by permitting the well-known economies of large-scale
production to operate.

This chapter can be summarized in a few basic propositions:

In a purely competitive society the interaction of the
forces of supply and demand determines value or price. But
this statement is scarcely more than a truism. To give it content we must clarify our thinking about both supply and
demand, and watch them interact with each other and with
price over long and short periods.

Demand is characterized by a decline in the amount demanded as desire is satisfied, and by its elasticity (or inelasticity).

Supply is characterized by an increase in the amount produced as costs rise, and by its elasticity (or inelasticity).

In the short run supply is fixed; price therefore depends more on the state of demand than on the costs of production.

In the long run, price and cost of production tend toward equality; that is, costs, or the forces of supply, play a greater role than demand.

The monopolist adjusts price, volume of sales, and costs in such a way as to get the largest possible gain.

The purpose of this type of analysis is not to appraise the value of an object, but, rather, to see what happens to a given price when some significant change, like the application of a tax or bounty, occurs.

And that just about ends basic training in the theory of value on a competitive market that sells only consumers' goods.

5. THE PRICE OF LABOR, LAND, AND CAPITAL

THE SECOND GREAT topic of economic analysis under its theory of value is the distribution of income. Study of this subject might be expected to throw light on why Mr. Jones has a five-digit income, while Tony gets $973 a year, but, as was revealed in the preceding chapter, economic science is unable in these matters to reach precise figures. It can say that this, that, or the other economic event may take place if high salaries or profits are decreased, or low wages augmented; it can find reasons for disparity of incomes; it can suggest ways of increasing the income of any class of income receivers. But it cannot put actual price tags on their services.

Economists usually speak of four groups of income receivers. Each group represents one of the four agents or factors required to produce goods and services. The four factors of production are:

1. Labor, meaning almost any kind of labor, head, hand or back. Labor may be pleasant, as it presumably is for various types of artists and professionals, but it is frequently distinguished from physical or mental play (like tennis or chess)

by its disagreeableness. "Labor is the use of the body for other than pleasure," as one of my bright sophomores put it. The reward of labor is named wages.

2. Land, meaning almost any gift of nature, like a waterfall or an Adirondack lake, as well as land itself. Again the sophomore speaks: "Land is God's gift to man—it does not imply only dirt." The reward of land goes to its owner, of course; its name is rent.

3. Capital, meaning a variety of things not always too clearly defined or differentiated. It may mean investment funds, but it may also mean the physical things bought by investment funds, like the machine in a factory or the stocks held by a retailer for sale. Like rent, the reward is a property income, and is named "interest."

4. Entrepreneurship, which refers to the special productive service of the policy-making person or board of any business establishment; to the special contribution of the big boss—his judgment, ability to combine land, labor, and capital in the most fruitful proportions, labor-management skill, inside knowledge, market information, lucky hunches, sixth sense about business affairs, good contacts with persons informed on business and political matters, discretion, poker face, ability to pick good lieutenants, aplomb when testifying before legislative committees, and the like. The entrepreneurial reward is named profit.

The classification of the four factors of production is not thoroughly satisfactory. Who, for example, in a modern corporation, is the entrepreneur? The Chairman of the Board, the President, or the stockholders who must vote on certain basic policies? Why is such a sharp difference made between land and capital? Why does capital have such widely different meanings? Is not one of the most productive assets of any civilization its accumulation of knowledge, its discipline, its ability to absorb inventions into its culture? And where is all this listed among the productive factors? It is doubtful whether any economist is thoroughly happy about this four-leaf clover of productive agents, but it is the best we have and we shall use it.

Some of the nineteenth century replies given to the question of who gets what income (in short, the theory of distribution) should claim our attention, even though the replies have been superseded. They are inherently interesting and still linger on in current theories.

There were several wage theories in the Ricardian era—about 1825 to 1850—but perhaps the most basic and striking one was the subsistence theory. This theory held that wages would always be a sum required to enable the wage-earning class to keep alive and reproduce itself. Never more, never less. A member of the House of Commons in a parliamentary debate relating to the price of wheat (hence bread), reflected then-current economic thought when he said that the proposed legislation had nothing to do with the working class. Whether wheat went up or down in price, the worker would still get only his crust. One rather obvious trouble with this theory is that the word "subsistence" is very elastic. What is mere subsistence to a modern working-class family in New York City would have been undreamt of riches to a family out of Dickens.

As a sort of companion piece to this doctrine was the famous Malthusian theory of population. Thomas Robert Malthus (1766–1834) argued that an increase in wages would call forth a considerable increase in wage-earners' babies—the better you are fed the more babies you have and the more of them survive. For a while this might be true, but presently there would be more babies than baby food; for the human race if properly fed grows faster (says Malthus) than food supply. Ultimately the overpaid workers would again have underfed children because of the competition for foodstuffs. And population would again decline. The theory hasn't worked out very well because our control over nature has exceeded anything Malthus could have dreamed of and because birth control has become more or less respectable. His theory has been and still is the center of controversy: whatever its defects, one must at least concede that a finite world cannot support infinite additions to its population; whatever its merits one must at least concede that the world has not had to face the issues that Malthus presented in the way he presented them.

A second recipient of income is the landlord. His income is rent. How the early economists hated landlords! They represented a decaying feudal aristocracy, opposed to progress, opposed to the changes being made by the rising industrial classes. The landlord was something of a parasite in the eyes of the busy, thrifty, manufacturers who were just beginning to consolidate their strength, and therefore also in the eyes of the economists, who championed their cause. His share in the distribution of income, rent, was a sort of parasitic share, defensible only because private property was defensible, not because the landlord did anything to deserve his rent.

By *rent*, the economist meant then, and means today, the amount that is paid for land only or for some other gift of nature. It does not mean the hire of a driv-urself car or rowboat by the hour, or of a house for twenty years.

Roughly, and perhaps a little too simply, rent was the difference between the produce of the worst land worth cultivating and any piece of better land. If a nation "wants" a billion bushels of corn a year and if to grow that many bushels a nation has to resort to fifth-grade land, then fifth-grade land yields no rent. But the four better grades do. And each higher grade yields higher rent than the preceding grade. If fifth-grade land yields ten bushels an acre and first-grade land yields forty bushels, then the rent is equal to the difference between the two yields, and the landlord is able to claim a sum of money equal to the difference in value between ten and forty bushels. We must, of course, assume that the difference in yield results from the land only; turned around, this means that all farmers used exactly the same amount of labor, fertilizer, skill, and so on, per acre.

The same idea is applicable to city land. If, with the same investment of capital and wage bill, you can make more money by putting your store at 37th Street and Broadway than in one of the more pastoral sections of Staten Island, then obviously you turn over a greater sum to the owners of land in the busier parts of Manhattan.

This simple and, on the whole, common-sense theory can be made more complicated by taking into account the differences between extensive and intensive use. Obviously you do not put the same kind of store in the heart of Manhattan that you do in the outskirts of Staten Island. You cultivate the rich Manhattan site more intensively; that is, you build a higher building, employ more salesmen, supply a larger variety of services, carry more stock, and advertise heavily. And this kind of activity requires amendments to the simple statement of the rent theory given above—which fact we may here recognize but need not pursue farther.

The general rent theory was anti-landlord because it suggested that the landlord, who exercises neither thrift, foresight, industry, nor his back, gets an income merely by virtue of ownership. Moreover, he benefits from an expanding society. As population increases and as worse and worse land comes into cultivation, each parcel already cultivated is promoted, as it were, into the next higher grade and gets a higher rental. The landlord made no productive effort and therefore really deserved no reward. And this brings up another idea of the nineteenth century that dominated economic thinking.

During part of the century, economists thought a lot about the role of pain—or, better, absence of pleasure—connected with production. The idea sprang from the mind of Jeremy Bentham, who figured out a pleasure-pain psychology particularly suitable to economic thought.

The essentials, when adapted to economics, are that the labors of production are disagreeable while the act of consuming is pleasant. The world is most economically run when the pleasures of consuming goods and services are greatest relatively to the pains of production. And each pain must have its reward. Wages reward the pain of working. But the landlord feels no pain at all.

Interest on money lent (our third form of income) was thought of during the nineteenth century and later, as a reward for a pain undergone. Nassau Senior (1790–1864) diagnosed the pain of interest as the pain of abstinence—that is, the kind of pain you get from not spending all of your pay check straight off. It is the pain produced by practicing the sometimes difficult virtue of thrift. Since the thrift of many people eventually finds its fulfillment in the creation of capital, in productive instruments like locomotives, steel mills, telegraph networks, the virtue is productive and worthy of reward. This theory was ridiculed by those who wrote ironically about how the Rothschilds, Astorbilts, and others were suffering the tortures of the damned because they were saving so hard. The theory was then revised in various ways. One revision takes into account the concept of preference—time preference: "I want my ice cream *now*," sobs the four-year-old, and presumably adults feel the same way, too. Whatever guise the theory takes—and it has taken several guises and disguises—some sort of emotional cost clings to it, even if the cost is not downright pain. The latest and most fashionable revision is that of the late John Maynard Keynes. To him interest is "the premium which has to be offered to induce people to hold their wealth in some form other than hoarded money." [1] It is a kind of bribe we take to induce us to part with liquid forms of wealth and allow them to be frozen.

Much of the pleasure-pain psychology has been dropped out of modern economics. The subsistence theory of wages is no longer accepted. The rent theory can, if one wishes to look at things that way, be applied to other factors than land and, in any event, needs more careful statement to have validity. Today, standard economists think of incomes as nothing but prices. Smith's income of ten thousand a year is the price of his services, not much different from the price of a banana. If the interest on your capital is five thousand annually, it is so because that is the price people are willing to pay for the use of the money you have saved or inherited. There is no difference in principle between the price of labor, land, and capital and the price of a pork chop that is eaten up. In all cases price is the result of the interaction of

[1] S. E. Harris, Ed., *The New Economics: Keynes' Influence on Theory and Public Policy* (New York, Knopf, 1947), p. 187. The quotation is from an essay written by Keynes himself and included in this volume.

the forces of supply and demand. But the nature of demand and supply is a little different. It is in the peculiarities of demand and of supply for land, labor, and capital that we find a reason for distinguishing between the prices of these and the prices of things we use up. Let us look at some of these peculiarities, first of demand, then of supply.

The demand for land, labor, capital is a special kind of demand—or, rather, the demand exists only in a special group of the population, namely, the managers or the entrepreneurial group. In the last chapter we studied everybody's demand for an infinity of things that could be directly used up like food, or worn out like diapers, or that, like perfume or fireworks, agreeably stimulated the senses. Here we study the demand of a few people for a very few categories: land, labor, capital. The demand*ers* are the managers, or entrepreneurs. It is true that many of us who are not entrepreneurs are in the market for the *labor* of servants, or *land* to build houses on. But it will make things easier if we forget about that, and think only of the demand of factory owners, store owners, bankers and the like, for the land, labor, and capital used strictly for business purposes. We should, however, realize that many of us who are not ordinarily entrepreneurs may have our entrepreneurial moments. If he rents out a house he owns, even the most absent-minded, up-in-the-clouds college professor is partly an entrepreneur, and many demure spinster schoolmarms think about their stocks and bonds as shrewdly as the most hardened businessmen. A large class of entrepreneurs, frequently overlooked, is the farming class. When all is said and done, however, the group of demanders on whom we focus our interest in this chapter is a much smaller group of demanders than that of the last chapter.

The demand for land, labor, and capital is then a derived rather than a direct demand. We want bananas because they are nutritious and taste good. The average businessman or entrepreneur does not want workers or machines for such reasons, but because workers and machines are needed to produce things that they can sell to us. Many of us stop eating bananas only when some sort of inner voice tells us that to eat more might have consequences. Entrepreneurs never stop hiring workers for this simple biological reason, or because workers no longer please them, or because it would be more fun to use their money on some other factor of production or on candy. The factory owner stops hiring workers and renting land and buying capital largely because he thinks that the demand for his product does not warrant an expanded output. The same general idea is true of land and productive machinery. The amounts bought are always related to the amount of the finished product that the con-suming public will and can absorb, or, at least, that entre-preneurs think will be absorbed.

Within limits, each agent of production (land, labor, capital) may be used in place of the others. The ground for an airport may be leveled as in China during the Second World War with shovels, baskets to carry earth in, and swarms of unskilled laborers; or as in this country, with bulldozers, steam shovels, trucks, and relatively few workers, most of them highly skilled. Either way may be cheap or dear, depending on many things; but what I want to call attention to here is that labor and capital are often inter-changeable. The same thing applies to land. If land is cheap, a thousand-bushel wheat crop may be grown on a hundred acres without much use of fertilizer or managerial skill or labor. If land is dear, fertilizer, tender care, and scientific knowledge will be used to grow the same crop on half the acreage; that is to say managerial skill, labor, and capital are substitutes for land. In short, demand for one factor of production may often be converted, if price is too high, into demand for another.

Entrepreneurs will ever be watchful to keep down costs, and in doing this they will be constantly comparing the usefulness to them of less labor, more capital, more land, less capital. This is partly a technological question, of course, for technology often dictates the only reasonable combination of the factors of production. A bus or truck, for example, has one seat, one wheel, and one set of pedals; three drivers operating these at the same time would wreck the vehicle. But technological considerations are not always the determining ones. Often the determining factor is purely economic; it is cheaper to use more men than additional machines, or more fertilizer than additional acres.

Some economists have intimated that the reward of each factor is equivalent to the marginal product of the factor. We can understand this better if we take a concrete case. A factory is geared to use somewhere between 80 and 120 men, the employer already has 80 men, and his figures show he could probably use five more advantageously. They cost him $50 a day, but their production increases his income by $60 a day. The employer is satisfied with the results of hiring 85 men and thinks perhaps it is worth hiring five more. These, too, cost $50; but this group of men adds only $51 to his income. He is still ahead of the game though he has now almost reached the margin. Considering the kind of plant he has, its internal organization, the state of demand for his product, its price, and the costs of raw materials, he sees that five *more* men would not yield $50, so he stops hiring men because wage and marginal product have become approximately equal and because hiring more threatens a loss. It must be made very clear that each quintet taken on is quite as efficient in a personal sense as the previous quintet or any other group employed. They at last become inefficient, in the eyes of *this* employer, only because his factory is overbalanced with labor.

But to return to the original proposition. At some point, it no longer pays the entrepreneur to take on additional land labor, or capital, not only because of the general state of demand for his product, but also because he has worked out the best combination of the three factors for his firm. In short, his demand for the factors stops when he has reached a certain state of balance.

Demand for entrepreneurs presents something of a puzzle. Demand for them is quite different from the demand for labor or land or capital or bananas. The entrepreneur is the demander of land, labor, and capital; but who demands the demander? He cannot be hired like a workman, or even like an exceptionally gifted executive, for he is the big boss who hires even the gifted executive. Some economists get around this by saying there is a "social demand" for the entrepreneur. What I suppose they mean is that if opportunities for making a profit arise, such as the outbreak of war or the unfolding of a real-estate boom, new and additional men will spring up to get the new business. The quality of this "social demand" seems to be quite different from the demand for the other factors of production. Indeed, standard theory is rather weak on the subject of the entrepreneur and his share, profits.

One way to treat the profits puzzle is to argue that profits do not really exist. They are illusion. This, of course, does not mean that the entrepreneur gets no reward at all. He can evaluate his services as a sort of supermanager at ten thousand or fifty or a hundred thousand dollars a year. This amount may be looked upon as his wage; and if there is that much money left in the till he can award it to himself. From one viewpoint this would be a cost of production and not a profit, provided that the self-award is in line with salaries paid elsewhere in the economy for work of equal responsibility and requiring an equally "big" man. But if, after awarding himself an appropriate wage, there is still some money left over, then that is a profit.

Now according to some theorists, such profits under competition are exceptional and temporary. The reason is that great profits in any industry attract entrepreneurs away from less profitable industries; more goods will then be produced by the new firms; more goods means lower prices and that means extinction of profits for everybody. Thus the lasting reward of the entrepreneur, as entrepreneur, is his wage of superintendence rather than his profit. But this, admittedly, can happen only in a static society in which competition is keen in all industries, and in which any newcomer may set up shop. A large number of contemporary economists think of profit as being a reward for uninsurable risks—risks unlike those of fire or theft, which are insurable.

The entrepreneur-in-the-flesh—not the abstraction of theory—often gets other rewards to swell his total income. He may own the land on which he builds his store or his factory. His bookkeeping should take account of the fact that part of his total income is rent, part interest, and part entrepreneurial reward. Unless he does this, he has no way of knowing whether or not he would be better off if he sold his property, invested the money in government bonds, and accepted a soft job on the city payroll.

So much for a quick look at demand for the four factors of production. It is a derived demand, it seeks the virtue of productivity; it is affected and limited by the substitutability of one factor for another. It is a concept that does not fit the entrepreneur precisely.

There are even greater differences between consumers' goods and the factors of production on the supply side than on the demand side. If people want more consumers goods, for example radios, and are willing to pay more for them, the forces underlying supply will quickly respond by increasing the number of radios. Increased price does not, however, as certainly call forth more land, labor, and capital.

The quantity of land, for instance, is not appreciably increased by high prices; it is fixed. Some land can be "made" or redeemed by irrigation, filling-in, pushing back the sea with dikes, and so forth; improved transportation may "bring" some land "nearer" a given center and may relieve population pressure on that center; still other things can be done, but, speaking broadly and strictly, an increased demand (or price) does not call forth *new* land. It may, of course, call forth new sellers of old land, but that is something else. Other important gifts of nature, like waterfalls, caverns, magnificent scenery, are similarly fixed in quantity. Thus, the rents paid for the use of land are more vigorously affected by the state of demand than by variations in supply. This explains why, when demand improves, fortunes can be made out of relatively small parcels. There is no way of increasing the land area of Manhattan Island, and that is why land values there have not merely gone up—they have become fantastic. On the other hand, inability to shrink the amount of land available locally when demand falls helps to explain why families that once were rich can now be pathetically "land poor."

A higher wage for labor may call forth a larger amount of labor, but not necessarily so; that depends. If my income is so small that my wife and children have to work, contrary to family principles, any appreciable increase in my wage will take them off the labor market—even if their wages go up at the same time. Higher wages may call forth certain new wage earners, of course, but the total number at work may decline. Nonindustrial workers in the tropics who formerly could be induced to work two days a week may now work only one day if wages are doubled. In parts of Africa, where something of the kind once occurred, the government, in collaboration with employers, placed a tax on natives; the effect of the tax was to confiscate part of the wage, thus driving the natives back to work. More experienced industrial workers in the temperate zones usually work out their full week even if wages are increased, but there is a long-term tendency for them to seek a shorter work week.

It is, of course, easy enough to increase the number of workers in any given vocation by the offer of higher wages. We may lure people into welding jobs or teaching by increasing wages in these vocations. But this may be at the expense of other vocations. A general increase in the supply of labor results from an increase in population, and it is not easy to discover an acceptable and constant relationship between high wages and increasing population.

Interest is the income associated with capital, or ownership of capital. Although the first thing likely to come to the economist's mind when the word "capital" is uttered is a machine of some sort, economists do not really think of interest as a payment for the use of the machine. They think, rather, of the rate of return on investment funds, or of a payment for saving. Capital can be defined as something produced by man but not consumed by him—at least, consumed only indirectly by being used up when it helps to produce other goods. It is something saved out of the things produced in order to help produce more things. Interest may therefore be considered as a payment for saving and for making the savings available to investors.

The supply of capital or savings involves a number of tricky ideas as well as new and untested theories. The upshot seems to be that all but extreme changes in the price of capital —rate of interest—do not much affect savings. For purposes of security, and for other reasons, we save something even if we get no reward at all in the form of interest. We seem to save about as much whether the rate of interest is 2 percent or 3 percent (a 50 percent increase, let it be noted). On the other hand, if we could, without increased risk, get a very high return, say 9 percent, we would probably save appreciably more than we do.

So now, again, we have studied the forces of supply and demand; this time, the peculiarities of the supply and demand for the factors of production. These can be translated into curves which are used as the basis of analyzing problems, as was explained in the last chapter on the prices of goods consumed.

We can summarize this chapter by saying that, in standard theory, incomes, whether from land, capital, or labor, are the prices paid for the use of these factors of production by the entrepreneur. Such prices are determined by the interplay of the forces of supply and demand, as in the case of the prices of things we consume. But, as we learned in the preceding chapter, to say that a price is determined by supply and demand is a facile half-truth. We must study the anatomy of supply and demand for each factor if we are to have any insight into the process of price determination.

6. RECENT TRENDS IN STANDARD THEORY

THE LAST THREE CHAP-
ters have presented the
hard and traditional core
of standard economic theory. Before 1930 any book written
on the modest scale of this one might have ended its discussion of standard theory here. But the past quarter century
has been productive of so much new writing and of so many
new theories that we must stop to give them consideration.

In a rather good sense, standard theory is more disorgan-
ized and asymmetrical than the last few chapters have suggested. There has been a wholesome questioning of old
ideas; some principles, like Say's law (p. 43) have been
thrown out. The result is that standard theory is today in a
rather yeasty state. Indeed, the distinguished Professor J. R.
Hicks has spoken of the possibly total wreckage of the
greater part of (standard) economic theory. But the chaos
and possible wreckage are generally welcomed; standard
economists themselves are—most of them—delighted with
the new vitality of their science.

The most important recent development is that standard
theory has, through John Maynard Keynes (1883–1946)

unreservedly recognized the profounder forces at work in economic depressions. The magnitude of this development cannot be thoroughly appreciated unless one realizes how reluctant standard theory was, until Keynes, to extend to boom-and-bust full recognition as an especially important phenomenon in economic life. The older standard theory prevented economists from viewing depression as anything other than a disagreeable situation that would soon straighten itself out—and straighten out sooner if men would only let economic laws go to work without interference. As a result of Keynes's influence economists are appearing who take, as the central issue of economic thought, fluctuations of income (or the business cycle) rather than the theory of value. (Justice will be done to this very great innovation in standard economic thinking in Chapter 12, which discusses business cycle theory in detail.)

Keynes has also plowed up the field of interest. To him the rate of interest has little to do with the pains of saving, but rather with the desire to keep property in liquid form, that is, not tied up in investments, but kept in the convenient form of money. He has, with his American counterpart Alvin Hansen, stirred up controversy on the subject of the "mature economy"—whether capitalism is getting stiff in the joints and needs large injections of governmental spending to keep it spry. He is generally credited with having brought economics back to its first tasks in the day of its greatest glory, of Adam Smith and Ricardo, when economists were not only scholars but also public men who influenced government policy fundamentally. Certainly many governmental economists on the Continent, in England, in the United States, and in the secretariat of the United Nations and its specialized agencies are Keynesoid, and some of the statistical work of these agencies is now adapted to the Keynesian categories.

Ranking second in importance to Keynes's work is that of a group of students who have specialized in questions of an imperfect market and of quasi-monopoly. The names are Piero Sraffa, Joan Robinson, and Edward Chamberlin. From their pens we have statements, theories, and diagrams that justify us in questioning the basic ikon of classical theory: a freely competitive economic society. Professors are even asking whether economists might not as well begin with an economic system based on monopoly or partial monopoly and consider instances of perfect competition to be the exceptions. Why not, indeed? To be sure, this means a complete reversal; for, as preceding chapters have shown, the great generalizations assume perfect competition to be the rule and imperfect competition exceptional. In the United States 250 large companies control about two thirds of our industrial facilities. Elsewhere the situation resembles that in the United States.

The new theories make certain useful amendments to the principle of diminishing returns (p. 7), which does not successfully explain why entrepreneurs often stop producing before the point of diminishing return is reached. Less theoretical and more closely related to everyday experience are the discussions of market imperfections caused by brand names (like Beautyrest and Coca-Cola) and by the loyalty of consumers to those names. Resistance to substitution is acknowledged to be greater than was originally assumed by standard theory. Even though Suds-O and Ah-Foam are substantially the same soap, consumers of each—often influenced markedly by the appealing quality of the soap-opera heroines—will consider their favored brand to possess superior properties not found in the other. Manufacturers, operating under conditions that permit of branding, come into the market with quite different thoughts and strategies than those who sell completely undifferentiated goods on a completely free market. The imperfect competers have also shown that, in an industry in which there are only a relatively few suppliers, as in the automobile industry, analysis of the price-making process is quite different from what it would be if any old loft could be quickly and cheaply converted into an automobile factory.

When all these things are taken into account in price theory, we get something considerably more sophisticated than was discussed above, in Chapter 4. The simple supply-and-demand curves there exhibited become formidable diagrams containing curves of average revenue, marginal revenue, marginal cost, and many other items. Sometimes the demand curve is kinked; this partially symbolizes a dilemma in which many large sellers of highly advertised goods, like breakfast foods or soap powders, find themselves. It might occur to one of the dominant breakfast-food barons that he could make more money if he either raised his price (and sold less), or lowered his price (and sold more). But he is effectively blocked from pursuing either course of action because: (a) if he adds a few pennies to his price, his rivals do not follow, and he loses most of his customers; (b) if he knocks off a few pennies, his rivals *do* follow, and he has no more customers than before. Either way he loses and therefore the price stays rigid.

Imperfect competition has, in short, considerably amplified the narrow concept of price determination discussed in Chapter 4. These ideas have been applied to a variety of

problems including those of the labor market and foreign
trade with much ingenuity and some fruitfulness.

The remaining tendencies of the past quarter century are
of less interest to the ordinary reader, perhaps, than the two
great ones discussed just above (business cycle; imperfect
competition). They demand a more purely philosophical
interest than does the work of Keynes and of the imperfect
competers, and are not easily related to daily life. They are,
however, important, and they do relate to daily life. They
are therefore reviewed here, even if only summarily.

Economists are moving away from the pleasure-pain psychology to which I called brief attention in the last chapter.
It will be remembered that the standard economics of the
nineteenth century had, through the influence of Jeremy
Bentham, assumed explicitly or implicitly, a sort of pleasure-
pain equation: pain of work equals pleasure of consumption.
A special case is that of labor pain plus pain of abstinence
equals cost of production.

Now economists were thoroughly aware of the fact that
the theory of a basic pleasure-pain balance had limitations
and that certain applications of the principle were bizarre.
Much criticism came from outside economic spheres as well.
The science of psychology was discarding the search for
pleasure and avoidance of pain as mainsprings of human behavior. Students of the human mind pointed out that much
work was pleasurable, not painful, and that consumption of
spinach was often engaged in to meet the dreariest of biological needs, not because the organism was forever on the
qui vive to find new delights.

Economists are increasingly unwilling to look for real

pains behind the price tags on goods. Many of them have thrown away the idea of diminishing utility and are using instead such ideas as preference, choice, indifference. Out of this the latter-day classicists make up first indifference curves and then new demand curves—most of which look like the old ones and are used the same way. The gain—if it is a gain—is that the new demand curve is supposed to be rooted in the undeniable fact of human choice among commodities, not the psychological theory of declining utility or the pleasures of consuming. Indeed, the moderns are stating that their work has no connection with Benthamite psychology and that the mind can be completely dropped out of economics. It is, they say, obvious that people choose among the things offered in a market, and it is obvious that people have preferences among goods. This is about all that economists need by way of psychological theory, they say.

Another innovation is the more general use of concepts and mathematical devices that bring out clearly the complete interdependence of prices and their mutual determination. Our work in the last two chapters provided no clear way of describing a situation in which my demand for butter is altered by a changed price for meat. If my food budget is limited—and for most of us it is—and if meat goes up very much in price, I am likely not only to consume less and cheaper meat but also less of something other than meat. I may give up butter entirely, substitute oleo, and use the money thus released to keep my consumption of meat up as high as possible. Thus, a rise in the price of meat changes my demand among types of meat and extinguishes my demand for butter. And, of course, thousands may do what I do, and the price of oleo will then go up. And maybe butter will go down in price. And so on, in a chain reaction. Now this is really a way of saying that prices determine prices. So we discover that not only supply and demand, but also prices, determine prices.

With the mathematical approach it is theoretically possible to portray such complexes as declining purchase of butter when meat has gone up in price and requires a share of the income previously assigned to coffee. The almost infinite number of simultaneous equations assumed in this type of analysis takes account of all goods, their prices, and the demand for them; it is a mathematical way of saying that prices form an interdependent universe, each price being a planet or star; when any one of them is disturbed, all are disturbed. This is a most useful concept and accords better with the world of reality than the isolated little diagrams we studied in Chapter 4.

The new economics gives importance to a type of cost which we have barely mentioned: opportunity cost. In Chapter 4 we spoke of a farmer who would not sell his underpriced product because the opportunity of using the product himself was more valuable to him than the small cash he could get by selling in a low-price market. This type of cost can be and is given much greater importance in a system of theory that discards costs arising out of the pains of labor or of saving. Lionel Robbins, a proponent of this kind of economic thinking, describes it as follows:

The conception of costs in modern economic theory is a conception of displaced alternatives: the cost of obtaining anything is what must be surrendered in order to get it. The process of valuation is essentially a process of choice, and costs are the negative aspect of this process. In the theory of exchange, therefore, costs reflect the value of the things surrendered. In the theory of production they reflect also the value of alternative uses of productive factors—that is, of products which do

not come into existence because existing products are pre-
ferred.[1]

It should be clear from this chapter that standard theory
has, in the past quarter century, wandered from its earlier
concerns into new and interesting territory. In doing so it
has attempted to correct some of its deficiencies. How really
divergent this new theory is from the old will be better
appreciated by the reader after he has read Chapter 12 on
the business cycle, and compared it with the rather thin
supply-and-demand analysis of the two last chapters.

[1] Lionel Robbins, "Remarks upon Certain Aspects of the Theory of Costs,"
Economic Journal, XLIV (March, 1934), p. 2.

7. EVALUATION OF STANDARD THEORY

THE LAST FOUR CHAP-
ters have presented a rapid
outline of standard theory
—a tour of its world in less than eighty pages. We now pass
on to a brief evaluation of that type of theory. In estimating
the merits of any kind of economic doctrine we should generously consider two points before applying yardsticks of
worth. First, economics is a new science. Adam Smith's
Wealth of Nations appeared 175 years ago. But Copernicus'
revolutionary treatise on astronomy was published about 250
years before that; Galileo's great experiments were completed
350 years ago; Newton's work goes back to 1687, nearly a
century before Adam Smith. Thus, the astronomy and physics of the modern world have always been several laps ahead
of the social sciences. Second, economics is probably a more
difficult science than any of the natural sciences. To Albert
Einstein is imputed the statement that physics is child's play
by comparison with politics. Such a statement may well apply
to economics. Perhaps like Toynbee's eskimo, whose rude
culture stems from the overchallenge of a harsh environment, economists have been overchallenged by a refractory

subject and have been able to develop only a rude science.

Despite handicaps, economists have done much thorough work. Standard theory has—to say the least—taken on many of the preliminary jobs. It has made useful categories, defined terms, pointed out vulgar errors. It has, with the man in the street, seen that supply and demand determine price, but it has also seen that supply and demand are themselves complexes. These it has sought to break down. If it has perhaps stressed too much its theory of value, it has also held that concept up to be viewed in many lights. It has, apart from its strictly theoretical work, accumulated a vast amount of descriptive material about the economic universe and has, in many cases, suggested sound public policies. Several of its practitioners have helped to perfect the science of statistics, which has become an indispensable tool of the social sciences. Many severe critics and dissenters themselves concede that the hard core of all economic thinking has been developed by standard theory and that others have only added, extended, embellished—in any event, have only built on foundations already laid.

Standard theory also has its great weaknesses. Pointing them out is not always an easy task. For this, there are several reasons. First, there is no longer available to us a body of complete and rounded doctrine as there was fifty years ago —no single great man or book to go to for the last word. The great men of standard economics today, like Lord Keynes or Lionel Robbins, have not been able to bring together a thoroughgoing "Principles of Economics," written under a unified command. The closest thing to a basic book of principles is the college sophomore's textbook. The best of these manuals—some of which are admirable—fall far short of the "Principles" done in the grand manner, by

Mill and Marshall. To appraise them is to appraise something that none will accept as a final summing up—that is, they are just textbooks.

A second difficulty facing the critic is that standard theorists have tried to correct almost every defect that has been called to their attention. The correction may be a mere patching up, reminding one of the anxious mother one always finds in psychologists' case histories. This mother goes to a consultant about her nervous little daughter and learns that the reason for the child's disturbing symptoms is parental pressure for good grades in school. The mother tries faithfully to act upon this information and now sternly represses her tendency to exhort or scold her daughter when she comes home with low grades. But the mother has not really given up the high scholarship complex. She merely finds new ways of applying old pressures: by extravagant praise when the child brings home a tolerable paper—framing it and hanging it in the living room; by unnatural silence when a bad paper is shown; by overhearty "we"-jokes when mistakes in addition are discovered in homework. In short, no real change from any discerning child's viewpoint; to the mother, however, the changes are great, and she can prove it! In similar fashion, standard theory has amended its behavior or found areas of silence. To many critics none of this has been too convincing. Much of it is old vinegar in new jugs; but the new shapes resist effective criticism.

Further to confuse matters, there is also a tremendous contrast between any economist spinning fine his theories in a world of abstraction and the same man rolling up his sleeves and doing an earth-bound job, such as investigating monopoly for a Senate committee, writing a memo in governmental offices on wartime rationing, or estimating the increased revenue to be brought in by a new tax. From the very beginnings of highly abstract theory—that is, from Ricardo—to the present, economists have worked on two levels: a down-to-earth realistic level concerned with immediate problems, and a lofty, abstract level of remoter issues. On the former they have usually shown themselves to be hard-working craftsmen, filled with scholarly humility; on the other they have sometimes spoken like arrogant casuists.

It is dangerous to make sweeping generalizations about standard theory—except the one just now made. There is nothing monolithic or close-textured about it that makes broad statement applicable to the whole. But let us have done with the difficulties of criticism and get down to criticism itself.

Among the chief criticisms made of standard theory is that its method holds it in bondage. That method has been partly described in the last few chapters and here it can be restated in a form more useful for the purposes in view. The method of standard economics is close to that of the geometry we studied in high school. There, a large number of theorems were deduced from a few axioms. Among the axioms of standard theory are:

1. The wants of human beings are insatiable.

2. Goods and the factors of production (for example, land) are scarce in relation to the insatiable wants of men.

3. Because of 1 and 2, human beings must make choices; that is, they are compelled to decide which few of their many wants shall be satisfied.

4. These choices, presumably, are not haphazard, but are made because the satisfaction of certain wants yields greater

pleasure than the satisfaction of others, or because certain choices lead to greater profit or least loss.

Out of such axioms (if they are axioms), supply and demand curves are built up, as are various cost and revenue curves, and all are combined into diagrams, simple examples of which were given in Chapter 4. These can be and are elaborated considerably beyond the point that most of us would care to go—not to mention the fact that similar things can be done algebraically. The pages of many current economic publications look like pages in textbooks of trigonometry and calculus. Now these more complicated figures and mathematical chains are used in answering various questions, such as: Is it more profitable for an American corporation to sell all its patented can openers in this country at a medium price, or to sell part of them here at a high price and part in Europe at a low price? If we assume that the supply-and-demand curves are correct (which is a whale of an assumption), if we assume a fairly simple and stable world without tariffs, Marshall plans, exchange control, dollar shortage, inflation, depression, and if we also assume no mixed motives on the part of the can-opening corporation officials, then an answer of sorts may be found by use of axioms, equations, or diagrams.

But, the critics ask, is any question so circumscribed, so simplified and so decontaminated, worth asking in the first instance? Is there not always something like a Marshall Plan, or a war, or a depression, or a tariff, or exchange control? Do not corporation officials often have mixed motives—that is, motives other than maximum profit to rank-and-file stockholders?

The very problems selected by standard theory, it is alleged, can only be significant by great good luck, for one criterion alone guides their selection: can they be answered by the axiom-plus-diagram method? If they cannot, however important they may be to mankind they are discarded as problems to solve. So true is this, it is further alleged, that standard economics often becomes mere sporting in a grove; as much unlike the reality to be explained as chess is unlike modern three-dimensional subsurface and atomic warfare. To some extreme critics, the whole business is reminiscent of the subtleties of medieval scholasticism, which, if appropriate to the thirteenth century, are remote from the interests of modern man.

Standard economists are not unaware of this sort of criticism and, within limits, accept the justice of the allegations. They confess that they handle "static" analysis better than "dynamics"—which, whatever it means, seems to be a way of saying that they can handle single problems of their own choosing more easily than those thrust at them by a complex world. They are usually rather scrupulous about insisting that their conclusions should be applicable only to the universe of their abstraction, or about offering them only as hypotheses to be tested. They warn that their conclusions are but remotely applicable to the real world, or that they indicate only a vague direction, or are not at all applicable unless corrected to take account of certain large realities. This is all in conformity with sound scholarship and scientific integrity. But then, it is charged by critics, a dilemma imposes itself. Either standard theorists must confess that their qualifications and simplifications have emptied all meaning out of their labors; or they must, by some sort of unconscious process perhaps, forget their elaborate exclusions or disclaimers and go on to treat their findings as if these did have considerable application to the real world, after all. Thus, it is alleged, standard theory sometimes hedges, qualifies, and almost disavows its truth—so much so that what remains is less than a kernel of the truth.

This type of criticism sometimes seems to degenerate into a juvenile debate: Resolved, That induction is better than deduction. Standard theory defends the negative. The issue should not be drawn along these schoolboy lines, for every intelligent person knows that both induction and deduction, not to mention lucky hunches and even accidents—all contribute to human knowledge. The real issue is whether long and pure chains of deduction based on dubious abstractions, or ikons, are worth much. An ikon must be a very reliable one to stand the strains put on it by far-ranging deductions; and the question is whether the ikon of standard theory is strong enough to stand the strains put on it.

Other ikons are available to economists now. They will be sketched in forthcoming pages. Perhaps none of these is good enough. In that case new ones must be developed. It is worth noting that between 1800 and 1925 the ikons of all of the more nearly exact sciences changed a great deal more than did the standard ikon of economics. The ikon of the atom of physics and chemistry is completely different today from what it was about 1850. And with changes in the ikon of matter have gone changes in the ikon of energy. Other examples can be cited in biology and psychology. Only economics has had to limp along with its ikon of the late eighteenth century.

Another objection in the realm of method is that standard theory has not changed its early bias toward the physical sciences. Standard theory in its early days patterned itself on mechanics, which is today a modest department of physics. It selected a highly abstract and very precise fragment of the world of science as a model. The scope of that science is largely confined to levers, pendulums, counterpoise of weights with and without pulleys, and the like: things that can be satisfactorily and fruitfully understood without the perspective of history or a theory of development. The early classical economist took his pattern from a mere corner of science, a corner that deals with the ding-dong, wiggle-waggle oscillations of clocks, playground equipment, merry-go-rounds, and the like. It was valiant to pattern on mechanics and showed a commendable desire to imitate what was scientifically most highly developed in the first years of the nineteenth century. But in the meantime many have come to believe that economics would do better to pattern itself on the biological sciences, for economics is a study of mankind engaged in a special kind of activity. Yet standard theory still goes on accepting mechanics as its model science.

Another major critique often made of standard theory is its conservative inclination; this charge was made more often before 1930 than later. The blunt way of saying it is to allege that the traditional core of standard theory is an elaborate defense of what is; that it defends the present as the best of all possible worlds. Readers may wonder how such a monstrous charge can be leveled at the seemingly innocuous matter of the last four chapters. I therefore give below as samples a few of the reasons why, according to some critics, standard theory may be seen as having swerved from a completely detached pursuit of truth by the claims of interest.

1. The scope of standard economics, which rarely got away from the price-making process, was so very limited

that many issues of importance and less flattering tenor to the vanity of man and his institutions were ignored.

2. The history of the development of standard theory demonstrates that its great men were by class and family ties or similar bond of interest devoted to the cause of the then rising and later dominant industrial class.

3. The concept that there is a relation, under capitalism, between marginal productivity and size of income (compare p. 88) becomes, by ever so slight a shift, the conviction that everybody is paid exactly what he produces, and that everybody is therefore justly rewarded. It is, to be sure, conceded that with perhaps only one exception no economist of renown has ever actually insisted upon such an extreme statement; yet many economists have tolerated it or allowed it to be inferred with only ambiguous challenge. They have, in any case, built up an edifice which reaches toward this conclusion, though they stop short of actually grasping it. Indeed, this would be cited as an example of what was discussed a few pages ago, namely, that standard economics often seems to say one thing here, disclaims it there, but then seems to say it elsewhere after all.

4. "As a matter of fact," a few critics would say, pursuing the above argument on a different plane, "it is rather naive to attribute much productivity to either labor, or capital, or the landlord, or the entrepreneur." They would argue that the most importantly productive factor of any society is a vast combination of skills and moral qualities transmitted by that vague thing we name the cultural heritage. The chief food plants and animals of today were developed by neolithic man. The average American boy of sixteen, without specialized training, can probably fit better into a factory

job than a young Soviet peasant after two years in a technicum. But it is more than a question of technical skill. It is a matter of comprehending factory discipline, not spitting on the floor, using drinking fountains and washrooms hygienically, recognizing safety precautions and sources of danger and infection, cooperating intelligently with fellow workers, drawing on wide experience with machines as background for handling unexpected problems. In short, the American is steeped from birth in the lore and self-discipline of an established industrial culture; the Russian is a peasant who went to a technicum. Well, this cultural heritage is perhaps the most productive entity in our economic society, but does not fit in as a factor of production, hence is largely ignored. But after all, one may ask, what can be done with the cultural heritage? Do critics of standard theory expect us to give it an income? Is it not, because of its insubstantial nature, both recognized as primary yet also taken for granted, like the air we breathe? Perhaps the point that the critic is trying to make is something like this: Both in economic theory and in popular thought, the idea frequently crops up that there is or should be some sort of relationship between productivity and income. Hence each group in the population tries to show how productive it is, and economic theory aids and abets this class vainglory. Labor unions said that the great productive miracles of the Second World War could not have been wrought without labor; corporation officials said that, without their devoted effort, America could never have been the arsenal of democracy. Then the critic steps in to say something like this: "A plague on both your houses; you are both worms and braggarts. How can you say you have by your skill and ability armed the world? You have been mere instruments of the ages. Thousands of years and billions of men have lent you skill and wisdom. Part of this immense accumulation of the ages you convert into swarms of planes and droves of tanks and schools of ships and then you say, 'I did it!' You did something, it is true. And you, too, added something to the swelling heritage of the ages. But when you produce anything, whether a pea shooter or an atomic bomb, do not say, 'I made the greatest contribution.' You made only a fraction of a fraction."

5. The pessimistic foundations of standard theory stand in the way of the unfolding, abundant economic life that some people think could be achieved. The Malthusian doctrine, the law of diminishing returns, the niggardliness of nature, and other such are the important parts of the mechanism of the older standard theory. It is alleged that when put together and caused to rotate, the pole of the mechanism, like that of a gyroscopic compass, points invariably in one direction: toward the conclusion that under no other institutional arrangements can man be much better off than he now is, for nature is miserly and we are feeble and another dose of manure will not bring forth an additional grain of wheat. The critics feel that this pessimism at best is rooted in a debatable faith; at worst, in apology and prejudice. To be sure, there are limits to what the world can produce; and man will, at some point, have to realize that his material condition cannot be much improved. But consideration of these questions is held by critics to be postponable until what can clearly be done is done indeed.

6. Though pessimistic in some areas, standard theory has often exuded optimism in others. It has tended to magnify the degree of harmony between the search for profits and the public welfare—that is, optimistically to see fewer con-

flicts of interest than are seen by dissenters. Until recently, standard theory looked upon depressions as rather unimportant and temporary disturbances. Standard theory has overworked the expressions, "tendency" and "in the long run" —and a vast number of things in the economic world were believed to have a tendency to work out all right in the long run. It is only in recent years, through the sanction of Keynes, that cautious and Pollyannish statements about long-run tendencies have been at least partly discredited in economics. Keynes reminded his readers that in the long run they would all be dead.

7. Standard theorists assume that the economic mechanism is completely neutral and can be used to achieve whatever ends the society desires; that it is like a mason's trowel or any other tool, as adaptable to the building of a cozy home as to the building of a military fort. In short, the economic system is a means to any desired end. Dissenters would not agree to this. Ends, they would say, are often partly determined by means. Allied to this is the objection that valuations of the market place are too tacitly assumed to be the only possible valuations. Often we delusively impute excessive intrinsic worth to things (like orchids, perhaps) that have high value in the market place; under another mechanism of valuation, this form of self-delusion would not be possible.

Standard theorists are not without arguments of rebuttal. The earlier economists, Ricardo, James and John Mill, M'Culloch, Say, often working with such public men as Joseph Hume and Francis Place, took the more difficult side of many public questions, from repeal of the Combination Laws to Parliamentary Reform. They weakened the political power of a great landed oligarchy and were among the chief forces behind a general redistribution of its power. Standard theorists can point out that they have with moderate consistency advocated many measures opposing the narrow interests of some of the great capitalists: income taxes, estate taxes, free trade internationally, trust-busting and so on. Many of the younger men, particularly among the Keynesians, concede that standard theory did have its spotty decades and the odor of apology, but that Anglo-American theory of the past quarter century has undergone purification. Indeed, a number of evolutionary socialists—socialists who would follow the doctrines of Norman Thomas or the British Labor Party rather than Stalin—have found much to admire in the newer type of economics described in the last chapter.

One final point should be made before the subject is closed. Even if standard economics is or ever was apology, as charged by some dissenters, few individuals are guilty of deliberate and cynical mental prostitution. (There are, of course, black sheep in every profession.) The fault is an anonymous one and results from the great difficulties that arise when men study something of which they are part and in which they have a great stake.

Now to evaluate the "new economics" of the last chapter. The Keynesians, imperfect competers, indifference-curve and opportunity-cost savants have unquestionably improved standard economic theory by putting a study of booms and depressions in a place of importance, by giving greater recognition to the pervasiveness of monopoloid business activity, and by struggling against the hedonistic psychology of Bentham. And it has also been observed, just above, that the newer trends do not so easily lend themselves to a blind defense of this as the best of all possible worlds. Yet some important critics seem to feel they have missed fire.

First of all, critics find themselves unable to intone hosannahs of praise over the fact that neoclassical economists, between 1926 and 1936, at last admitted monopolies, quasi-monopolies, and depressions into the science of economics. After all, even dead-end kids know something about quasi-monopoly, the value of a trade name like Wrigley's, good times and hard times. The new work was received by some dissenters with a bored "At last!" rather than with delight at the new contributions made to theory.

Second, the new emphasis on imperfect competition and the business cycle does not make economics as realistic as it promises. Discussion is being carried on in planes of fantasy as elevated as ever. The problems dealt with, it is charged by critics, are problems that monopolies in real life rarely face, and that do not typically arise in such governmental agencies as the Federal Trade Commission or the Anti-Trust Division of the Department of Justice. Quasi-monopoly price is discussed as if collusion among businessmen were nonexistent. Mrs. Joan Robinson, among the first of the imperfect competers, has evaluated her own work much better than some of her followers have done. To her, the degree of abstraction in theories of imperfect competition is "distressingly" high: her own method of analysis, far from being a sharp tool is but a "knife of bone" or a "hammer of wood" (her own words). As for its new business cycle theory, there is only partial correspondence between what Keynes sees and what has been seen by American students who have been working on the facts of the business cycle for forty years. This point will be more completely developed in a later chapter.

A third criticism to be made of the new economics is that it is a series of bold amendments with no new underlying social philosophy to hang onto—though the reader should be warned that this is my own criticism, rarely touched upon in the writings of others. In an earlier chapter I made much of the fact that the great economists of the past had developed a most ingenious theory of economic organization. We noted then that men, unfettered by government regulation, motivated by price and profit considerations, and allowed to pursue their natural bent, would unconsciously and automatically impose a beneficent and harmonious pattern on our economic activity. Adam Smith held that men by pursuing their selfish interests unwittingly promoted the general interests of society, as if "led by an invisible hand." This belief was the outcome of a thoughtfully and consciously embraced social philosophy, and of explicit assumptions about the nature of man.

But now the imperfect competers and the Keynesians are telling us that the invisible hand may lead us not only into the green pastures of a prosperous world dominated by fruitful competition, but also down into the valley of depression and into the shadow of monopoly. Today we are told that men do not "naturally" compete, but build up instead all manner of monopoloid situations; that supply is not to demand as a hole in the ground is to the earth taken out of it; that things do not come out even, and that without governmental intervention we are as likely to have unemployment as full employment—perhaps more likely. Briefly, then, until 1930, standard theory held that men by unconscious act, through competition and in response to natural law, and their own human propensities, organized the economic world satisfactorily. Now standard theory denies that man's unconscious act tends toward satisfactory organization; on the contrary. But no really fundamental reasons are given for these new conclusions. The denial is probably in better accord with the facts, and should be put down as improvement. And yet it is an improvement that inspires doubt in some minds for it has not been accompanied by a reexamination of the foundations of theory and of what lies under the foundations—which is what so complete a reversal seems to demand. There is no new ikon; there seems to be only a repudiation of the old.

What is it that makes us sing the praises of vigorous competition, yet often persuades us to settle for imperfect and lethargic competition? Is the invisible hand leading us where we do not want to go? If so, why do we let ourselves be misled? If the basic, natural laws of Adam Smith, laws that presumably directed economic activity harmoniously, have been found inoperative, what similarly fundamental laws are there to replace them? In what kind of broad economic pattern, or gestalt, do imperfect competition and monopoly and depression fit congruously with spurts of keen competition and prosperity? Does our economy have a split personality? If so, is it manic-depressive, or what?

Standard economists who work with the very latest of their theories no longer seem to have an ikon or care about one—no longer, in short, find need for a general theory of how economic life is organized. No longer have a central core of social philosophy. Their theories are not held together by a hedonistic utilitarianism, like those of their spiritual predecessors, or, to anticipate later chapters, by Hegelianism, like Marx's revolutionary theories; or by a quasi-Freudian psychology, like Veblen's dissenting theories. There are, of course, some qualifications. Such great standard economists as Schumpeter and Cassel do seem to see a kind of general form in our economic life which makes reasonable such things as business cycles and monopoloid business in our kind of world. In recent articles, John von Neumann, Oskar Morgenstern, and K. W. Rothschild have seemed to suggest that businessmen want to *win* rather than compete, and that the price-fixing process more nearly resembles poker playing than a search by the forces of supply and demand for a point of equilibrium. Out of such materials as these a new ikon may possibly be created. But none exists as yet. And the new developments in standard theory seem to have diminished value on that account.

Standard theorists do indeed have "models," but a show window full of models is not an ikon. A model is merely a set of assumptions, sometimes expressed in mathematical or diagrammatic form, into which an imaginary disturbance is introduced. The effects of the disturbance are then observed in imaginative experimentation. Through one model we can see what an assumed general monetary wage increase would do to real wages when we assume full employment; through another we see some theory of the business cycle working itself out. You can make any kind of model—even, I suppose, one to show what would happen to an oligopolistic egg industry if chicken farmers should decide to lose money on eggs while selling pullets at extortionate prices. But the capacity to trace in imagination and with ingenuity the repercussions of policies or disturbances under assumed conditions is no substitute for an ikon of the economic system as it is.

Part of the reason for the nonexistence of a unifying force in recent standard theory seems to be the absence of a basic concept of human nature. However false the pleasure-pain psychology of Bentham may have been, it had the virtue of holding the older economics tight together. Present attempts to drop psychology entirely out of standard theory leave economics without unifying integument. The only psychology left in the most modern versions of economic theory is that men have sufficient capacity of choice to buy only a few among the myriad things offered to them in the market, and that they seek, in any transaction, to maximize gains or minimize losses. This may be all right as far as it goes, but it is certainly not far.

If we understood individual men better we could probably understand economic life better. Many of the things which diminish our economic life—as monopoly, imperfect competition, depressions—are probably as deeply rooted in the nature of man as are those things that increase our economic life—propensity to exchange, division of labor, instinct of workmanship. The "new" economics has smashed the old ikon of Adam Smith, Ricardo, and Say. It does not yet seem to be searching for a new one, and certainly not where it can probably best be found: in the nature of man.

Thus we find that even the more recent developments of standard economic theory do not escape criticism. The best thing about the newer trends is that they have issued a strong challenge to the theory that came before. Out of this may come a genuine revolution in economic thought—not too late, let us hope, to save us from some of the disasters that threaten Christendom.

Here we end our formal study of standard economic theory. Its principles will arise again, however, in Part Four, where we shall discuss certain special topics like banking and foreign trade. For a while, our attention will be centered on the economic world of the dissenters. Let us now, through their eyes, watch man as he goes after worldly goods.

Part Three

DISSENTING ECONOMIC THEORY

8. INTRODUCTION TO DISSIDENT THEORY

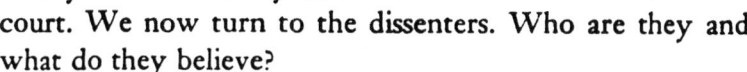

IN THE PRECEDING CHAP-
ters standard economic
theory has had its day in
court. We now turn to the dissenters. Who are they and
what do they believe?

It is not easy to say exactly who the dissenters are and
harder still to decide how much they must dissent, and from
what, to be in good standing. Malthus and Ricardo disagreed
sharply with each other, yet no student of comparative
economic doctrines would do otherwise than range both in
the direct line of orthodoxy. John Stuart Mill, mature and
married, repudiated some of the theories held by John Stuart
Mill, the young bachelor; but he, too, is classified without
reservation as orthodox. On the other hand Karl Marx used
the apparatus of the standard theory of his day like a confirmed Ricardian, yet none would deny him a high place
among the fully qualified dissenters. Among the moderns,
Pareto, Cassel, and Schumpeter have much of supreme interest to say to dissenters; but they, too, belong to the orthodox line. To confuse things still further, all dissenters accept
a good many of the basic concepts of standard theory. No

intelligent person and certainly no economist, would, for example, question the statement that, where the ideals of laissez-faire prevail, useful things tend to be dear if the supply is limited.

Veblen, a most competent and articulate American dissenter, once tried to distinguish his kind from others in words of learned length and thundering sound, but then rather weakly concluded his exposition by saying that the difference was a "spiritual" one. If Veblen was driven by the difficulty of his subject to use so meaningless a word in summary, lesser men will write thickly and readers will have to be patient.

On the whole it seems easier to name dissenters than to generalize about their dissent. There seems to be broad agreement that certain names belong together in the category. What holds them together as a group is not always so widely agreed upon. Thus, it is quite safe—because of consensus on names—to put down as dissenters Marx and his forerunners and followers. Among the forerunners are gentle dreamers who would have paled at the thought of stamping Utopia into existence with iron heel. One was Fourier, an unmarried fuss-budget who dreamed of a world of apartment hotels connected with subsistence farms, within which each individual would perform tasks for which he was best suited. Among the more interesting conclusions of his philosophy of vocational guidance was that children of about ten should wash dishes and attend to sewage disposal because pre-pubescents love dirt. These clean-up teams were to be named "The Little Hordes," and they were to march first in all parades. Although he is remembered for these startling ideas and for the influence he had on the founders of Utopian communities in the United States, as Brook Farm and the Oneida Community, his great contribution to dissident thought was his cosmogony.

Substantively, Fourier's cosmogony was sometimes fantastic. The oceans were to evolve into lemonade as man himself moved to higher levels of civilization. Ferocious animals were to become the tame servants of man; he predicted that lions with elegant manners would draw carriages across France in a day. Some of his ideas were less extravagant. I have already spoken of his concern with what have become parts of our daily lives, namely vocational guidance and multiple-dwellings you can eat in (which we name apartment hotels and which he named phalansteries). He predicted rightly the coming of the era of "guarantism"— that is, the age of womb-to-tomb social-security legislation, partially realized in this country, more fully realized in other English-speaking countries and elsewhere. Though the substance of his cosmogony was unrestrained, the underlying method commands respect. He is one of the first of the economists who sees the rise, disintegration, decline, regrouping of human institutions, and sees this process with the eye of the economist. He sees change or evolution in economic process. The present is understandable to him because he also understands—or thinks he does—the past and future.

But I have been led to digress by the bizarre yet seductive ideas of an eccentric and not-too-important bachelor. We return to the task of listing the dissenters. We already have Marx, forerunners and followers. We can add some of the economists produced by the British Fabian movement, Sidney and Beatrice Webb, for example. The American, Thorstein Veblen, belongs. A few economic historians like R. H. Tawney support dissent rather than orthodoxy. Other names should be mentioned to fill out but not complete the list: Werner Sombart, John A. Hobson.

Now we have the men; what ideas do they hold in common? We can safely say of all of them that they either disagreed fundamentally with the method of the orthodox economists, or they made their center of interest to be a type of economic problem generally neglected by standard theory, or that they did both.

This said, one finds one's self hard-pressed to say much more that is applicable to all dissenters. It is, however, fairly easy to list half a dozen points that are common to an important and determining number of them. As one might expect, the positive theories of the dissenters are the reverse of the coin considered in the last chapter, namely the criticism made by them of standard economic theory. Here is a little list of the things one might expect a dissenter to do or be concerned with, though perhaps no single dissenter does all of them.

1. Most contemporary dissenters give a good deal of attention to the complexities and infirmities of the human mind. Veblen, the best example, took his psychology most seriously and developed an economic man of most subtle and tortuous behavior—one rivaling the creations of Freud, Jung, or Adler. The reader recalls that standard theorists hold to the simple pain-pleasure psychology of Bentham. Or, if they are dissatisfied with that, they repudiate psychology altogether, except the hypothesis that men are capable of making a rational choice between the competing claims of two commodities. Dissenters hold the Benthamite psychology to be faulty and the procedure of attempting to cast psychology out altogether as self-deluding. Econo-

mists, either by what they say or do not say, are always making assumptions about human nature, so dissidents believe, and when these assumptions are made unconsciously and not carefully examined they lead to error. But there is more to it than just psychology. The issue is, to use Crane Brinton's phrase in his *Ideas and Men*, one of anti-intellectualism versus rationalism. The standard economists are children of the eighteenth century enlightenment, who believe that men can reasonably control their environment. The dissenting economist has little faith in man's reason. He looks upon human beings as bundles of conflicting wants and competing fears whose minds are dark, unexplored caverns. The rational part of man is like the small, visible part of an iceberg; the irrational part, like its submerged base, is several times as large. The standard economist believes that man can order his economic life to conform to his reasonable aspirations; the dissenter believes that man is pushed around by his economic institutions, by his habits, by his environment, by all kinds of forces that are stronger than he.

2. The dissenters believe that a large and telling number of economic activities involve unequal bargaining power and that, therefore, coercion is an important ingredient of economic life. Adam Smith assumed in man a strong propensity "to truck and barter," and postulated in him a love of equal exchange. Dissident theory assumes in man a great love of unequal exchange and a strong propensity to get something for nothing. Standard theory speaks of competition rather than coercion as the dominant mode, and assumes that competitive activity—with negligible exceptions—is carried on within the limits imposed by law, morals, and human decency. Coercion, on the other hand, is given great

recognition in dissident theory. It speaks much, for example, of international warfare with economic ends in view, of the ruthless building of economic empires by "robber barons," of the economic power exerted by monopoly.

3. The dissenters study economic process rather than economic equilibrium. Thus they study the business cycle, or speculate on the larger outcomes of current economic activity—whether it tends toward state socialism or international socialism, or cultural regression or progress, or a long era of warfare. When I spoke of Fourier and his oceans of lemonade I referred to this concept under the name of cosmogony: a study of the origins of the economic system and of its current drift. Veblen, a dissenter, thought of his economics as being evolutionary in contrast to standard theory, which is mechanical and static. Standard theory has, in recent years, under the influence of Keynes, bent somewhat in this evolutionary direction, but the longer history has centered on normality, on equilibrium rather than process; and even Keynes is more at home in an equilibrium than a process.

4. Many dissenters concern themselves but little with the ikon of a freely competitive, normal society. For a given problem the ikon may sometimes be considered useful, but for many purposes other abstractions give better results, they think; for example: the ikon of a changing capitalism —early capitalism, late capitalism—each stage dying as it fathers the next and each having characteristics of its own.

5. Many dissenters would classify economics with the biological rather than the physical sciences. In a variety of ways (their more explicit interest in psychology, for example) their economic theory is man-centered rather than market-centered. This does not mean that they are more

humane, but that they observe more carefully what men do
rather than what prices or commodities do. Dissenters are
filled with wide-eyed wonder at the things men do to get
a living; the others are mainly interested in what markets do.
There may be a historical basis for this, namely, that standard
economics first gained recognition when the physical sciences, particularly the subscience of mechanics, had begun
to demonstrate their fabulous potentialities. Since then,
among orthodox theorists, there has been a tradition that
economics was not unlike mechanics. Dissent sprang up on
the continent of Europe, away from the mechanically
minded British.

6. Dissenters are unwilling to accept for economics a narrow scope as is implied by the limiting phrase of standard
theory: "disposal of scarce goods." Anything a man does to
get a living, from erecting a log cabin to gambling at Monte
Carlo, from bribing a cabinet officer to selling the army
decayed meat, is of supreme importance to him. These are
not exceptional economic activities. They are part of a total
scheme. In trying to embrace such activities under a unified
system, they seek aid from political science, anthropology,
psychology and the other sciences of man. They are accused
of galloping through whatever fields interest them, and of
trampling down the boundaries between economics and
other fields of knowledge. Thus, if they do in fact make
contributions to knowledge, the contributions are as likely
to belong to social philosophy or sociology or history or
social psychology as to economics. At least that is the view
of standard theory. To dissenting economists these are all
soft impeachments, which they own, for they say there are
no sharp boundaries among the social sciences. Just as the
physical sciences can no longer be sharply distinguished

from each other, so the sciences of man are all of one piece.

7. Many but by no means the best-known of the dissenting theorists rely oftener on the inductive method than standard theorists. They study economic phenomena historically, statistically, objectively (as they think). They count, they pile up mountains of facts and figures. They criticize standard economists for bringing a whole battery of doubtful premises to bear on any problem, from which they arrive at conclusions by the sometimes doubtful rules of traditional logic.

8. Dissident theory does not believe that economic society is organized as standard theory teaches. The fundamental idea in standard theory is that private vices become public benefits; that self-interest, through the process of competition, transforms itself into a socially useful force (compare p. 44). This transformation results—according to standard theory—in a very great harmony between human needs and private profits. The profit seeker gets what he wants (profits), by giving the world what it wants (food, clothing, shelter, luxuries). Dissident theory denies this as a fact and repudiates it as an assumption. It sees no mechanism by which first things come first: simple food, minimum clothing, and housing. On the contrary, much of the energy of our society goes into producing second things first. A recent example was to be found in the charge that an inordinate amount of labor and materials went into new bowling alleys and roadside cafes while young couples steadily employed might whistle for modest homes of their own. The greater part of the human race goes short of its needed 3,000 calories daily, while the shops of the world are filled with the most frivolous stuff imaginable. In short, by whatever forces economic society may be organized, there is no great harmony

between them and the process of satisfying human needs. It is partly for this reason that many dissenters made early studies in the distribution of income, or economic surveys on housing, medical costs, standards of living, and the like, all of which demonstrated that no comfortable view could be taken, even in a rich country, of the adequacy with which the economic system was meeting the most fundamental needs of the human organism. All these studies have shown a large gap between the standards of minimum human decency and fact. It is perhaps true that under a thoroughgoing competition a harmonious relationship between the profit-making process and the process of satisfying human wants might exist. But under conditions as they really are, the two processes diverge often enough to cast doubt on the whole theory of beneficent economic organization—or even that there is much organization of any sort.

To be sure, there is a measure of organization. Few biological phenomena are devoid of some sort of "natural" balance, or recognizable form. Human warfare imposes pattern. Oceans and forests have structure. There is enough water for all the fish and enough land for all the trees. A certain balance of nature is maintained by the fact that big fish eat smaller ones, that large trees shade saplings to death. The economic world has somewhat similar methods of regulation. On the whole, however, dissenters find at least as many forces working against a spontaneous harmony in economic affairs as may be found working the other way.

9. Dissenters seem always to be a little unsympathetic toward the complexity and indirection of economic life. They brood on the contrast between the forthright technological process and the roundabout financial process. They are not sure that they always see the virtues of credit,

of stock exchanges, of speculation, of certain brokerage operations. How do such things make radishes grow better, or improve the skills of garment cutters, or give us more efficient heating systems in our homes? They know the usual replies to these questions and accept some of them; but, on the whole, they are not completely convinced, and they seem to measure economic achievement with an engineer's yardstick.

10. Some of the dissenters bear a similar relationship to economics that psychoanalysts do to psychology. The psychologies that stem from Freud have sometimes been named "depth psychology." This appears to mean that underlying levels of the mind—compulsions, wishes, and prohibitions —are given much weight in the understanding of personality. Thus John Doe's dream or slip of the tongue may tell the depth psychologist more about John Doe than any thoughtful statement of self-appraisal that John is able to make about himself, or than might be revealed in ordinary psychological tests. In about the same way, dissident economists might seize on certain small, often disregarded facts to tell them much about the essential nature of the economic world we live in. The fact that the Anti-Trust Division of the Department of Justice has never been well supported by funds might strike the dissenter as more important in the understanding of economic life than the assumption of standard theory that long-run cost equals long-run price. There are other similarities. Depth psychology shatters illusions and arouses resistance in students as they try to learn. So does "depth" economics. It is not surprising that in recent years several books have appeared seeking to demonstrate similarities between the economic dissenters and the Freudians.

Both groups deal with modern civilization and its discontents.

With these general statements as background we go on to study two of the dissenters. The first case study will be of Marx; the second, of Veblen. The method we adopt here is rather different from the method we used in studying standard theory. There we studied certain great topics, like price formation and distribution; here we study the theories of individual men.

9. WHAT MARX MEANT

KARL MARX WAS BORN in 1818 and died in 1883. This means that in 1950 one living American in twenty was on this earth during part of Marx's lifetime. Stalin, though only a very little dictator then, was already four years old when Marx died. One needs to remind one's self of Marx's relative contemporaneity when one considers how great his influence is today. Though the sword (and the pistol behind the ear) has been used in his name, he himself used only the pen. If there had never been a Russian revolution or a Soviet Union, or even a social democratic party, his theories would have placed him high among the dissenters—or, for that matter, among economists of any persuasion, for even bitterly anti-Marxian economists recognize his genius.

As an economist, he built up a system as rounded, involved, abstract, subtle and hard-to-understand as any two or three orthodox economists put together. During his lifetime and after his death, disciples perfected the Marxian system. Among the greatest were his colleague Friedrich Engels and later Lenin (who turned theories into reality after gaining control of Russia for the Communist party). It is to these three that I shall principally refer when I speak of the economics of Marx.

Marx was both an economist and a propagandist, or revolutionary. The two roles were fused into a consistent personality. We cannot study the one without studying the other. Yet it is possible to lay stress on the economist and to keep the revolutionary in the background. By doing this in the next dozen pages we can free our minds from the psychological resistance that his name quite understandably arouses in a nation at war with Communist aggression. We also need to remember that Marxian theory is not synonymous with the policies of the Soviet Union. Many Marxians are bitterly anti-Stalinist: the Trotskyites, for example, who for decades have warned Americans of the Soviet peril. Trotsky's mantle appears to have fallen on Tito, and here again we have an example of one kind of Marxist who has won the fierce enmity of a second kind. There is every reason to believe that many "good" Marxians, but "bad" Stalinists, have been liquidated within the Soviet Union and its satellites, or are now experiencing the horrors of concentration camps.

We shall understand Marx better—indeed, any economist better—if we try to figure out what were his hopes and aspirations for the human race. How did he believe man could fulfill his destiny? Orthodox economists, we have already intimated, believed that men realized themselves by trucking and bartering, by disposing economically of scarce goods under current institutions, by constantly comparing amounts of pain with amounts of compensating happiness, by exercising personal liberty, natural right, following natural law. To Marx, most of this was chaff. Without playing the dangerous role of amateur psychoanalyst we have every right to assume that Marx was consumed by the inner fire of

a most uncompromising Utopianism. He saw men not as
cautious, penny-counting shopkeepers, but as potentially
little lower than the gods. Since men were obviously much
lower than the gods at that moment, how were they to develop upwards toward their fullest potentialities?

To Marx the basis of his kind of spiritual development was
material and primarily economic. His theory breaks with
Christian tradition in that he did not think man could love
his neighbor as himself or do unto others as he would be done
by, unless economic conflict with its accompanying poverty
were made to vanish from the face of the earth. So long
as acquisition of economic goods involved—as he thought
—exploitation, war, knavery at large, and the existence of
a more or less permanent working class opposed to a more
or less permanent wealthy class, so long would all the nobler
human endeavors and sentiments, from friendship and love
to art and science, be soiled by economic considerations.
Marx proposes, in a manner of speaking, that we simplify our
lives by taking steps to abolish economic conflict. And you
abolish economic conflict by abolishing poverty. And to
abolish the have-nots, you have to abolish the haves—not
because sharing their wealth will level things off better.
Sharing the wealth, or sharing income, is not an essential
idea in Marxism. The haves will be liquidated only if and
because they stand in the way of organizing the more productive society envisaged by Marx. A cooperative society
that centrally plans its economic activities—the socialist state
—will yield a larger product. The real point was to abolish
the political power of the haves and their alleged master
class psychology.

He saw, perhaps more clearly than many of his contemporaries, that the rapid development of science and tech-

nology in the dynamic middle years of the nineteenth
century held out the hope of freeing the world from its
long curse of hard labor and low productivity—hence poverty for the masses. Fourier, though of the older generation,
was still fumbling with the idea that lions, not machines,
could be induced to supply power for the French transportation system—and no doubt many riders on the PLM are
under the impression that the Fourieristic doctrines must
have won out. Ricardo, Malthus, and others were so pessimistic about man's economic destiny that they inspired
Carlyle to use the phrase "dismal science" as the synonym
for social science.

For Marx, economics was, in a kind of backhanded way,
a hopeful science. In the agricultural, low-productivity past,
there had been, he said, a reasonable basis for serf and lord,
slave and master. But mankind now had iron slaves and the
tireless muscles of expanding steam. Abundance for all lay
within the realm of probability. But something was going
wrong. Steam and science, iron and technology had plunged
the working class into even greater misery than before—
for the first generation of factory workers was indeed a lost
generation. Capitalism seemed to him a more wasteful type
of economic organization than man might reasonably hope
to have. The physical basis was here. Yet reasonable expectations had been disappointed. There was no obvious movement in the direction of a better and easier life for mankind,
and, on the surface, no signs pointing toward Utopia.

Marx might, like many of his contemporaries, have sought
to usher in an Utopian state of affairs by advocating freer
education for the workman, or the creation of model factory
villages, or a gradual program to be enacted by the parlia-
ments of the newly industrialized countries. He might have

enlisted the aid of the churches. But he laughed at such
methods. He laughed at them because, in his view, the obstacle to immediate realization of a heaven on earth was the
inefficient and wasteful capitalist class, the class that in bourgeois democracies is heir to masterhood traditions and institutional benefits of an earlier age. Government, press,
education, and the church were, he said, owned lock, stock,
and barrel by the capitalist class; by the enemy. The enemy
was satisfied with the positions he held, the disposition of
his forces, and the tribute he was able to levy. No hope of
budging him or working out a permanent peace based on
the capitalist's willing abandonment of rights and benefits
enjoyed.

As for local Utopian communities, to Marx they were
childish. The system of production in an industrial era,
whether under the proposed cooperative or present capitalist state, was necessarily large scale, often nation-wide or
world-wide. High standards of living could never be
achieved by subsistence farming, even if it was hooked up
to Fourier's fancy phalansteries. Large-scale operations were
essential to a heavy volume of production, and exchange of
goods between specialized regions indispensable.

Thus, Marx concludes, if you look at things on the surface, there is no basis for hope of Utopia, despite the iron
horse and the power of insubstantial steam. But if you look a
little farther and a little deeper . . . "Come with me
through three fat volumes of *Das Kapital*," he seems to say,
"and I will show you that the house of capitalism is falling
down because of its inner weaknesses and that a brave new
world is building up."

It is of the essence of Marxism that this capitalist world is
plunging toward Utopia, even though we are unaware of it,

just as the physical earth is turning and plunging through space without our being able to feel its motion. The foundations of capitalism are invisibly crumbling—invisibly, that is, to those who do not, like him, know what symptons to look for. And, to pile up metaphors, capitalism carries within itself the seeds of its own destruction. A species of economic termite is gnawing away at the sills. Capitalism is decaying; Utopia is rising up. That in broadest outline is how Marx's subconscious went after his Utopia, since he could not get it through government, church, education or model factory communities. Our next step is to find the Marxian termites in the sills and the seeds of the alleged decay.

The basic thing to grasp about capitalism, Marx says, is that under its institutions there is a considerable and inevitable gap between the current wages of labor and the value created by labor. How does Marx support this bold assertion, so fundamental to his other conclusions? Marx's first step is to develop again, partly in Ricardian fashion, the then-dominant theory of labor value. This, the reader recalls, is the theory that the value of any product is related directly to the number of hours of labor congealed in it. That is the cornerstone of the edifice. Marx meets naive objections immediately. Obviously the things made by labor must have utility to have value. An undesired commodity like a fur-lined bathtub would never sell at its full labor value. In the case of a really useful thing like a boat, only the socially necessary labor-hours confer value. By this he means in part that anybody who builds a freighter in the desert and then transports it overland to the sea cannot hope to be rewarded for the extra work required by so awkward a system of production. Large boats are built at the water's edge—that is "socially necessary."

How this discrepancy between wage and value works out can be shown in an imaginary case. Assume that a man's felt hat has both theoretical economic value and an actual market price that are correctly symbolized by the words "ten dollars." Assume also that it took a total of ten hours of labor to produce the hat, beginning from the time the rabbit was caught until the time the consumer's initials were stamped in the hatband. These ten hours are to cover everything, even the small emanations of past labor absorbed by the hat from the machines, chemicals, and kettles used in manufacture. A hat-making tool or acid or any kind of tangible capital is congealed labor; a little of that stored-up labor rubs off on each hat made. When Marx assumed that it took ten hours of labor to make a hat he meant ten hours of every conceivable kind of labor: current, recent, previously congealed, unskilled, skilled, managerial, artistic—as well as labor used in transportation to market, storage, retailing, and so on.

Let us agree with Marx that a hat takes ten hours of labor to make, that it sells for ten dollars and that therefore the value created by all labor used in manufacture is a dollar an hour. "Good," says Marx in effect, "but now we shall find that the workers employed actually were paid an average of only 60 cents an hour" (or 30 cents, or 80 cents—the exact figure, so long as it is appreciably less, does not matter). Why does the worker get less than a dollar an hour? Because he was robbed by the employer? Marx does have some harsh things to say about the employer's being an Old Money Bags, and about capitalism's dripping with the blood of workers, but this sort of thing is not the basic explanation. The basic explanation is economic.

The reason the wage is 60 cents an hour instead of a dollar is that 60 cents is the true value of an hour's worth of labor power. So? Why, then, the dollar-an-hour story with its intimation that the worker was robbed? Oh! That dollar applied to something else. There are really two things involved:

1) Value added by one hour's *labor* = one dollar
2) Value of one hour's *labor power* = sixty cents

We are talking about two different things—value added by labor and cost of labor power. To understand the two equations, you must think of a human being who belongs to the labor force as you would a machine: he costs so much to bring into the world; in a normal lifetime he consumes 60 million calories, as a truck consumes x gallons of gas; he yields 80,000 hours of work, as a truck is able to deliver y ton-miles—and so on to complete the analogy with depreciation, repairs, replacement, and all that. Now, all the costs of producing, maintaining, and replacing a worker, divided by the number of hours he can work in a lifetime, figures out in our assumed case to 60 cents an hour. Just as we can say that each ton-mile over the total lifetime of a truck figures out to two cents. Thus, when the worker gets 60 cents an hour for his *labor power* he is, in one sense, getting the proper reward for his time. He is being reimbursed for past and current labor congealed in *him*. Add up the money value of all the hours of labor required to produce, maintain, and replace a workingman; divide by the number of hours he will work in a lifetime. The figure you get is 60 cents. That is what he is paid for his *labor power*. The employer is under no business obligation to pay more; he has paid the total costs of production of the labor power he has bought. But when the worker actually goes to work, he adds one dollar's worth of value to whatever he is producing: one whole dollar's worth, not 60 cents' worth. Why?

Why not? the Marxians might say by way of reply.

This concept of getting something extra out of one of the factors of production was not foreign to economic speculation in its earlier days. A school of French economists known as the physiocrats (flourished about 1750) based their principal theories on a similar concept applied, however, to land rather than labor. Land, they said, yielded an economic super-plus: a net product, to use their phrase (*produit net*). Agriculture and mining yielded something special-extra they said. The physiocrats were wrong about land. But the Marxians believe they were right about the super-plus; and it is produced by labor, says Marx. He named the super-extra, "surplus value," a phrase which has become a most provocative one in the modern world.

Marx also gives a direct and positive reply to this question —though I do not mean by this that it is convincing. All through his economic theory he makes a distinction between use value and exchange value. There is no particular relationship between the two, he says. The exchange value of bread, for example, is about 17 cents a loaf today; its use value is incalculable, for it is the staff of life. In our example we may say that the exchange value of labor is sixty cents an hour; its use value is a dollar. And the capitalist is able to appropriate this difference. And there is no reason to believe that use value and exchange value should coincide. Marx develops this point fully and interestingly. I am reluctant to burden the reader with an expanded statement, however, because it is precisely here that Marx is least convincing. It cannot be said that he has made his point or that he has been able to convert even sympathetic readers. This is a crucial spot in Marxist doctrine. If his analysis here were unequivocal, then most of his other propositions would have to be accepted as true, with all that that implies. It is one of those things you either believe or don't believe.

The difference between what a worker consumes and what he produces, I have said, goes to the capitalist. He is not cheating the worker or demanding a kickback as straw bosses sometimes do. Sixty cents is the proper rate. He is simply paying the worker an amount equal to what the worker must expend to keep going efficiently. But why does not the worker see what is going on, and demand the surplus value for himself? Well, the worker does not see this clearly because our economic process is rather complex and obfuscating. But, anyhow, the capitalist is in a strategic position to appropriate that surplus value. Our institutions are such that the worker is not now in a strong enough situation to take what—according to Marx—might rightfully belong to him.

To Marx the important economic point here is not so much that the working class is being exploited, whatever slogan-value the concept may have in propoganda. Marx is, in a sense, hard-boiled about the "injustice" visited upon the worker, and rather admires capitalism for the productive miracles it has achieved. Marx's real interest in surplus value is that it is the lever to pry open the door of Utopia—the very thing he was looking for from the start. Surplus value not only belongs morally to the worker, but will destroy the capitalist system. Under capitalism the worker is never paid enough money to buy back all he produces. Thus, wares pile up and find no market. Gluts cause depressions; depressions cause misery; misery causes revolutions.

The process is a little more intricate than has been sug-

gested just above. Marx is not a pure and simple underconsumptionist. He assumes that technical progress will go on
apace and that production will employ fewer and fewer
men. This will be hard on labor, but it will also be hard on
capitalists. Surplus value, according to Marx, can come only
from living labor. Mammoth labor-saving machines cannot
produce surplus value, for surplus value is a kind of biological reversal of the law of the conservation of energy; surplus
value means that the value of the labor poured into the human organism is always less than the value of the labor that
can be drawn from it. This law is Marx's economic fundamental. This basic fact—a fact for Marxians only, of course
—is not true of machines, buildings or land. Thus the capitalist cannot exploit a turret lathe, a factory, or a coal mine. He
can exploit only an employee. When he gets rid of an employee (competence assumed), he gets rid of the only agent
of production that can be exploited, and thereby lowers his
income. Even when he substitutes labor-saving machinery
for workers, he loses—at least in the long run. He loses because only human beings can yield surplus value; and, in the
long run, surplus value is the only substantial and enduring
source of the employer's income (or profit).

Marx here recognizes the paradox that, although surplus
value can arise only out of human labor, employers rush to
get rid of their profit-returning workers and to substitute
for them batteries of expensive labor-saving machinery. He
removes the paradox by saying that any *individual* employer
who keeps ahead of his fellows by using new labor-saving
machinery cheapens his costs and may make a large differ-
ential gain. But when the others catch up with him—and
competition forces them to do so—they all ruefully discover

that they are now worse off than before. Now they all use
less labor to make surplus value for them, and the innovators
have lost their initially favorable position. Thus, what inno-
vating employers really want—on the Marxian theory—is
the jump on their competitors, not a reduction of the number
on the payroll. The decline is an inevitable outcome, but is
not the end sought; indeed, it defeats the end sought.

But there is a way of sustaining income, after all, Marx
tells us, at least for a while. By expanding his existing plant,
or building new plants, the capitalist can again employ more
men; by employing more men—or, rather, by employing as
many as were employed before the innovations—he can collect as much surplus value as he did in the past. In other
words, each dollar invested in new capital now brings in
less; but, since more dollars are being invested, incomes remain the same. The ratio of income to investment is always
going down, but the total amount of income is the same, because the same number of workers is employed in the expanded plant or branch factories. Workers are now spread
thin in a large number of expensive factories. The capitalist
is thus constantly driven to make new investments. To do so
he must frantically build new plants—here, or in Europe,
Cuba, China, Saudi Arabia, South America—where incidentally he comes into conflict with capitalists of other countries
on the same mission, a rencontre that (Marxians say) sometimes has serious consequences, like world wars.

On Marx's view, then, capitalism is at first a dynamic—
even in some ways admirable—force that equips the world
with machines, railroads, ships, communication networks,
and the like. At some point, however, the world's workshops
are built. After that, the continued rapid, remorseless build-

ing, building of new and often redundant equipment, becomes sheer madness from a community viewpoint. Over a long enough period it is a losing race.

Fewer and fewer men relatively will be employed and paid wages; more and more things will be produced—or, at least, will be producible, because of the vast amount of machinery in existence and because of its extraordinarily high productivity. Less and less *relatively* can be bought back by the working class. There will be gluts. Capitalists will produce too much to dispose of profitably. Workers will be too poor to buy. It will take months or even years to absorb the surpluses produced. This partly explains—to Marxians—the recurrent depressions with which we are so familiar. According to Marx they will get bigger and deeper and worse and longer. To get out of a depression, the price of capital goods will have to be scaled down, or capital goods will have to be destroyed. War is doubly useful to capitalism here, for it destroys factories and surpluses; but peaceful means may also be used, like burning surplus coffee, or plowing under every third pig (as followers point out).

The capitalist can expand for a long time, but at some point the waste and futility of overinvesting, overbuilding, overproduction, underconsumption—with attendant crises and wars—will be plain to all. When that time comes, capitalism will have decayed. Everybody will be sick of it. Society will be turned over to, or be taken over by, the working class under revolutionary leadership. Surplus value will become the property of the workers themselves, not of the owners of capital—indeed, there will no longer be any capitalists. Perhaps violence will be required to achieve the final step; even so, the era of violence is but a moment in a long, evolutionary process—like the period of labor in childbirth. Both are the final, decisive, traumatic events in a long process of gestation.

The main process described above will be accompanied by secondary movements, some described best by Marx, others by Lenin. One will be the disappearance of the middle class. Marx feels that we members of the middle class are doomed to extinction. As the process of capitalist development goes on, larger and larger industrial plants are needed for reasons spoken of above. To go into business for one's self requires more and more money. Monopolies and large-scale enterprises develop. The difficulties of starting business on nerve and a shoestring, or of hanging on after starting, increase. The time will come when there is no business except big business. During this period of evolution the middle class will, increasingly, find business opportunities closed. It will be driven into the ranks of the working class or of what Marxists describe as the paid flunkeys of capitalism: corporation lawyers, labor management experts, government employees, and so on. Some fine day (before the revolution) society will be neatly divided into only two groups: a few capitalists with their loyal henchmen and many workers. After the revolution, society will be classless.

Another secondary movement is imperialism, the reaching out of monopolies beyond national boundaries to pick up all raw materials and markets not already nailed down. This process, to be described more fully in a later chapter on foreign trade, will, by inciting warfare, further contribute to the disorganization of capitalist society.

A by-product of Marxism is its effect on almost all fields of knowledge. Marx held government—even democracy— to be the exclusive possession of an economically dominant oligarchy; although this is denied by most students of government, the concept has been used by some in their study of political science. Marx laid emphasis on the role of economic forces in history. This has for many scholars changed the study of history.

In the domain of biology, the greater importance of nurture over nature has long been a matter of thoughtful concern to the Marxist, and he has always been on the nurture side. The Marxist has had to deny that men reached the top in business, government, or even the professions, by inherited ability alone, or by native qualities of character or racial superiority or any inborn qualities. On the whole, Marxians must say, the big jobs are passed around by the elite to to its own members; and they are able to fill the jobs to which they are called because only they have the educational and other opportunities for training. The undernourished child of a dull-minded workingman, according to Marxist doctrine, could do as well if he were properly fed, and trained. To much of this many non-Marxists agree. But the point to be made is that in the Soviet Union today a most extreme position is being taken in the nature versus nurture debate. So extreme is this position that the validity of much American research in genetics is being denied by Russian scientists. American science does not minimize the importance of nurture, by any means, yet, apparently, we do not recognize its role sufficiently to please the Russians. I recall this to the reader merely as a crowning example of how deep and how far Marxism can leave its traces in every department of knowledge.

Out of the above discussion we are able to disengage what might be named the Marxian ikon; that is, the basic plan of the economic system. The Marxian ikon is dynamic—indeed, it is a moving picture rather than a static ikon.

Roughly, here is what we see in this cinematic ikon. Out of the ruins of feudalism a driving, restless class arises to build up a new culture, capitalism. It is industrial and urban, as feudalism was agricultural. It seizes—as all economically dominant classes do in the Marxian system—the control of government, of the church, and later of the press and system of education. It performs miracles of production, applies and encourages science. It fosters democracy and, in its conflict with the landed aristocracy, concedes to the working class certain rights it never before possessed. But it still exploits the working class; that is its functional (rather than moral) weakness. For out of this exploitation come the forces that will lead to its decay. In due course of time, this industrious, dynamic class will disappear. It will disappear because it blindly pursues its own logic to the point of self-destruction. The verdict of history will always be favorable to capitalism. Its historic mission was to build up a tremendously productive economic machine, which, however, it never learned to control. The future therefore belongs to the working class. Q.E.D!

Something like this is the basic ikon that Marxians have of contemporary economic society. It resembles a plant that grows, bears fruit and dies, rather than physical forces seeking equilibrium, as standard theory so often suggests. The ikon is of the whole society, rather than merely the economic part of it. Marx cannot separate the economic part of society from the rest of society, as standard theory often seems to do. Everything hangs together in an all-embracing pattern. But there are clearly erroneous ideas in this ikon, to be discussed in a later chapter.

The easiest way to summarize this chapter is to formulate the kind of questions that Marxism seeks to answer:

How can we get a fundamentally better economic system than the one we have—not just small improvements, but great ones?

Granted that capitalism is more productive than feudalism or any other economic system thus far known, does it produce as much as can reasonably be expected, having regard for the new inventions and the newly harnessed energies?

Why is capitalism so restless and dynamic—always expanding, unlike anything under feudalism—sometimes expanding fruitfully, sometimes compulsively and to little purpose?

Why is monopoly increasing? What causes capitalism to be changing so radically from the small, competitive industry of the Napoleonic era, to its present form—almost a negation of the professed objectives of capitalism itself?

What is the relationship between the economic system and the other institutions of society? The school? Church? Press? Government?

Why are there depressions?

Are wars related to the capitalistic method of producing and distributing goods?

Are depressions and wars likely to increase in frequency and severity under capitalism?

Since capitalism is not logically organized for survival what comes next?

Some of these are good questions; some are obviously loaded. Many of the answers are not convincing, even to those as far to the left as socialists are. I have heard the distinguished American socialist, Norman Thomas, say that Marx and socialism had little to do with each other, and that

Marx's chief value to socialism was not his economic theory but his having made the working class feel that history was on its side. British socialism would, I think, take about the same position on Marx.

10. THORSTEIN VEBLEN

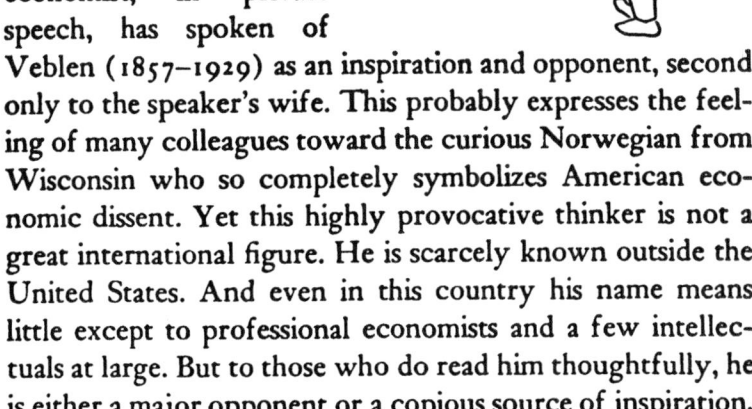

A NOTED AMERICAN
economist, in private
speech, has spoken of
Veblen (1857–1929) as an inspiration and opponent, second
only to the speaker's wife. This probably expresses the feeling of many colleagues toward the curious Norwegian from
Wisconsin who so completely symbolizes American economic dissent. Yet this highly provocative thinker is not a
great international figure. He is scarcely known outside the
United States. And even in this country his name means
little except to professional economists and a few intellec-
tuals at large. But to those who do read him thoughtfully, he
is either a major opponent or a copious source of inspiration,
or, ambivalently, he is both.

Veblen meets even more of the canons of dissent than
Marx, for he is completely a dissenter. Marx used standard
theory diabolically, to get his ends. Veblen spurned the
received doctrines as well as those of Marx: to him they all
just fell short of being completely useless. Unlike Marx, he
was not an activist. No movement or organization or even
school of thought rallies around his name. Early in his adult
life he was a professional philosopher. Later, uncommitted

by any brand of economic doctrine, he turned his attention to the economic world around him. This he looked at with level gaze and wrote down what he saw—wrote down what he saw with a misanthropy of Swiftian proportions.

Veblen's economics, though it is a rounded system,[1] has no theory of value. This is a tremendous departure from both standard theory and Marx. Price—if his readers were unduly concerned with trifles—is determined variously: sometimes by the forces of supply and demand, as the books said; more often by "what the traffic would bear." Price was fixed by a general process of collusion aimed against the underlying population, whether worker or consumer, in the back rooms of saloons or in paneled board rooms. But price is a dismal and tiresome subject to Veblen. Since the economic world, seen through his eyes, is fairly chaotic, the organizing function of price cannot be great, as standard theory asserts (see p. 42); and price formation loses much of its interest if it is not looked upon as the basis of economic organization. What *is* interesting to him is the kind of people human beings are—the sort who run the cock-eyed economic system they have. And to Veblen, it was *they*—a world he never made—for he had the ability to watch his fellow men as if he were not of them.

The most cursory study of human economic behavior reveals to Veblen a surprising state of affairs. Presumably mankind wants certain things like plenty of food, adequate housing, serviceable clothing, and the like. Presumably, too, mankind would wish to conform to a principle of parsimony in getting these things, that is, would like to get them with

[1] Since the opposite has often been asserted, the reader who wishes to pursue this matter is referred to an excellent article by Karl L. Anderson, "The Unity of Veblen's Theoretical System," *Quarterly Journal of Economics*, XLVII, No. 4 (Aug., 1933), 598–626.

the least expenditure of effort and the least waste of resources. And yet, as he looks around and considers the
mechanism actually devised by mankind to realize the desired ends, he finds no sleek, highly productive machine but
an awkward contraption, held together with flour and water,
scarcely more efficient than a fantasy by Rube Goldberg.
His discovery is like that of the psychoanalyst who finds in
his patient a great yearning for a husband and the esteem of
acquaintances, yet in her actual behavior, spitefulness and
hostility engendered by the unconscious fear that she might
get the very things she says she craves.

This is quite different from the findings of standard theory, which sees, at least in the ikon of a freely competitive
society, and therefore to some degree in society itself, a
well-organized efficient economic machine, where scarce
land, labor, and capital are efficiently disposed of by rational
entrepreneurs, where competitive prices ensure that everything will be devoted to its highest uses (compare p. 42).
Veblen sees half the human race starving, which means that
goals have been only half achieved; he sees waste of natural
resources, underproduction, and a great contamination of
the "instinct of workmanship," all of which prove to him
that the means used to achieve professed ends are halfhearted.

Why this unredeemed discrepancy between goals and
achievement, between ends and means? The main trouble
seems to be in man himself, the curious kind of animal he
has turned out to be, either because of his instinctive equipment or the civilization to which he belongs and conforms,
or to a nauseating mixture of both.

Man has, according to Veblen, two basic tendencies or
drives: constructive and destructive ones. Love, childbear-
ing, and science are among the general manifestations of the

constructive propensities; superstition, vain ritual, and love of hierarchy are among the general manifestations of the destructive propensities. The economist is primarily interested in certain other manifestations of the basic drives: making goods (constructive) and predation (destructive). During most of the history of mankind, including the present, we have had in our midst both the makers of goods and the predators. The economic system, could it have been directed by the makers of goods alone, would be rather efficient and serviceable; but the predators have always had a part in economic life, usually a very large part, and have clogged up the works. They have, through the ages, hampered and even sidetracked the forward movement of the constructive propensities by injecting into the mechanism such corroding liquids as superstition, ritual, hierarchy, love of waste, belief in luck or in divine and natural rights.

This age-long pulling and hauling between the two groups is by no means mitigated in the world of today. Conflicts are perhaps attenuated, at least within the boundaries of the great modern nations: there are no Wars of the Roses, or feuds resulting in bodily contacts between Burgundian lords and Orleanists. On the other hand, we do have monopolists, promoters, speculators, bankers, corporation lawyers, advertisers, salesmen, public-relations experts, statesmen, and the like, who place their dubious gifts at the service of the economic system. Since their talents are prompted in large part by the destructive psychological drives, their share in the productive process is in large part destructive. That is, they are the predators. This group comprises the money-makers, as opposed to the makers of goods, who are animated by the constructive propensities. To them the perfect economic action is not the beautiful

exercise of the instinct of workmanship, but the getting of
something for nothing. The money-makers are not much
interested in production. They are interested in the arts of
acquisition, in rights, sanctity of contract, the spin of the
wheel, the streak of luck, in status, hierarchy, and ritual.
Not only do they themselves inhibit the economic process,
but they also infect the entire society with their economically barren interests. Being a dominant class, they are the
envy of other classes, and there is a general tendency to
emulate that class, even among those who by necessity or
native endowment respond largely to the promptings of
the constructive tendencies. Though the workers are makers
of things they dream of "making money." They, too, love
to waste within their straitened incomes, gamble, get something for nothing; and, through their trade unions and otherwise they withdraw from industry part of their efficiency.
Thus we have a most imperfect system of production. Here
and there, in this factory or that operation we do find mar-
velous productive efficiency. But the system generally is
blighted by the pervasiveness of the destructive tendencies.

Now, between those who are primarily money-makers
and those who are primarily makers of goods, there is a
psychological gulf. There always has been a gulf between
the makers and predators. To Veblen all this is not exactly
a class struggle in the Marxian sense, though there are resemblances. There is now, he says, a widening gulf because
of the influence of the machine. Under feudalism and most
other isms of the past, the cleavage between the two groups
was held within bounds of a sort. Under capitalism, however,
which uses industrial machinery and promotes the development of science, the cleavage is and becomes deeper and
deeper. For the cultivation of science and the tending of

the machine nourish the realistic and constructive propensities in mankind while they starve the aggressive propensities
and destroy superstition. Thus, the machine-tenders (factory and transportation workers), engineers, scientists, and
all whose work develops the constructive tendencies, will
discover a progressive atrophy of their destructive traits.
The money-makers, of course, will develop, as before, their
aggressive traits.

In this state of affairs, several things can happen. Tension
between the people who like to make money and those who
make things will develop to the point at which there is overt
struggle. Out of this struggle, if the makers of goods win, we
may get either an industrial republic modeled on the patterns
of Utopian thought; or we shall get, if the makers of money
win, a reversion to a system of status, something like fascism.
(Veblen pointed out this possibility years before fascism
had appeared in Italy). Another possibility is that the money-
makers, imbued as they are by strong attitudes of national
glory, will wage nationalistic wars. Whatever happens, we
may be sure that capitalism as we know it will disappear.
When it goes, we may have instead an Utopian industrial
republic, or something else. The something else will be a
long season of warfare or a system of what today would be
named neo-fascism something like what George Orwell describes in the currently popular book, *1984.*

To many readers this division of society into an aggressive and financial class on the one hand and a constructive
class on the other may seem to be based on poor observation,
both of human society and human nature. Yet others
than Veblen have seen similar phenomena in cultures that
had never had significant contact with the modern free-
enterprise democracies. Miss Cora du Bois has found a tribe

on the island of Alor, north of Timor, that practices this
Veblenian dichotomy with startling faithfulness. The story
comes to us through Paul Einzig's book on *Primitive Money*.
The currency on Alor includes kettle-drums (*mokos*) and
brass gongs:

On Alor all the hard work is done by the women. Men have
no time for gardening or other similar physical labour, for they
have a full-time job on hand by looking after the highly involved financial system. Indeed, this division of labour is in
force to such extent that a woman who shows an interest in
finance is referred to as a "man-woman," while a man who finds
time for gardening or gathering wood is referred to as a
"woman-man." . . .

By far the most important part played by *mokos* and gongs
is in the sphere of credit. The total circulation of *mokos* in Alor
serves as a basis for an inverted pyramid of credit structure not
unlike that of our modern communities. On Alor, wealth consists essentially of a series of outstanding credits, not of accumulated property. Natives are busily engaged in looking after their
drum and gong investments, or are trying to find drums and
gongs to repay their debts. Those owning a number of these
valuables are not happy unless and until they have succeeded
in lending them—if only in order to protect them from being
seized by their creditors. It always requires an immense effort to
force debtors to pay, and festivities which provide occasion for
it are the scenes of furious haggling between creditors and
debtors.

When the creditors assemble in the debtor's house in order to
collect the drums and gongs the latter owes them, their own
creditors in turn are also present in order to lay claim to the
drums and gongs the moment they change hands. The result
is that in addition to the quarrels centring on the liquidation of
the principal debt, there is also a series of subsidiary quarrels
being waged on the side.

To form an idea of how fully this credit system dominates
the minds of the natives, Cora du Bois quotes a number of speci-
mens of their poetry in which there is very frequent reference
to the none too poetic subject of relations between debtors and
creditors.

"The lack of standardized currencies, the contest devices and the chicanery associated with wealth, the difficulties attendant upon feasts, the competitive system in which only a fraction of the male population can be successful, all contribute to the frustrations and irritations of gaining prestige," Cora du Bois remarks. "In addition, no one can relax his efforts once the goal has been reached. There are too many socially recognized pressures to permit him to withdraw and still maintain his status rating." [2]

It was characteristic of Veblen that he approached non-economic problems as an economist. The titles of some of his essays and books are not in the strictly economic tradition: *Instinct of Workmanship*, *Theory of the Leisure Class*, *An Inquiry into the Nature of Peace and the Terms of Its Perpetuation*, *The Higher Learning in America*, *The Place of Science in Modern Civilization*. Yet these varied subjects he treats with the compulsions of an economist. On the other hand, much of the traditional subject matter of economics he either neglects, or takes for granted as a truism, or touches upon lightly, or with audacious phrase sets in a new and disturbing light. For example, the "development of the American continent" is, to him, a "disemboweling" of the good earth. Loan credit, usually considered a highly productive thing by standard economics is dubiously so to Veblen except in so far as it transfers the control of capital from passive to active hands. He has a complete theory of the business cycle. We have already mentioned his theory of price: what the market will bear, primarily, though supply and demand play their obvious roles. I do not remember that he has anywhere a theory of distribution, but the basic principle of such a theory is easy to deduce: how much you

[2] Paul Einzig, *Primitive Money* (London, Eyre and Spottiswoode, 1949), pp. 95 ff.; Einzig quotes Cora du Bois, *The People of Alor* (Minneapolis, Univ. of Minnesota Press, 1944).

can get away from the other fellow—though Veblen would never have written so grubby a clause.

Most of his writing in the more strictly economic field consisted of his criticism of standard economic theory. He made enemies of those he criticized, but never opponents. He robbed them of their weapons because he would not fight their way. He simply pinned his colleagues to a dissecting board, carefully traced a muscle or other organ to its source, then explained coldly: "You see how curiously this tissue is fastened; how weak the sinew; how unnecessarily complex the method of attachment; how futile this tendon—a useless encumbrance; yet it all holds together in its freakish way and is paradoxically serviceable to the organism; on the whole, an interesting though defective specimen, gentlemen, and most certainly another example of Nature's inscrutable ironies." Then he would throw the whole thing into the waste pail, wash his hands, and quietly slip out of the laboratory. This was not in the tradition of the great economic debates, in which an opponent took the other seriously, spoke to him rather than to the reader, attacked his specific conclusions but never his general intellectual myopia. Veblen had few friends among economists.

He attacked their Benthamite psychology, their imputed ignorance of scientific method, their inability to see what bearing Darwin's theories had on economics, their contradictions, their limited scope and their eternal preoccupation with the theory of value, their blindness to the "opaque" facts of the economic environment, their fixation on eighteenth century doctrines of natural right, their Panglossian satisfaction that all was for the best in the best of worlds.

Veblen has exercised both a very great and a very slight influence on American economic thought: great in the sense that most economists of domestic growth between the ages of 45 and 70 have had their train of thought seriously arrested by his work; slight in the sense that many of them, after making a minor adjustment, if any, have allowed their thoughts to move on as before. His distinction between makers of goods and makers of money is used as a tool of analysis by only a very few, Wesley Mitchell being the most distinguished one. This is the heart of Veblenism; it is his ikon, just as a perfectly competitive society is the ikon of standard theory. Yet it has been disregarded by many whom he has otherwise strongly influenced.

His record under the minor categories is more impressive. One of his ideas on consumption, for example, has become a commonplace of the general theory of consumption—such as it is and what there is of it—not only in this country but elsewhere, namely that the wasteful use of goods confers a distinction on the user. He has spurred on inductive and statistical research. Though himself primarily a theorist and often a very abstract one, he pressed with a strong left hand for greater attention to facts, the irrefragable, "opaque" facts. Many of those on whom his influence is clearly visible today—again Mitchell is at the head of the list—are "statistical economists," an inadequate phrase, perhaps, but one usually intended to set a group apart from ordinary standard theorists. They are empirical, pragmatic, nontheoretical, but in a partial sense only. They are likely to be experts in one of the subdivisions of the economic realm—experts on labor, coal, transportation, social security and the like, or else economic historians.

For this urge toward fact-gathering Veblen must, however, not be given unalloyed credit. Part of it is in the spirit of the times; with social security, broad income taxation,

public assistance, and other kinds of governmental intervention demanded first by depression and then by war, facts
and figures have become an administrative necessity and
have stimulated inductive research in economics.

Veblen is the victim of a semantic prank. During the last
decade or so of his life, some of his followers described his
work as "institutional economics." Max S. Handman has
been credited with first using the phrase. The root word,
"institution," in its various forms and parts of speech, rapidly
spread as a way of designating Veblenian economics and the
teachings of those whom he influenced. It was not a very
good word, for it put emphasis in the wrong place, but I
have never run across any evidence that Veblen objected.
His writings suggest that he thought of his economics as
"evolutionary" rather than "institutional." At any rate, "institutional" became fixed, although it was perhaps more appropriate as a description of some of his disciples, like R.
Hoxie, than of himself.

Now, all this would be of little importance had not the
word suffered degradation in current economic writings.
"Institutional" has come to mean "descriptive." Writers of
manuals for the classroom state in their prefaces that the
institutional side of the science has not been neglected; the
reader will, for example, (they continue) notice that one
chapter is devoted to banking theory and the next to an institutional study of banking. Now, what does this mean?
It means that the writer has described the Federal Reserve
system and spoken briefly of the history of American banking in one of his two banking chapters! Thus, the tricks of
language have been unfriendly to Veblen, for they have
made him the victim of the following illogic:

Veblen is an institutionalist;

Institutionalism means any kind of economic description;

Therefore, Veblenian economics is any kind of descriptive economics.

Allan Gruchy, who has made a specialty of American dissenters, has suggested the word "holistic" to describe those economists now being covered by the word institutionalism. This is an excellent suggestion, but there is nothing to guarantee that that word might not be misused—that it might not, twenty years hence, be applied to any sort of a revolving economic statistician or historian.

Veblen strongly influenced many younger American economists during his lifetime. He died in 1929. But the spreading of his influence was rather suddenly halted for a variety of reasons. One was the reinvigoration of standard theory by some of the trends discussed in Chapter 6: the economics of imperfect competition, Keynes's ideas on the cause and cure of the business cycle, and abandonment of the pleasure-pain equilibrium. The work of Keynes was particularly attractive. He promised a sure-fire cure for depressions—something that could not be resisted by those young graduate students who were in their disappointed twenties when the century was in its depressed thirties. Many who might have been counted upon to be Veblenians —other things being equal—have become Keynesians instead.

But Keynes's promise of full employment is not the only thing that has told against Veblen. If you accept his system you have gone as far as you can, and you are lost. All you can do is to sit at a dead end waiting for one of three things to happen: more frequent wars, reversion to a system of status, the appearance of an industrial republic following Utopian hopes. Since it seems to go against human nature to wait for Armageddon without lifting a finger to help prepare one's side for victory in that final battle, one tends to adopt a more activist attitude—and by so doing, one denies Veblen's basic teachings—for he was a determinist. His books have the remorselessness of Greek tragedy. Man being what he is and his institutions being what they are, his destiny is clear. To be sure, Veblen suggested more than one destiny for mankind, but human beings had no control over which fate would overtake them.

But wait—there is one thing that can be done: to let one's curiosity, one's "idle curiosity," slowly, honestly, painfully, study mankind as it tries to get its living. Perhaps something might come of that, but Veblen did not believe many people would be willing to undergo such terrible self-discipline.

He died as he lived, an unhappy man, unhappy perhaps because he believed that "history records more frequent and more spectacular instances of the triumph of imbecile institutions over life and culture than of peoples who have by force of instinctive insight saved themselves alive out of a desperately precarious institutional situation, such, for instance, as now faces the peoples of Christendom." [3]

[3] T. Veblen, *The Instinct of Workmanship* (New York, 1914), p. 25.

11. EVALUATION OF DISSIDENT THEORY

IN MAKING OUR AP-
praisal of the economics
of dissent we must be on
our guard against preconceptions that we ourselves may
bring to the task. Those of us who are more or less in revolt
against our economic institutions and contemporary culture
at large shall recognize in Marx and Veblen kindred spirits,
and shall approve too heartily and too uncritically of their
findings. Those of us, on the other hand, who like our modern society as it is, may find Marx and Veblen so repugnant
to our moral feelings that we shall be unable to discover any
good in them or to sift out their economics from their propa-
ganda or misanthropy. To take an Olympian position of
even-handed judgment free from Utopian or ideological
bias (see p. 16) is to try for perfection, but surely there can
be no harm in trying.

First we take up the merits of our dissenters. We can get
at their more obvious merits by running backward through
the sausage grinder of criticism some of the same materials
which, in Chapter 7, we ran through frontward. The faults
pointed out in standard theory and avoided in dissident the-

ory are, in a sense, virtues. Thus we can perhaps praise the following:

1. The scope of the dissenters is not narrow; the dissenters have long taken account of the business cycle, the great role of monopoly in economic life, and the rise and decline of social institutions.

2. Methods of dissenters are more varied and less completely based on the method of mechanics and mathematics. They study the present and even the future in the light of the past; they have, we observed, a cosmogony; they seek to achieve greater realism by induction (statistical investigation; regard for the "opaque" fact). It can even be alleged that dissident theory really works more like the natural sciences than standard theory does. Since Darwin and Einstein —not to mention the matter-is-energy scientists who preceded Einstein—the natural sciences are quite different from what they were when Ricardo and others set the pattern for standard economics.

3. The dissident ikon is not based on the concept of a nonexistent, perfectly competitive society dominated by group harmony. However wrong Marx may have been in his oversimplified view of class conflict, he at least had the germ of a truth, namely, that not all economic agents are pulling together to achieve a harmonious result. The dissident ikons we have examined are comprehensive enough to include and plausibly explain: the business cycle; why businessmen as a class seem to favor exportation over importation; monopoly; evolving and changing capitalism.

4. Dissident theory certainly cannot be accused of insisting that we now live in the best of all possible worlds. There are, certainly, no apologetics in dissenting theory.

5. Dissenters seem to have a fuller understanding of

human psychology and to base their economics upon it. Veblen's psychology is probably better than Marx's, but even Marx saw a much more complex human being than Bentham and Ricardo, or their latter-day followers. The reader who may wish to go more deeply into this problem should read R. Osborn's *Freud and Marx: a Dialectical Study*.

Now for some of the faults. It is obvious that Marx's Utopian bias caused him to combine his variables in such a way as to get the conclusions he wanted without regard to the rules of evidence or science. A theory that marches so directly toward the Utopian goal so obviously desired by its author may be correct, but is certainly suspect. We must at least tentatively assume that what he found out was determined by what he wanted. If it is a vice of standard theory that, as some have alleged, it selects its material with an uncritical and unscientific loyalty to the authoritarian agencies of society, then it is equally a vice—a methodological vice—of Marxism that it selects its data with a view to the abolition of present authority.

Some of Marx's faults spring from his virtues. For example, he made his study realistic by insisting upon the phenomenon of conflict. But he limited himself too narrowly; inordinate emphasis on the class struggle seems a distortion of whatever is valuable in the idea of conflict on the economic plane. It is true that he spoke of internecine struggles among capitalists and among members of the working class, but for him struggles between man and man paled into insignificance before the struggle between the classes. A more accurate view would probably reveal the greater significance of an all-pervading conflict for economic goods or economic advantage—a conflict that differs from both the class struggle of Marx and the Eton-playing-field competition posited by standard theory. His labor theory of value, on which so much of his argument is based is never submitted to proof.

Though I have indicated praise for Marx's cosmogony, or, rather, cosmogonical approach, I had a mental reservation which it is now high time to share with the reader. His cosmogony was founded on purely philosophical—worse, metaphysical—grounds, not on science. It is true that a cosmogony concerning even the more concrete physical world of natural science also leans toward the metaphysical, but science does provide a few checks against sheer fantasy or the errors of Utopian bias. Not so in Marx's case. He was a Hegelian, a Hegelian invert, to be more accurate, and his cosmogony was directed toward a preconceived end. The glaring example is his belief that the capitalist class has a "historic mission" to develop the techniques of production and to endow the world with a full equipment of factories, steamships, telegraphs, trucks and tractors; then, when most flourishing and best-equipped, the world would become the property of the working class. This historic mission he often invokes as the reason why capitalism cannot reform, will run its course, and must eventually abdicate. Often it looks as if all of history had developed with only Marx's goals in mind, as if everything that had ever happened had taken place in order to prepare the way for his industrial cooperative republic. This seeing of a goal in history is teleological, and science is allergic to teleology.

It is not so easy to find similar faults in Veblen. He came fifty years later, after Darwin, and his cosmogony had better models to pattern by. This is not to say that Veblen is right or without contradiction or flaw. He was certainly not dispassionate, and the Olympian calm found in him by his uncritical admirers is denied on every page he wrote by his sadistic prose. His work is somewhat marred by Utopian bias, for he, like Marx, wanted an industrial, cooperative republic of some sort. Nevertheless, he comes closer than Marx to the ideals of science.

There are definite, tangible faults in Veblen, however. His psychology, for all its strength, is vulnerable at one important point. He argued that the discipline of the machine on the worker would develop the latter's constructive propensities. This was no minor point in his scheme, yet it is one that finds no support in modern psychology. It was no minor point because this theory is the only door left open by Veblen for humanity's escape from its present state of want and warfare to better things (see p. 157). But modern psychology offers no evidence that the machine process has any special power to instill in man a greater reliance on his constructive propensities.

It is also charged that Veblen, with "audacious charlatanism"—to use Eric Roll's phrase—pushed fruitful ideas to ridiculous extremes. He seems to say, for example, that business and financial activities *always* hinder production, and that the cleavage between making money and making goods is absolute. This would have to be put down as an extreme view. A similar point is his discussion of the economic basis of beauty. Rightfully he makes the point that beauty is imputed to some things only or primarily because they are expensive or "in style" (being stylish costs money), or are otherwise associated with wealth, leisure, and decorous waste. But this fruitful idea sometimes gets pushed too far.

His contempt for the standard economist's supply-and-demand theory makes him ignore completely the pricing process, except to ejaculate occasionally the phrase "what the traffic will bear." Perhaps he felt that standard theory was already overcultivating the field of price determination, or that the field was of secondary importance, anyhow. If so, it might have been gracious of him to explain to his colleagues why he was ignoring a subject that was so highly esteemed by them.

The best that can now be said of Veblen is that he gave a stimulus to the development of a more realistic kind of economics. Some of his more ardent admirers believe he has not yet come into his own, and that his real stature will be appreciated only in future decades.

And that is remarkable when one considers that Veblen's work consisted so largely of untested hypotheses and therefore stood in exactly the same vulnerable position as the standard theory of his day!

One very telling criticism can fairly be made of all dissenters, Marxian, Veblenian, or otherwise. They have not yet developed a truly reliable science of economics. Even if one were disposed to concede their claims that they are more realistic than standard theory, or that their ikons are more nearly related to the things represented, or that their cosmogony clarifies economic processes, or that their methods promise to be more fruitful, one would still have to admit that they are only on the threshold of understanding economic life.

It is important to point this out, because one may sometimes get the impression from dissenters that they are ridding economics of bad philosophy, poor psychology, and a casuistic method, and that they are substituting science for all this. Perhaps this is true, but if it is, the science is still in the most undeveloped state. William James, who can scarcely be described as a foe to the science of psychology, observed in his mature years that psychology was but "a string of raw facts; a little gossip and wrangle about opinions; a little classification and generalization." This, he concluded, "is no science, it is only the hope of a science." Economics, too, is only the hope of a science, and dissenting theory has not been able to push it beyond this point.

It is often said that though dissenters have done useful critical work, they have not built up a complete and rounded system. This is a little different kind of accusation from the one made just above. One can have a rounded system without having a science. And one may reasonably ask why it is important to have a rounded system if it is unscientific—I am assuming, of course, that economics should aim toward science, not primarily toward the field of values as do aesthetics or ethics. Well, the charge of lack of system is widely made and should be examined. It is perhaps a loose rather than untrue accusation. It is loose because it does not take into account the fact that individual dissenters, like Marx and Veblen, have developed very tight systems. *Das Kapital*, particularly, is rounded and complete—if anything, more nearly perfect formally than anything standard economic theory can show after generations of patching up and revision—but not necessarily more nearly true. Allan Gruchy, in his *Modern Economic Thought* has convincingly shown to many of his readers that current American dissenters are bound together in ways to suggest the emergence of a school or of a body of systematic doctrines. Veblen, too, has a fairly well-rounded system.

The accusation is also loose when it assumes, as it usually

does, that dissident economists have found no way of answering the questions that standard theory would like to have answered. Dissident theory sees the economic world differently. It therefore often asks questions that are different from those of standard theory, and doesn't care a fig about those that trouble the standard economist. And, of sourse, it takes pains to answer questions that standard theory considers unworthy of asking in the first instance. Here is a modern version of the medieval debates about how many angels can stand on a pinhead; or can God, being all-powerful, make a wheel turn and stand still at the same time? These are interesting and perhaps important problems if you take a certain view of the world and of what lies beyond it. But to most of us, sinful creatures of the twentieth century that we are, some issues raised by the medieval schoolmen are unworthy of debate. For similar reasons, dissenting economists sweep aside grandly and even sometimes contemptuously, the questions raised by their standard brethren. On the other hand, they study meticulously things that standard theory considers trivial or, at best, beyond the scope of economics.

The accusation of lack of system is also loose if it carries with it the assumption that dissenting theory is totally destructive and repudiates almost everything ever developed by standard theory. Such an assumption is absurd. For thousands of years reasonable men have known that scarcity causes high prices. This is Biblical truth, amply demonstrated by the story in Genesis about Pharaoh, Joseph, the seven lean years, and the willingness of Egyptians to barter all their possessions for a few bushels of wheat. Mark Twain endows Huckleberry Finn with the knowledge that, if quantity is increased, prices go down (other things being equal).

No dissenter repudiates this verity. Most dissenters admire much of the demand-and-supply analysis of Marshall. Some acknowledge the usefulness of the multiple-equation approach of Walras and Cassel (pp. 100, 101). A little of this kind of learning is to them not a dangerous, but a most valuable thing. Dissenters, however, soon discover a point of diminishing return in the study of this kind of business, and they believe there are more things beyond supply and demand than are dreamed of in standard theory.

There is, however, some sort of justice in the accusation of lack of system. Standard theory has, by contrast with dissident theory been hashed over and mulled over by successive generations. There has been a secular cumulation of economic knowledge, stone upon stone. It is true, as was stated in Chapter 6, that recent emphasis on the business cycle and imperfect competition has destroyed the symmetry and hanging-togetherness that characterized standard theory before 1930. But even in its presently disrupted state, standard theory has probably a more obvious pattern than dissident theory.

No such process of cumulative piling-up is easily distinguishable in dissenting theory. What is perhaps sound in Marxism has been thrown out with what is unsound, and, speaking too unqualifiedly, no body of economists, other than political followers of Marx has sought patiently to utilize what is good. Marx came, made a splash and vanished —vanished from the field of academic economic theory in democratic communities, that is. He is, of course, very visible elsewhere. Something like that may be said of Veblen except that he is not highly visible anywhere. There has been little attempt to salvage the good, to test it, retest, apply to new problems.

To this statement there is an exception. For more than thirty years a group of public men and economists have worked together in a research organization named the National Bureau of Economic Research, Inc. During most of its existence the leading spirit was Wesley Mitchell, who was much influenced by Veblen. The current director of research, Arthur F. Burns, is in the same tradition. For thirty years the Bureau has made meticulous inquiries into the nature of our economic system. It is perhaps true that the general outlook of dissident theory and its attitude of revolt from the methods of standard theory have determined the Bureau's major projects and attack on problems. Yet one cannot possibly say of the Bureau that it is a custodian of active, current dissent. It has merely tried to look at our economic system in steady appraisal and to report what it found without Utopian or ideological bias. The best among modern dissenters have no higher goal.

Our conclusions from this chapter must be that dissident economic thought, despite its waywardness, has left us many fructifying ideas. To those who, uncommitted to any system of economic thought or way of economic life, wish only to understand economic phenomena or find promising paths toward understanding a great field of human behavior, dissident theorists have much to offer. But they, like standard theorists, are neither custodians of the whole truth, nor free from bias and error.

Part Four

SPECIAL PROBLEMS

12. BOOM AND BUST

INTRODUCTION

As the industrial revolution developed, and the monetary economy spread, economists began to cultivate special interests within the larger framework of general theory, interests like foreign trade, money, banking, taxation, and, later, labor problems, agricultural economics, public utility regulation, monopolies. Economists today are mostly specialists, either as teachers, government officials, business advisers, or functionaries in the United Nations and its associated organizations. In thus specializing, economics follows the general trend in all fields of knowledge.

The implication should not be left with the reader, however, that interest in special topics is entirely a modern phenomenon. Decadent Rome was very much interested in what today we would call agricultural economics, probably because of soil exhaustion. The economists of the Middle Ages, if Thomas Aquinas and Albertus Magnus count as economists, were much concerned with usury and just price —indeed, that was economics to them. The century before Adam Smith yielded many competent studies on foreign

trade. The German Kameralists who flourished in the eighteenth century and earlier were much concerned with taxation and other problems of public finance. Ricardo's great
work was entitled *The Principles of Political Economy and
Taxation.* One fourth of the book is devoted to a discussion
of various kinds of taxes.

We are going to study a representative list of special topics
in this section: money, banking, taxation and the public debt,
foreign trade, the business cycle. I selected these after looking at a dozen or more current college textbooks on elementary economics and discovering that all of them treated
these subjects at least. Most textbooks include one special
topic that will be omitted, namely, labor problems. In a book
that tries to economize the reader's time and effort, that
topic seemed to be the most expendable.

The basic pattern in the chapters to follow will be the
same as that of the preceding parts of the book: first, how
does standard theory see this thing?; second, how does dissenting theory see it? The actual execution of this plan will,
however be a little different. The topic under discussion in
each succeeding chapter will, within the limits of the chapter
itself, be subjected to double scrutiny. At some point each
chapter will break somewhere, to show that dissident theory
begins and standard theory ends. The chapter on taxation
and public debt is an exception. I am not aware of any
sufficiently great divergency of viewpoint based on the
standard-dissident cleavage to be worth reporting.

UNEMPLOYMENT AND DEPRESSION

If we consider the economic achievement of our nation
over the decades and particularly since 1940, we have many
reasons to feel a complacency that no other country at any

other period of history has had the right to feel. During the war we produced guns *and* butter. Our population rose to a Standard of Life, as the British say with capitals, that equaled or excelled anything heretofore known, even by Americans. Since the war there has been no long period of serious unemployment; except for small groups that have been by-passed, like teachers, and those who have felt the full shock of the housing shortage, few have had reasonable grounds to complain too bitterly of their lot, economically. This does not mean that there are no poor people at all or that there have not been abuses, extremes of wealth and economic power, dubious policies, trends that point to trouble ahead. But it does mean that the institutions which we wrap up in a semantic bundle named "capitalism" have triumphantly demonstrated their ability, in the United States, to produce and distribute wealth more effectively than has ever been done before.

The sense of great satisfaction that the ordinary man might derive from this fact is, however, spoiled by the great anxiety that he feels about the brittleness of his prosperity. Depression has always been just around the corner in our thoughts. We enjoy our good fortune uneasily. Capitalism in America has licked problems that no other form of economic organization has ever been able to master. But it has one great disadvantage: it goes into recurrent tailspins. Stalin is still counting on these as his secret weapon.

Except perhaps to the very young, little needs to be said about the social and economic evils of a depression. Many of us who are over thirty experienced some of these evils first hand: unemployment, business failure, sudden loss of fortune, social unrest, careers halted, hopes for higher education disappointed, marriage delayed or entirely circumnavigated, bad teeth from wrong diets, and countless other miseries and frustrations. Unless relief is given adequately and in time such things may lead to revolution. Some qualified observers have gone so far as to trace the Second World War ultimately to the depression of the 1930's. A prosperous Germany, it is argued, would never have accepted Hitler. And without Hitler there would have been no war.

Cannot this great imperfection of capitalism be remedied? Can we not stamp out depressions? The purpose of this chapter is to see what two great economists have to say on the subject: first, the standard theorist, John Maynard Keynes—though it must be conceded that Keynes represents standard theory with the "new look"; and, second, Wesley C. Mitchell, as a representative of dissident theory.

When the history of the economic doctrines of this period is written in the perspective of time—say about A.D. 2050 —one of the chief things to record will be that in the 1930's and 1940's economists as a class finally gave serious attention to the study of depressions. It is true, of course, that dissident economists have been giving them serious attention for a century and a half; it is also true that here and there a nondissenting, or standard, economist had made a specialty of boom-and-bust theory. But it was not until after 1936 that Anglo-American economists as a whole began to think of the ups and downs of business as something important enough to put at the center of economic theory rather than at the edges.

Historians will probably give the British John Maynard Keynes credit for this shift of interest. As a great economic showman with a perfect sense of timing, a coiner of quotable phrases, a glamor boy of the dismal science, he moved depressions toward the very center of economic theory. But historians of economic doctrines will perhaps also record that, on balance, the work of some of Keynes's American contemporaries, particularly Wesley C. Mitchell, came earlier, was more durable and less conducive to error.

How can we explain the amazing fact that standard economic theory, until 1936, relegated so important and visible a phenomenon as depression to a tail-end position in their mystery? The answer probably is that coming to grips with the problem posed by alternating periods of prosperity and depression would destroy their ikon of the economic world. We saw, in the third chapter of this book, that standard theory had developed the concept of a world automatically organized by price, competition, certain basic human drives and the like. Among the corollaries of this theory of economic organization was the inevitability of the full employment of resources (land, labor, and capital). It followed from the ikon that, if factories were idle or men unemployed, then somebody would be smart enough to make a profit by bringing them together—and therefore somebody *would* bring them together and make the profit and the idleness of economic factors would be short-lived.

Now, of course, it was observed that this did not always happen. When it did not happen the event was considered a departure from "normal" or from "equilibrium"—an aberration or oversight that would soon correct itself. If it did not soon correct itself, then perhaps the tariff ought to be lowered, or inter-Allied debts should be canceled, or perhaps the unemployed workmen were holding out for too high a wage or the owners of the machines were holding out for monopolistic profits. In any event, the ikon of a self-regulating economy that ordered things to their highest

uses and called out the full employment of resources was
much too precious to discard just because some occasional
maladjustment cast doubts on its validity.

There were, of course, economists, standard economists,
who thought about these things a little more profoundly.
Jevons had wondered whether good and bad crops did not
have something to do with good times and hard times: and
bad crops, he felt, might be related to the periodic reappear-
ance of sun spots. Schumpeter believed that capitalism
encourages innovation; innovation attracts imitators; innovation and imitators appear, he explains plausibly enough,
in wavelike surges and are reflected in an uneven economic
rhythm. Others spoke of keen competition at a peak of
prosperity between consumers and entrepreneurs for all the
products and resources of the economy; the tremendous
bidding up of prices on both sides would lead to a crash.
Despite the acuity of insight of some of these special inquiries, none of them shook anybody's faith in the basic
ikon, partly because the theories themselves were not iconoclastic.

Then, in 1936, in the midst of depression, came Keynes
and he *was* iconoclastic. He published in that year his book
on the business cycle. It had a curious title: *The General
Theory of Employment, Interest and Money*. Each word in
Keynes's title is interesting but the most interesting of all is
the word "general." What is its significance? In his brief,
opening chapter—a *chapter* less than 200 words long—he
says, in effect, that standard theory, for more than a century
had been studying a special case only. The special case is
economic equilibrium when there is full employment. There
are, he intimates, several other "possible positions of equilibrium," among them being, as readers later find, positions

of chronic unemployment or depression. Hence the phrase in his title, "general theory." Keynes proposes to discuss more than one position of equilibrium, not just the one postulated by standard theory. He promises a more *general* theory than that offered by his predecessors.

This two-hundred-word chapter is meant to be provocative, and it is. It seems to make a clean break with standard theory and its ikon. To Keynes, the study of depressions is no longer the postscript or afterthought of economic theory; it is the basic idea which molds the remainder, and his followers (who are legion) have been using his ideas to clarify such special subjects as banking theory, foreign-trade theory, public finance, and so on. A large part of what is significant in the Keynesian doctrines is negative—intentionally so. It is negative, or destructive, in the good sense: in the sense that before offering his positive ideas, he demolishes obstructive dogmas of nineteenth century standard economic theory. One of these is Say's law, already referred to in preceding pages. A depression, he says, is not a temporary disequilibrium that soon rights itself in a laissez-faire economy; on the contrary, a depression may itself be a case of equilibrium. In other words, the underemployment of resources (which includes unemployment of men) may turn out to be long enduring and incapable of automatic readjustment. To get out of this situation, overt steps may have to be taken (by government, perhaps). In putting forward these negative propositions Keynes was able to make them stick where others had written in water. He succeeded for several reasons: he published in a timely year, 1936, in the midst of a depressed period, when interest in such a book was high; he had already won, through earlier works and deeds, great prestige in government, business, and academic circles;

his known sympathies, unlike those of Marx and of neutral
dissenters cursed with a long historical perspective, lay un-
deviatingly with our democratic institutions.

When dissenters criticize standard theory they are overly
serious and much too highbrow. Keynes was serious but
not too highbrow in criticism. Dissenters accuse standard
theorists of being followers of Locke, taxonomic, nonevolu-
tionary, hedonistic, utilitarian, of being arrested in the rational eighteenth century, of not having emancipated
themselves from outworn concepts of psychology, natural
law, of being Newtonian rather than Darwinian. Standard
theorists do not like to have all these names flung at them.
Keynes made none of these accusations. He said only: "Hey,
fellows, haven't you forgotten that there is an unemployment equilibrium as well as a full-employment equilibrium?"
No accusations that dark philosophical sins are being committed. He spoke their language. This cannot be overes-
timated. His partial repudiation of standard theory was
phrased in the cadences to which standard theory is accustomed. Readers were not rubbed the wrong way by historical studies, statistical tables, anthropological evidence,
psychological theories, or other changes in the methodology
of economics. Instead, Keynes's writings are full of the
equations that reassure so many economists and his propositions can comfortably be turned into little diagrams roughly
similar to the ones of Chapter 4. In all of this Keynes was
doing only what came naturally to him, but if one had cyn-
ically planned a campaign to break through the resistances
of standard theory, none could have been better planned.
The unconsciously adopted strategy worked marvelously,
and Keynes won a large fraction of Anglo-American economists to his doctrines.

His positive theory is an underconsumptionist theory. Not all individuals, he says, spend all the money they get. Everybody who can saves something, the poor saving less, absolutely and relatively, than the rich. This tendency to underconsume may cause trouble. Men's habits of consumption are fairly stable and predictable, Keynes says, and, in rich societies the gap between what is received and what is spent is large. The residue is, of course, saved. If we could somehow make everybody spend appreciably more of his income when incomes rise and save less of it, depression would be milder and, in the extreme case, nonexistent. The Keynesians state that depressions are worst in the rich countries, where individuals save, or try to save, a lot.

If, then, we could make people spend *all* their incomes we would not have depressions. This statement suggests a method of control: make people spend all their money. But Keynes recognizes that you cannot put people in jail because they won't spend their whole income. There are special problems, too, for those who have monster incomes to spend year after year after year. He therefore looks elsewhere for a means of applying his principal controls. But something can be done about spending, even so. Keynes advocates greater equality of incomes—not by any means complete equality, just greater equality. Allied to this idea is his refutation of the argument that a cut in wages will solve the problem of depression—an argument that had been made by many economists during the early 1930's.

When Keynes wrote, a striking characteristic of capitalist countries had long been the extremely unequal division of the national income. In the United States it was true, as hostile critics of capitalism never tired saying, that the richest 5 percent of the population were getting one third of the nation's entire income; that the upper 1 percent were getting a fifth of the whole; and that the lower half among income receivers got less than a fourth. These figures varied somewhat from year to year, of course, but the general pattern was a clear and established one, not only for the United States, but also for other capitalist nations. The Second World War has completely disrupted this pattern in the United States and probably in other modern industrial countries as well. Simon Kuznets, an able student of income statistics, finds that relative equality of income has gone very far in the United States. Since 1946, Kuznets's studies suggest, the top 5 percent have received only 18 percent of the total national income (compared with 34 percent in 1929); and the uppermost 1 percent have received less than 8 percent (compared with almost 20 percent in 1929). This is a change indeed! It is a great but peaceful social revolution, and it is doubtful whether the Soviet Union, after a violent social upheaval and three and a half decades of professed economic egalitarianism, can truly boast of a similar accomplishment.

Keynes died before this new income pattern became visible. We can only guess as to how this big fact would shape his thinking if he were alive. Would he say that depressions are things of the past? Would he say that an end of the Korean War and of rearmament might plunge us back into a skewed distribution of incomes again, and thus back into depression again? We cannot know and must therefore return to consider what Keynes actually wrote rather than speculate on what he might have written today.

Normally, Keynes said, less is saved out of low or medium incomes than out of very high incomes—not only absolutely but also proportionately. If, then, we did a rather effective

job of bringing down the highest incomes and raising the
lowest through very sharply graded income taxation, a
much larger part of the total income of the nation would be
spent on food, houses, clothes; and a smaller total saved—
often pointlessly saved as we shall see presently. According
to the Keynesians, this lively spending would keep business
activity humming and would prevent depression. This, then,
is the mechanism to be used to make people spend a larger
part of their incomes; or, more exactly, to cause a larger
share of the total income to be spent on the products of farm
and factory. But Keynes does not put all of his faith in increased consumer spending, and does not advocate going
too far in equalizing incomes. After all, there must be some
saving and some investment in a dynamic society. And after
all, investing in new capital goods (like locomotives or steam
shovels) also keeps the wheels of industry turning. Let us
see how Keynes handles this part of the question: spending
on capital goods.

Since it is characteristic of our world that consumers do
not spend all they get on food, clothing, shelter, and other
consumer's goods, there is an unspent quantity lying idle
in our economic system. This we must follow up. Whenever you and I decide to save more out of our income we
run the risk of subtracting by that much from the income
of somebody else. When we cut down expenditures on
cigars or on a new dress for our wives, we reduce the income
of tobacconist and of the modiste. To be sure, this may be
compensated for somewhere. Our savings may fall into the
hands of some borrowing manufacturer who pays us interest and buys a new machine with our savings. This can
happen directly or through a bank which uses our savings
account as the basis for a loan. Either way, our money pays

for the machine, and is in turn transferred to those who market and make the machine; and these, in turn, pass our money along to tobacconist or modiste. If this happens, our savings flow back into the general income stream and are spent by others just as effectively as if we ourselves had spent the money on cigars and clothes. But sometimes our savings get dammed up, or flow into a kind of economic backwater, and are not spent by anybody. That's bad, says Keynes.

Whether our savings are effective, in that they are invested by others, or whether they are abortive, in that they merely subtract from other incomes, is not for us as consumers and savers to decide. This is a decision made by entrepreneurs. If entrepreneurs decide to invest actively, the savings of individuals return to the income stream of the society. If they decide not to invest actively, our savings are withdrawn from the income stream; or, to put it differently, what we have saved is lost to the business system as a whole, though not necessarily to us as individuals.

From this it follows that prosperity depends upon a strong propensity to invest as well as upon vigorous spending by consumers. When businessmen are investing heavily, the stream of income is high. There is little if any unemployment. The country is prosperous. But let us be clear about the meaning of the word "investment." Investment here means building new plants, adding to equipment and inventories now in existence—not mere acquisition from other holders of old stocks and bonds. It means the new investing of the entire economy, not the swapping around of the same investment among different owners—which is what happens if you "invest" by acquiring the house I have owned and lived in for ten years. The total national income, then, de-

pends on the total amount newly invested. In one place
Keynes puts it this way: "The amount of consumption-
goods which it pays entrepreneurs to produce is a function
of the amount of investment-goods which it pays them to
produce." [1] The total sums paid by consumers for consumption goods and by entrepreneurs for investment goods are,
of course, equal to the income of a nation—at least in the
simplified case, which leaves out certain transactions that
do not interest us.

Since heavy investment of this kind increases the national
income (makes us all better off), while light investment
diminishes the national income and makes us poorer, how
can we keep investment high—high enough to absorb all
that savers in advanced countries feel able to save, and therefore high enough to guarantee prosperity?

One way to increase investment is to keep interest rates
low. If I can borrow money at 2 percent and make it earn 8
percent in a new venture, I am more likely to invest than if
I have to borrow at 7 or 8 percent. I can never be sure that
it will actually bring a return of 8 percent, of course; I must
act on my best judgment. Incidentally, the best rate that any
new investment can be expected to yield is formidably
named the "marginal efficiency of capital." This is part of
the Keynesian dialect; no one had ever used that phrase
before. The government policy suggested is that the competent authorities should do what they can to keep interest
rates low as an antidepression device. And this statement
completes a basic Keynesian chain: a low interest rate stimulates investment; much investment increases the national
income; a high level of national income means a high level

[1] From an article by Keynes in *The New Economics,* ed. Seymour Harris
(New York, Knopf, 1947), p. 193.

of employment. Which brings Keynes to the place he
wanted to get to when he began.

He did not expect a low interest rate to perform miracles,
however, even if combined with the other reform spoken of
above, namely, a partially equalized distribution of income.
Something else would, in most cases, and in developed
countries particularly, have to be added to his elixir of prosperity. And that something else, he suggested, might be
investment by government itself—government spending, in
other words. He seemed to feel that the great investment
oportunities of the nineteenth century for private capital
were over, at least in the advanced capitalist nations; and
that in this new day, governments would have to spend
heavily when private capitalists were bashful about investing
—that is, whenever the marginal efficiency of capital seemed
too low to them, even if interest rates were also low. This
application of the Keynesian doctrines puts the stamp of
approval on such things as the old WPA, and on TVA's (if
built in depression).

Keynes came to this country in the early Roosevelt days
(June, 1934) and gave his benediction to many of the spending programs of the New Deal, though he later decided that
more should have been spent. According to Frances Perkins,
then Secretary of Labor, a meeting between Roosevelt and
the economist turned out to be somewhat disappointing to
those who might have believed that the two great spending
advocates would greet each other like brothers. Roosevelt
complained that Keynes was too theoretical, and Keynes
that the President should have known more about economics.[2] The President later remarked to Miss Perkins, "I

[2] Frances Perkins, *The Roosevelt I Knew* (New York, Viking, 1946), pp.
225, 226.

saw your friend Keynes. He left a whole rigamarole of figures. He must be a mathematician rather than a political economist." Perhaps the most interesting thing about this interview is its date, 1934, two years before Keynes published the book partly summarized above, and several years before its message was generally absorbed by economists. In other words, Keynes in 1936 appears to have rationalized policies of control discussed generally in preceding years and actually in operation, rather than to have originated new ones. Indeed, the idea of using public works as a counter-cyclical device is much older than Keynes. In 1907 the French Minister of Public Works had argued for spending in depressions; and in 1912, Sidney and Beatrice Webb had spoken in similar vein. The International Labor Organization, formerly of the League of Nations and now of the UN, has given consideration to the countercyclical timing of public works since 1919.

The Keynesians also hold increased exportation—which may involve a governmental stimulation of exports—to be a force having effects similar to those of public expenditure for roads, dams, and so on. Thus their doctrines would support as antidepression devices Marshall Plans and other plans recently called for by President Truman on the international level. Keynesian theory thus supports what most of us know practically, namely, that the Marshall Plan is good for American business.

Keynes has an interesting subtheory about investment, a sort of booster theory. It may be named the multiplier concept, introduced into economics by R. F. Kahn, a colleague of Keynes's. The multiplier idea goes like this: If, say, to increase the national income in a depression the government spends a billion dollars on new roads, in ultimate effect the billion will be multiplied three or four times. The reason, as was suggested on p. 187, is that income is passed along and can be used several times. The money the government uses to buy new cement for new roads finds its way into the pockets of new workers employed to produce the new cement; the workers spend the money for more groceries; the grocer in turn spends the money partly on new stocks for his shelves and partly to increase his own consumption. Theoretically this could go on forever, and one billion dollars could increase the national income by some infinite exponent. Actually, there are leaks on the way, and the initial billion will add only a very few billions to the total national income. Perhaps three billions.

These are some of the leading Keynesian ideas. One way of summarizing them in part is to look at some of the things that occurred in the United States during the Second World War and after. What happens in the field of public spending in wartime is something like what happens under Keynesianism, except, of course, that in wartime to savor the roast pig of full employment we have to set the world on fire. But from many economic viewpoints the public spending of warfare is equivalent to the public spending advocated by Keynes. Public spending brought prosperity, pulled us out of the depression, and raised our level of living. Certainly all this was in conformity with the expectations of the Keynesians. And then after the war, as has already been noted above, a succession of "public works," from European reconstruction to the new war in Korea and a monster rearmament program, kept that prosperity alive. It is indeed a curious thing that international politics has made us into involuntary Keynesians, almost since the date of the publication of the famous *General Theory of Employment, In-*

terest and Money. Keynes seems to have been a prophet as well as an economist.

Keynes's theories, the policies that have been suggested by his theories, and some of the proposals put forward by his more exuberant epigones, all have come in for much criticism from many quarters. Our conservative friends do not like the income-equalizing suggestions, or the apparent contempt for a balanced budget. To be sure, Keynes himself did not advocate a truly communistic sharing of income, or complete indifference toward balanced governmental budgets. But substantial and cautious citizens feel that his theories move far in these directions.

Noncommunist Marxians have praised Keynes and have found in his work a partial confirmation and rediscovery of their theories, for at some points Marx and Keynes come up with curiously similar answers. A striking similarity is that both men look upon depression as a period in which capital disappears (by deterioration, destruction, and so forth). When enough has disappeared, new investment becomes profitable again. The Russian Communists, on the other hand, will have nothing to do with Keynes. In one significant publication, the Keynesian formulas for stamping out unemployment are dubbed "a theoretical figment, which is used for demagogic ends." [3] In another it is stated that "Keynes transformed economic theory into a powerful weapon of economic policy to be used by the bourgeois state against the toiling masses." [4]

[3] Translation by I. Trachtenberg (of an article in *Mirovoe Khozyaistvo i. mirovaya politika*, Nos. 4–5, 1946, supplement, pp. 18–20) in *Science and Society*, X, No. 4 (1946), 405–409.
[4] Taken from a translation by E. E. Domar, Johns Hopkins University, of an article on Anglo-American economic theory written by A. Ayzenshtadt, Soviet economist, *American Economic Review*, XXXIX, No. 5 (September, 1949), 934.

Economists who on balance are pro-Keynesian, have many small disagreements with him and with each other. This means that doctrines of the master are being refined; broad statements are being qualified; certain kinds of errors are being corrected. There are several neo-Keynesian schools. Indeed, few if any Keynesians follow Keynes slavishly today. His legacy is one of viewpoint and method and emphasis rather than of infallible theory. But the critics of whom I now speak stay within the Keynesian frame of reference and use his methods, concepts, and categories.

The position of the non-Marxian dissenters on Keynes is partly one of welcome. They are glad that, through Keynes, standard theory is seriously attacking the question of boom-and-bust. It was a tremendous gain to make clear that economic theories and policies appropriate to a period of full employment were not necessarily applicable to a period of underemployment. And since, over the years, there have been longer periods of underemployment than of full employment, the new theories of Keynes make better contact with reality than the older ones of standard theory. But the dissenters' welcome is only partial. An important fraction of the nonconformists feels that Keynes with his multiplier, marginal efficiency of capital, propensity to consume, liquidity preference, and the like, is adding to the jargon and folklore rather than to the science of economics. They see in his work the same overreliance on deduction, on analogies with the science of mechanics, on dubious categories, on unrewarding definitions, that marred the work of Ricardo and his followers (compare criticisms of standard theory, pp. 106–110).

Such criticism concerns method only, and good method is partly a matter of opinion. But questions are also raised in

the realm of fact. Arthur F. Burns, successor of Wesley
Mitchell as Director of Research of the National Bureau of
Economic Research, finds that several important conclu-
sions of Keynes are unconfirmed by statistical investigation.
Burns writes:

[Keynes's] theory is that a collapse of investment brings prosperity to a close; that this in turn is caused by a collapse of
confidence regarding the profitability of durable assets; and
that the contraction which follows is bound to last, say, three
to five years, since recovery is possible only after stocks have
been worked off, and more important still, after the "fixed" capital of business firms has been reduced sufficiently to restore its
profitability. But can this theory be easily reconciled with the
fact that orders for machinery, orders for other durable equipment, and contracts for different categories of construction
often reach cyclical maxima at widely scattered dates? Or with
the fact that even a sharp decline in investment orders is ordinarily converted into a fairly gradual decline in investment
expenditure, which moreover starts several months later? Or
with the fact that the stock of durable goods in a growing country is virtually free from any trace of business cycles, increasing
as a rule during contractions of business activity as well as during expansions? [5]

It is further objected by dissenters that Keynes, like many
of his great predecessors, with whom he compares so favorably, uses "theory" to defend a program for the times. That
is what Adam Smith did; he felt that governmental restraints
were bad, and developed a theory to justify removing them.
Ricardo did the same thing. He wanted cheaper wheat for
England and a breakup of the power of the landed aristocracy. His theories were oriented to those ends. Keynes,
animated by lofty motives, wanted to do something about
the paralyzing depression that followed the First World

[5] A. F. Burns, *Economic Research and the Keynesian Thinking of Our
Times* (New York National Bureau of Economic Research, 1946), pp.
20, 21.

War. His theories supported a program that works well
enough if applied, whether by design or the pressure of
events; but this does not mean that they shed much new light
on the economic process, or on what happens in the business
cycle.

The staunch pragmatist may here exclaim, "But if Keynesianism works, it must be true!" Not all things that work are
true. Shaking a watch will often make it run again; but from
this one does not deduce that the real trouble with the watch
has been diagnosed. The North Star was a reliable guide to
sailors long before astronomical "truth" as we now know it,
had been revealed to man. There is, as a matter of fact, considerable doubt as to how long or how far we can profitably
go in using public spending and other Keynesian devices to
frustrate economic depression. The rough-and-ready governmental Keynesianism of recent years, partly planned and
partly imposed, has already brought us a serious measure of
inflation—which means, for millions of people, loss of half
the real value of their bonds, insurance, pensions, loans (like
mortgages); and for other millions, completely undeserved
gains. It has also brought controls more onerous and more
numerous than those envisaged. To be sure, much of this
can be attributed to war; on the other hand, war is a public
work; and what has been going on in recent years is not
too bad a preview of what would go on if mammoth public
works were dedicated to the constructive projects of tran-
quil times. We know the evils of unemployment. The evils
of full employment may be lesser ones, but we still have
much to learn about them.

Finally, dissenters plant a huge question mark over the
issue of practical policy making. This concerns feasibility.
To get the full force of this objection we must assume that

the world returns to a period of serenity somewhat resembling that of the 1920's. There would be no wars or rumors of wars; and in capitalist countries, some of the governmental interferences that we have come to tolerate in the permanent emergency of the last two decades would be modified. There will, of course, never be a return to the economic freedoms of the "aspirin age," but we might run into a period in which prosperity is not kept alive by rearmament and half-war. Now, in this paradise regained assume the dramatic events of 1929 to occur again: markets collapsing, brokers leaping from high windows, crucial index numbers plummeting. Under these circumstances would or could governments swiftly take action to prevent a long depression?

The answers of the dissenters vary, but some of them believe that government action would be slow, grudging, and would come only in response to ominous unrest. Minimum action would finally be taken, and the goal would be to hold things together rather than to achieve the goal of full employment. Part of the reason for pessimism would be that legislative bodies act too slowly and that, in a country like ours, drastic anti-depression laws might have to be validated by the Supreme Court before they would be conscientiously enforced. This is democracy at work, and democracy is the form of government that reflects and is most congruous with the economic freedoms we believe in. There is a definite relationship between type of government and type of economic organization. But even if things could be speeded up on the legislative plane, there would be other difficulties, perhaps more serious ones, in the eyes of many dissenters. The economic concepts of deficit spending, countercyclical taxation and unbalanced budgets are so much at variance with the prudent and thrifty businessman's habits

of thought, and with the principles that govern his account-
ing methods, that large segments of the community are likely
to manifest considerable resistance to a thoroughgoing
Keynesian program. Equally significant is the fact that depression is not an unmixed disaster. Many persons living on
fixed incomes or pensions would benefit by lower prices,
easier-to-get domestic service, and the misfortunes of other
economic groups. Cousins of the Wall Street bears are found
throughout the business community; at every whistle stop
some sort of speculator may be found who takes his profit
on the downturn, not the upturn. Even labor leaders may
see a silver lining in the dark clouds of bad business weather.
One of them told me several years ago that he hoped the
next depression would come soon and that he prayed it
would be a "lollipalousa." His reason for expressing hopes
so contrary to the apparent interest of the rank and file was
that *his* union would be able to ride out a depression while
a rival union would probably founder. Thus, people who
have or think they have something to gain and little to lose
through hard times could not be counted on to telegraph
their senators about stopping a depression.

These reasons against feasibility are, in the main, political
reasons. Against them it can be argued that economists have
no right to reply to economic proposals with political objections, which are beyond their scope and jurisdiction. If
the government, or powerful pressure groups, or an indifferent public, refuse to take the proper economic medicines
—well, that is their lookout, and they can keep having their
depressions until the last trumpet. Many dissenters are not
quite satisfied with this argument. If a sick man is indeed
unwilling to take the remedy prescribed by his doctor, further study of the case is indicated. Perhaps the patient ought

to be moved for observation to the psychiatric ward, where fuller diagnosis is made possible. Perhaps the Keynesian diagnosis, too, is incomplete.

What positive theory of boom-and-bust have the dissenters to offer? One theory, that of the left-wing dissenters was presented in Chapter 9. This theory—the Marxian—was based on a labor theory of value, on surplus value, and on the instability of an economic system in which employers receive that surplus value.

We also noted that Veblen had a business-cycle theory, but without particularizing. It is best summarized in the following quotation:

To Veblen, then, the important factor in determining the character of a business period is the relation between current capitalization and anticipated earning capacity. When prospective profits rise, business has a season of prosperity, during which capitalization expands rapidly. But rising costs always undermine the basis for anticipating high profits and then capitalization is left higher than prospective profits warrant. The latter situation characterizes depression.[6]

In the work of Wesley Mitchell, nonsocialistic yet dissenting American theory on boom-and-bust finds its most adequate expression. This we shall now examine.

The approach of Wesley C. Mitchell to the problems of depression is a contrast to Keynes. Mitchell began studying them in 1908, and published a book on the subject in 1913. Fourteen years later, before the great depression, he published another. Again a long silence, nineteen years this time, his third book came out in 1946 in collaboration with Arthur F. Burns. In 1948, a year after Keynes, Mitchell died. A posthumous book is to appear. During the period between

[6] Wesley Mitchell, *Business Cycles: the Problem and Its Setting* (New York, National Bureau of Economic Research, 1927), p. 44.

1910 and his death, Mitchell encouraged his students and colleagues to carry on studies related to business cycles. On much of their work he was able to draw for his later publications. In short, he painstakingly studied a persistent problem of economic life over a period of forty years. Keynes devoted only a very few years to the study of depression and prosperity; a few years in the thirties, when the problem was acute.

Keynes begins his work by stirring up a vast dust cloud, as he tilts his lance against the wizards of standard theory. He then proceeds to the task with much of their apparatus. Mitchell—at least most of the time—grandly ignores standard theory. He does not use the concept of supply and demand. Neither word appears in the indices of the 1927 and 1946 books! In Keynes's *General Theory*, "supply" and "demand" each gets slightly less than a whole column of the index.

Mitchell uses a phrase that Keynes does not use: "the business cycle." This phrase is important and suggests a sharp difference between the two men. Keynes works with the idea of equilibrium: sometimes you have equilibrium with full employment, sometimes you have equilibrium with massive unemployment. To Keynes the economy seems to operate on plateaux of varying elevation. Each plateau is a case of static equilibrium. Mitchell's word "cycle," on the other hand, suggests movement, rhythmic ebb and flow. Prosperity, or the expansion of business activity, slowly recedes until there is depression, or a period of contraction. Then there is gradual revival, leading again to expansion. There is flow; the concept of equilibrium is absent. The word "business" in the expression, "business cycle," is also important, and suggests a different viewpoint from that of

Keynes. Mitchell, like Veblen, accepts the idea of a frequent disharmony between the process of making money (business) and that of making goods (industry). The rhythms of our economic life result from money-making activities; they are not *economic* fluctuations; they are not *industrial* fluctuations, they are *business* fluctuations, or cycles.

His definition makes this clearer:

Business cycles are a type of fluctuation found in the aggregate economic activity of nations that organize their work mainly in business enterprises: a cycle consists of expansions occurring at about the same time in many economic activities, followed by similarly general recessions, contractions and revivals which merge into the expansion phase of the next cycle; this sequence of changes is recurrent but not periodic; in duration business cycles vary from more than one year to ten or twelve years; they are not divisible into shorter cycles of similar character with amplitudes approximating their own.

A business cycle, as its name implies, is a complete circuit. It has several phases, often described as:
1) Revival (getting out of the depression);
2) Expansion (the boom phase);
3) Recession (heading downward after peak);
4) Contraction (the depression).

When these four phases have run their course, we start all over again, like sitting several times through a movie. Not *just* like the movies, really, for the next show is never exactly like the last—or any preceding one. It may be much longer or shorter, more harrowing or less. We do not always go through a depression as long and deep as that of the 1930's, or through a high, wide and handsome boom like the one after the Second World War. Indeed, the best we can say is that business cycles resemble each other only just enough to persuade us that they really do form a species. They are siblings rather than identical twins. They are recurrent rather than periodic.

If these concepts are true, it follows that most readers of this book have lived through several cycles, that we are all living through one now, and that the more venerable ones among us have lived through many—as many as ten or more. These are proper deductions granting, of course, that readers have been behaving themselves and have been living in capitalist, money-using, industrialized countries. (There are no business cycles in Tibet or in the wokas berry culture of the Klamath Indians.) Cycles vary in length from one to twelve years and seem to "average" about four years in the United States, and a little more in Europe. The word *average* is placed in quotes to remind readers that there are several kinds of averages, that sometimes they are not very meaningful, and that it would be dangerous to plan to make stock-market killings on the basis of four-year pulsations.

Mitchell's approach to the problem is a little baffling and very insidious. He tells us about disturbances in the business systems of antiquity and the Middle Ages. He gives us a brief history of the use of statistics in economics, uses figures to measure the cycle. He assesses the reliability of business annals. He distinguishes the ups and downs of the cycle from the ups and downs of business due to seasons of the year— the bathing-suit industry is not dead because few swimming garments are bought in November.

He measures the cycle forwards and backwards and cross-wise. He makes charts of where it has hit hardest. He studies the degree to which it is an international sickness—apparently catching, like the Dutch elm disease. He gives us little gemlike summaries of what other people have thought about the business cycle. There is enough of this to weary many

readers, who wonder whether he will ever get down to
brass tacks: what, in short, causes the business cycle and
how, in short, can we stop it?

The reader is apparently put off again and again and again.
If, however, he is willing to take what he finds rather than
search for the answers he wants, he will be fascinated by
and return again to the long second chapter of *Business Cycles, the Problem and Its Setting* (or the similar chapter in
his 1913 book, *Business Cycles*). This is a chapter on the
structure of a modern money-making society. It reveals to
us his ikon—his map of the economic world. It shows the
influence of Veblen. What he says, in effect, is that there are
few organizing forces in modern economic society similar
to those postulated by standard economic theory. The
search for profits does have a sort of organizing force, it is
true, but it does not—and is not and never was intended to
—insure continuous, full employment. It would be repeti-
tious here to summarize more fully this chapter. The reader
has already got hold of similar or identical theories of economic organization from pages 154–157.

It does differ from Veblen in one important respect.
Veblen's theory of organization was also a theory of change.
The reader may remember how, in the apocalypse according
to Veblen we are supposed to go into either an Utopian
industrial republic, or into a regressive state, a kind of industrial feudalism (p. 157). There's nothing like that in
Mitchell, and it is one of his shortcomings that he is a static
economist, though not at all in the sense in which the term
is used and perhaps mis-used by standard theorists. This
paragraph, however, is an aside, and Mitchell gives us enough
in his ikon to improve our understanding of the business
cycle. Indeed, a thorough reading and comprehension of

his ideas on social organization make us suddenly lose interest in *the* cause of economic fluctuations.

What has so unexpectedly slaked our eager thirst for causes is the realization that, in an economic system like the one described—in Mitchell's ikon—business cycles just can't help happening.

The whole situation is a little as if a precocious child, observing that his father's mandolin is often out of tune, were to develop his solitary theories about why it gets out of tune. He might decide that it always gets badly out of tune after his father plays "Turkey in the Straw," or after the mandolin has been left open on the piano overnight instead of in its case on the shelf. One day he asks his father, who explains that there is no special reason. All stringed instruments get out of tune for all kinds of reasons. Strings sag under tension; pegs loosen up slightly and often get knocks; the materials out of which mandolins are made expand and contract and in different places and degrees. It is futile to state the reason for untuning, but an understanding of how a stringed instrument is made shows clearly that it must get out of tune. Our ikon of the instrument directly reveals its pitch-losing property. And so it is with Mitchell's business cycle. If you follow his neo-Veblenian description of how the economic world is put together, how productive activity is necessarily subordinated to profit-making in a money economy, you accept such derangements as the business cycle without wonder. He calls your attention to obviously and necessarily different rates of contraction and expansion in individual lines of business activity. He shows that there are few guiding or coordinating forces. He shows that the economic system is quite as indifferent to full employment as a mandolin is to being in tune. The economic system has no greater propensity to return to an equilibrium high or low than has a stringed instrument.

I must not, however, let this stringed-instrument analogy go too far lest it conceal one of the most important parts of Mitchell's analysis—and one which does seem to belie a little my last sentence about the economic system's not seeking automatically higher or lower levels of activity. The economic system has a kind of bouncing-back quality that the stringed instrument does not have. Each phase of the business cycle, Mitchell says, generates the next, almost as if the mandolin, after getting out of tune, were somehow to work itself at least partially back into tune again. To see how this happens we must follow a business cycle through its phases. Start at any point you like—at depression, let us say. Prices at last have fallen so low that consumers with money decide to buy, and some businessmen have come to believe that they will never be able to get new machinery cheaper. Interest and wage rates are low, hence favorable to renewed activity. In the home, furnaces or refrigerators have worn out; industrial equipment must at length be replaced, too, unless the factory owner is prepared to go out of business altogether. Firms have been strengthened and reorganized; their owners have come to accept the idea that they are worth less than they formerly thought they were and are ready to operate with less grandiose expectations. A condition like this may be reinforced by propitious events, like a local war far away somewhere, that stimulates orders for material without threatening a general debacle.

Once a revival starts, it tends to spread by cumulative process. A few new men are hired and get wage envelopes; these are spent for new things, and the demand for new things requires new hands to make them; spending further increases employment and new employment increases spending. Timid hope gives way to optimism. Profits are good because firms are producing enough to operate efficiently, that is, at low unit costs, and because wage rates tend to rise more slowly than prices. This process, sometimes with temporary setbacks, goes on and on until prosperity is reached.

But Mitchell's "prosperity" is not the same thing as Keynes's "full employment." In the 1920's, Stuart Chase wrote a book entitled *Prosperity, Fact or Myth?* He showed that despite a widespread sense of well-being, many groups, like the farmers and the textile industry, were having hard sledding. To them and the technologically unemployed, the prosperity of that seemingly golden decade was a myth. Well, it is that kind of fact-myth prosperity that Mitchell is talking about, and to which we are able to return by a self-generating process. This does not mean that full employment cannot be reached; it only means that full employment does not have to be reached when we speak of prosperity.

So now we are more or less prosperous again. Why do we not stay more or less prosperous? How do we lose our grip on this pleasantest phase of the business cycle? Prosperity brings stresses to the business system. Some of the laggard prices are beginning to catch up with the businessman and to threaten his profits: interest rates go up; rents go up; wages and even salaries rise. Less experienced or less competent workers have to be employed; more rejects are thrown away because greenies' hands are clumsy; to fill rush orders, overtime at time-and-a-half must be paid. There is, besides, a tendency for the price of raw materials to go up higher and faster than the price of consumer's goods. A few industries begin to feel these pinches severely. Strains are accumulating in many sectors. Some of the weaker firms may be failing. More cautious bankers may refuse to renew certain loans. Here and there a spectacular business failure may sound a shrill note of warning to overconfident businessmen. Sometimes untoward outside events (like a series of unprofitable harvests, or the destruction of an armaments market by the outbreak of peace) may add to the more ordinary stresses, and saturate the business community with gloom.

Now the cumulative process is reversed. Caution and gloom may give way to fear. Everybody is searching for a way to remain solvent in case the boom goes completely sour. This helps to make it sour. Orders decline or are canceled, workers are laid off. A process of liquidation sets in, then gathers momentum. Now we are in recession and only a step away from the depression—which is where we started —and then the whole process is repeated.

The above summary scarcely does justice to Mitchell's analysis of how this self-generating, cumulative process goes on. It is a mere suggestion of how he handles this part of the job, and gives no hint of the skill with which he weaves together many strands to form a pattern.

Mitchell's account of how one phase breeds the next is widely accepted by economists, but accepted as description rather than explanation. To Mitchell, however, the line between description and explanation is very fine, if it exists at all. To many his entire performance is disappointing, because he never fastens attention on any one or two factors (such as investment) as *the* cause. With Mitchell, there are no specific causes for depression, or prosperity, or business-cycle-as-a-whole, just as sophisticated men find no special cause for war. He suggests that, as capitalism evolves and changes, so may business cycles change. Their immediate and precipitating causes, their length, perhaps their severity and frequency, and some of their characteristic phenomena —all these are subject to change as our society changes.

Mitchell may, like Veblen, have had strong ideas about the long future of capitalist society, but he has not said enough about them to let us know what he thought. Unlike some of the Keynesians he has no stagnation theory tied up with his business-cycle theory. He does not say that investment is getting to be increasingly profitless, that future depressions will last indefinitely unless government intervenes. On the other hand the money economy is not likely, unassisted, to bring about lasting full employment. It rarely has done that, and was not particularly designed to do so in the first instance, except in the romantic minds of nineteenth century economists (and some of the twentieth century). He does suggest somewhere that a change in the direction of bigger and better business cycles may have been made in 1914 and he states that, as backward countries embrace more tightly the monetary economy, they place themselves more completely at the mercy of the business cycle.

What cures, or palliatives, does Mitchell offer for the business cycle—that is, for the unemployment, lost wealth and widespread misery of the depression phase of the cycle? He has no sure-fire cure. Indeed, his economic suggestions are about as thin as you might expect the musical suggestions to be from somebody who took as his theme: How to Prevent Mandolins from Getting Out of Tune. He notes that we no longer have such flimsy business phenomena as the Tulip Mania in Holland or the South Sea Bubble. Man's increasing economic knowledge and repudiation of certain kinds of insanely frenzied speculation have cured "busts" of that type. In his 1913 book, speaking of the pre-Federal-

Reserve banking system, he recommended among other palliatives reorganization of the banks (which, the reader will remember, was being done at the very time); he suggested countercyclical public works, or concentrating public works in depressions and postponing them in prosperity. He mildly advocated stabilizing the dollar. He advocated a deeper knowledge by more people of current economic conditions on the theory that, if more people understood better what was going on, the swings of the economic system might be narrower.

Mitchell took part in the economic planning of the First World War. His very early experience as a planner made a deep impression on him, and he emerged with the feeling that conscious guidance of economic activity could stabilize the economy somewhat. He spoke and wrote about this a good deal and was later asked by President Hoover and President Roosevelt to do work which was more or less related to the general question of governmental guidance of economic activity—in peacetime now, of course.

Since the business cycle may be viewed as the outcome of planlessness and lack of central purpose in economic life, the cure, or mitigation, Mitchell felt, would arise from conscious planning. In several places he has written about the advantages of national economic planning, but he also saw its limitations and sometimes seemed to view man's efforts pessimistically. People, he observed, are willing to accept economic plans only in emergencies (like war); under such conditions the plans are thrown together hastily and piecemeal. And piecemeal planning may, in the long run, be worse than none. The present state of development of man's social intelligence, the unreliability of the social sciences, the difficulty of social innovation, all militate against wise, comprehensive economic planning for the future. In short, and in words less elevated than Mitchell's, the ultimate obstacle to curing the business cycle now is that human nature gives little evidence of being ready to take a swift turn for the better. Man solves his problems slowly.

Mitchell, then, has no firm program. He seems to be motivated primarily by "idle curiosity," to use a Veblenian phrase. He is not much concerned with outcomes, and does not stop to look where his investigations lead. There is a kind of scientific indifference about Mitchell that is as rare in economists as it is baffling to some of his readers and many of his critics. This does not mean that he is devoid of interest in human welfare; but he appears to feel that human welfare is, in the end, best served by disinterested study.

The work of these two men gives thoughtful students of economic science much to ponder. Is man better served by vigorously endorsed programs of action that are made reasonable through theory than by long, hard study that does not particularly lend itself to a concrete program (although it may suggest one)? No final answer can be given, for any reply is founded on faith. Perhaps both pure and programmatic study are needed. If all men adhered to the Veblen-Mitchell approach, economics might become as remote from direct and immediate human concerns as astronomy is. To observe men's acts as one watches the stars in their courses, unable to alter them and forced passively to accept their motions, is a hard thing for human beings to do. On the other hand, inexpert intervention in human affairs may have worse results than mere drift.

Keynes and Mitchell are at the poles in their outlook upon current social institutions. Keynes thinks that the business cycle occupies a position in our society somewhat similar to that once occupied by smallpox. He is the discoverer of the vaccine. And now, of course, everybody will go for it. To be sure, there will be resistance to business-cycle vaccination, as there has been to smallpox vaccination in the past and still is today, but vaccine has won the day and so will the Keynesian cure. It is all very simple. Keynes's outlook is that of the eighteenth century enlightenment which held that men, by taking thought, would perfect their society as they learned more about it.

Mitchell represents an outlook that is infinitely more complex. The business cycle is not a separate problem, like smallpox. It is more deeply woven into the social texture. There are probably no real cures under our institutions, though there is the possibility of "symptomatic relief" as the antihistamine pillboxes say. Moreover, man seems unwilling to pay the full price required to solve his problems. He prefers to gloss them over or postpone ultimate solutions by making readjustments that can only be temporary. To Mitchell economic life is only one more example of Francis Bacon's observation that "it is common in principle to will contradictions." He brings to economics, and therefore to the study of business cycles, some of the brooding mystery of conflicting human desires and aspirations that has haunted all great students of man and his work. He studies the business cycle as a puzzling phase of our culture, as if he were an anthropologist studying the mores of a strange tribe. It is true that much of this is hidden behind a formidable wall of statistics. But it is there for those who care to look, often in books that are not about the business cycle, like his *Backward Art of Spending Money*. Mitchell's writings, taken as a whole, more nearly resemble in temper Sir James Frazer's ranging explanation of why one priest had to kill another to get his job in the sacred grove at Nemi, than Keynes's one-two-three-bang! discovery of the causes of underemployment equilibrium.

It may be that capitalism has already changed more completely since Pearl Harbor than we realize; and that the business cycle has changed with it. Keynes's remedies for depression, worked out in the 1930's, may be as outmoded in the future as the Maginot line, worked out to prevent an invasion in 1914, was outmoded in 1940.

Mitchell's meticulous studies and his superb analysis of how business activity itself, in a relatively free society, causes business cycles—those great studies may become the materials of history rather than of economics. When the wars now in the making have been fought out and peace restored (if ever in the calculable future) we can imagine that social forms not yet conceived will take shape. And in those the business cycle, as we know it, may not again appear. The possibility of a long season of war or of uneasy and fully armed peace did not figure in the writings of either man, and would perhaps have made them say different things.

13. MONEY

THE SIGNIFICANCE OF
money to modern man has
perhaps never been more
thoughtfully discussed than by Georg Simmel in his book,
Philosophie des Geldes. I can think of no better way of
introducing this difficult topic than by sketching out some
of his ideas.[1]

The entire basis of individual liberty, Simmel says, is
founded on money. Under economic systems involving
slavery or peonage and under feudalism there is little need
for money; there are instead, certain duties, claims, rights,
obligations of the master or of the vassal. In such non-
monetary economies, we find an intimate relationship between the producer and the product or service made ready
for the market. We see a similar intimate and unfree relationship in the family. The dependent sons, daughters,
maiden aunts, or grandchildren of a feudal lord (and they
were all dependent because of the economic organization
of feudalism) had to accept a daily and personal relationship

[1] My knowledge of German is such that I have never really been able to
get past p. 14 in Simmel's treatise. I have therefore relied heavily in what
follows on N. J. Spykman's excellent book, *The Social Theory of Georg
Simmel* (Chicago, Univ. of Chicago, 1925).

toward the lord if they wanted to live according to their station in life. They could not withdraw from the family and lead a separate existence in a tiny apartment in town, as is so often done today, not only because there were no apartments, but also because without money there was no easily divisible wealth or income. The lord's wealth consisted of a chateau, land, rights over villeins and cotters. Parts of things like that could not be mailed to a son or maiden aunt as a monthly allowance. The illiquidity of wealth tied people down to their possessions and to other people, in ways that necessarily blocked the avenues leading toward individual liberty.

In those stages of economic development the ordinary person was extremely dependent on a small number of individuals, most of whom were known to him. But after the introduction of the money economy a person becomes dependent upon numberless individuals, most of whom are unknown to him. He depends on completely anonymous Brazilian coffee pickers, Greek sailors, American brakemen. Money becomes the substitute for tribal bonds, feudal dues, certain family obligations. This ability to spread dependency thin through the loose bonds of money over countless unknown persons is a large step toward individual liberty. This new dependency is a dependency on function rather than on individuals. That is, we get our shoes shined by an anonymous bootblack, who bootblacks for anybody who will pay. The feudal lord had his shoes attended to by somebody in his service, who served only the lord and his family. Because modern man "is dependent on the function and not on the bearer of the function, he can change and select the latter according to his own choice. This gives him an inner independence, a feeling of individual self-sufficiency." [2]

Thus, money has paradoxically made men much more dependent on all other men at the same time that each man gains a greater personal sense of independence.

Money has also changed the meaning of private property. Until nations developed into full-blown monetary econo-mies, ownership and use went together. Simmel seems to feel that, until fairly recent times, personality was always min-gled with ownership. The medieval manor was for example more fully woven into the very core of the owner's person than modern corporation bonds are in the fabric of the con-temporary owner. Presumably this is tantamount to the assertion that that much-criticized but all-pervading institu-tion of the day, absentee ownership, is made possible by money, and is impossible where there is no money.

Because money is generally conceived as an end, it de-grades many things to means which are themselves really ends. Money causes man to treat the whole of his world in arithmetic terms. Modern man is essentially an accountant. Money develops that form of mental energy which we call intellect. Emotions, sentiment, feeling have a minor place in the monetary economy.

Thus, to Simmel, money is a good deal more than it is to most economists, particularly the older ones, who thought of it as a completely neutral medium of exchange, a standard of value, a store of value and a standard of deferred pay-ments. To Simmel it is a force that shapes the mental devel-opment of each of us and that makes possible forms of economic activity (organizing holding companies, for ex-ample) that could not otherwise be engaged in. Money

[2] Spykman, op. cit., p. 221.

dominates our type of society so completely that it is probably more correct to refer to our way of life as the pecuniary
culture, or the monetary economy, as Veblen and Wesley
Mitchell do, than to refer to it as capitalism, as Marx and
others do.

According to historical and anthropological studies, at
least a hundred fifty different objects or materials have been
used as money, among them arrow poison, beer, dog's teeth,
cracked gongs, pig's jawbones, rat traps, human skulls, and
woodpecker's scalps. Perhaps we can already begin to sur-
mise from this list that money does not have to be intrinsically
valuable, as gold and silver are, to serve its functions.

Money is not easy to define. There are, of course, plenty
of passably good definitions, such as: what is generally acceptable in the payment of debts; or anything that is generally acceptable as a medium of exchange. But these do not
do justice to the object defined. Money is a concept rather
than a thing. Money is not only, as my dictionary says,
pieces of metal in convenient form stamped by the public
authority, or pieces of paper that are substituted for the
metal. Nearer to the truth is the idea that money is a sort of
general claim on the community's present and future goods,
regardless of the material from which it is made, or the
metallic reinforcing it may have. The idea of its being a
liquid asset should also inform the concept; a farm is an
illiquid asset, a U. S. Savings Bond is highly liquid, therefore
much closer to being money than a piece of land. Checks
made out on checking accounts should also be considered
as money. When the word money is used in this chapter, I
shall usually assume under the concept bank money or
checkbook money, as well as money directly issued by gov-

ernments. The next chapter will pay special attention to bank money.

The search for the perfect definition will not teach us much about money. A better approach is to wade boldly into the subject by discussing two topics that have been among the chief concerns of standard theory in the monetary realm. One is the value of money, the other is the desirability of the gold standard.

Standard economic theory, in dealing with money, exhibits the same primary interest in its value as it does in the case of goods. Until now we have been measuring the value of other things in terms of money; now we have to talk about the value of money itself. Money is a useful measuring rod for economic quantities over short periods. But we all know from personal experience that over a period of years, money will buy different quantities of the same thing: a dollar equals two pounds of good steak in 1935, but only one pound in 1945. A study of the value of money is, in a sense, a study of the elasticity of our economic yardstick. To this we now proceed.

The value of money may be looked at from so many points of view that one hardly knows where to begin. Take the American dollar, for example. Its value from the viewpoint of gold has, since 1934, been an absolutely unvarying figure: one dollar = 13.7+ grains of fine gold. It is true that this is a partly fictitious value, since the ordinary citizen cannot, by an ordinary transaction, change his dollars into gold. But this ratio is very real to bankers, dental supply houses, jewelers, miners of gold and others. This gold value of the dollar is fixed by law and there is no significant black-market deviation from it in the U. S. (though the establishing of a black market in gold is a possibility). Thus, from one point of view, the value of the dollar is stable over long periods. It may, of course, be changed, and has been.

From the viewpoint of a Frenchman, the dollar is much more unstable. Taking the 100 franc note as his measuring rod, a Frenchman discovers that this sum has been able to buy amounts varying from about thirty cents to three dollars in the last dozen years. "But," somebody may object, "those figures measure the spread in the value of the franc, not the dollar." True, or, at least, almost true. The point is that, if you use a foreign currency as a yardstick, even if it is a yardstick of sand, the value of the American dollar has changed considerably. So far we find, then, that the value of American money may be looked at from the viewpoint of gold *and* from the viewpoint of a foreign currency.

There is a third way of looking at the value of money. How much will it buy at home? Or, what is its purchasing power? If its purchasing power is high then its value is high; if low, then its value is low. We are all aware of the fact that the purchasing power of the dollar has changed considerably in the last 15 years. Does this mean that the value of goods has gone up, or that the value of money has gone down? The answer depends on your point of reference, as in the case of the dollar-franc ratio, but most economists would be disposed to say that the value of money had gone down. And remember, in the United States at least, the gold content of the dollar has been exactly the same during this period. Measured by living costs, or purchasing power, the dollar has lost nearly half its value since 1933 and has carried the value of gold down along with it. Or, if you wish, gold has lost purchasing power, and dragged the dollar along. Either statement will do for our limited purposes. Thus, our

third way of looking at the value of the dollar is to look at
it from the viewpoint of purchasing power. It is from this
third viewpoint that the economist most frequently and
earnestly studies the value of money. Money is dear to him
when the cost of living is low; it is cheap when the cost of
living is high.

Under the purchasing power criterion of value, neither
convertibility into gold, nor gold backing, nor even gold
content, has a completely determining effect on the value
of money domestically. An excellent example is to be found
in the period 1933–1934. In that period our government
proclaimed that the dollar was no longer freely convertible
into gold and that it was devalued: that is to say, they
changed the gold content of the dollar from 23.2 grains of
fine gold to 13.7 grains, a reduction of 40 percent. Did its
purchasing power (value) decline? The answer is really
no, but there is a *but*. As a matter of fact prices rose—a little,
but so little (and so many other things were being done to
raise prices at the same time) that we are almost justified in
saying *no*. In any event, and this we can say without any *buts*,
the loss in purchasing power was not comparable to the loss
of gold. Thus we learn an amazing fact: you can—at least
in a large and economically rugged country like ours—cut
most of the gold insides out of the dollar and it will recover
from the operation almost as sound and strong as it was
before. So long as it stays at home. I do not say this can
be done often, or at any stage of any business cycle; but it
can be done. And that is remarkable. It helps to explain how
purely paper currencies can have value.

On the other hand, the value of the dollar, after a reduction of its gold content, does drop from the viewpoint of
the foreigner. To the French, Swiss, and others who were

on the gold standard, the dollar declined in value after the Roosevelt operation of 1933–1934.

Now let's sum up before we go on. First, the value of a dollar, or any other money, of course, can be looked at from three angles:

Value in gold
Value in a foreign country
Value at home

Second, these three kinds of values need not be closely related. For example, when the government took 40 percent of the gold out of our dollar in the early Roosevelt days, here is what happened:

Value in gold, considerably lowered
Value in foreign countries, considerably lowered
Value at home, not much change (This is the kind
    of value we shall study.)

Seen in its largest terms, analysis of the value of money at home does not differ from analysis of the value of consumer's goods or the factors of production: the key is in the words "supply and demand." But we have already learned that this phrase is only the beginning of economic wisdom. Unless we are able to snake out of this truism some of the concrete situations that cause changes in supply and demand, we have made little progress. This we shall now try to do.

The supply of money has a significant peculiarity: its "supply" can be tremendously increased without change in quantity. In this it is like a library book; it is passed along to other users, not consumed by the first holder as most commodities are. If a public library allows its books to be borrowed for three months at a time it will need many more duplicate and triplicate copies than if books are called in after two weeks. That is to say, the harder work done by the fortnightly book, as compared with the tri-monthly book, releases the library from the need of adding to its stock. This "harder work" may be named "increased velocity of circulation."

Money, too, has high and low velocities of circulation. There are times when men spend slowly, agonizing over each dollar of outgo. There are other times when men discard their money like canasta players getting rid of the high cards in their hands. Keynes—his name bobs up everywhere—observed the following after the First World War:

In Moscow the unwillingness to hold money except for the shortest possible time reached at one period a fantastic intensity. If a grocer sold a pound of cheese, he ran off with the roubles as fast as his legs could carry him to the Central Market to replenish his stocks by changing them into cheese again, lest they lose their value before he got there; thus justifying the prevision of economists in naming the phenomenon "velocity of circulation"!

The first peculiar thing about monetary supply then, is that increased velocity has the same effect as increased supply. Our next point is that cost of production is not always important in limiting supply. This, of course, is more true of paper money than of metallic money having intrinsic value. By comparison with other commodities and in relation to its face value, paper money costs almost nothing to produce, which is, of course, the undeniable attraction of the counterfeiter's art. The law of diminishing returns does not operate in precisely the way that it does in the production of corn or cotton. This being true, the brakes to production that operate in the case of most goods do not operate in the case of paper money. Yet there are brakes. Government ultimately controls the supply of paper money and does not manufacture it to make a profit (as makers of engraved letterheads do). Therefore the usual incentive to make goods—private profit—is absent. Moreover, it is the usual aim of government in normal and quiet times to preserve the current value.

Large, sudden, and arbitrary changes in supply and therefore value of money, transfer wealth unjustly from one class to another and inspire feelings of resentment against the government. One way to preserve stability in the value of money is to hold approximately constant the amount of money in existence. To be sure, governments are not always able or even willing to follow the policy of monetary stability. In wars, revolutions, and the aftermath of both, governments may decide that the evils of the printing press are the lesser ones.

Another brake to excessive production of paper is the gold standard or its effective present-day variants. This brake is becoming daily less effective through disuse. A government on the old-fashioned gold standard cannot keep on expanding its supply of paper money without increasing the amount of gold it holds. The supply of gold, like that of ordinary commodities, does depend on its cost of production. Producing gold requires blood and toil, tears and sweat. Costs of production operate to keep the quantity down. So long as paper money is really linked to gold, so long must some sort of safe ratio be maintained between amount of gold and amount of paper, and so long will new paper money, like new gold itself, be produced sparingly. That is why the British statesman Stanley Baldwin once said that the gold standard was as nearly "knave-proof" as anything in the world could be. Not because it provides a "backing" for paper money, but because it sets up a limit beyond which amount produced cannot go.

But sometimes even gold is not produced sparingly—we are using the word in a relative sense, of course. In the sixteenth century, gold (and silver) came from the New World in copious flow, by comparison with the period of the Middle Ages. Gold discoveries in California and Australia about 1850 caused a remarkable increase in the production rate. About fifty years later, a new surge of gold resulted from discoveries in South Africa, Alaska, and the Klondike. All three of these periods of gold discovery were followed by a decrease in the value of gold and of paper money tied to it. This diminished value was felt by the ordinary man in the usual way: an increase in the cost of living.

A word about demand. The reader will remember that the demand for goods was tied up with the principle of diminishing utility: one suit of clothes is absolutely necessary; a second is highly desirable, but the need is not so urgent; few men care about owning more than ten. But money seems to be different. The demand for money appears to be insatiable. One wonders perhaps what its heaven-sweeping demand curve looks like. In truth, the demand for money—for *money*—is not so great as all that. King Midas had too much gold. A nation that could produce only coins or paper money would gladly trade its product for just a little ham and eggs. All of us part with some of our money nearly every day. This alone shows that we want other things more than we want money. Demand for money is not the same thing as the desire to be rich, for two reasons. First, mere desire is never the same thing as effective demand, else every shopgirl's sigh would send up the price of fur coats. Second, we really don't want much money; what we want more is the things that money will buy.

Because money is only a means to something else, the demand for it is easily kept within bounds. Even rich men have little actual money; they have lovely homes, stocks and bonds, boats, automobiles, beaches, swimming pools, famous paintings—not large packages or oaken chests full of money in the literal sense. The demand for money whether in the form of cash or checking accounts at the bank is always limited by the desire to pass the money along: to pay debts, to invest it in claims like bonds that yield an income, to buy a factory, replenish a stock of goods sold, secure the necessities and comforts of life. The demand curve for money has limits.

The supply and demand considerations discussed above have been gathered together in what economists name "the quantity theory of money." Stated in its most naive form, the quantity theory tells us that when the amount of money in any society is increased, whether absolutely or through increase in velocity, prices rise; we assume, of course, that other things remain equal. When the amount of money declines, prices decline. This simple theory has been much qualified, amended and criticized, yet the essential idea is still considered a pillar of economic wisdom. The principle apparently operates even in societies that are culturally quite different from our own. Paul Einzig, in his book on primitive money, reports several cases in which the medium of exchange of primitive communities was quickly debased by European traders or explorers who entered the community with the same kinds of sea shells, beads, and so on, that were used by the uncivilized islanders as money.

The chief monetary phenomena of recent years have been the abandonment of the full and automatic gold standard, and a movement toward a managed currency. What does this mean to us as citizens?

Until 1914 the international gold standard was presumably conferring certain benefits on the human race. The gold standard died in that year, though it was temporarily revived later. Its benefits are now being questioned and monetary agnosticism has paved the way for a possibly total abandonment of the gold standard. The greatest benefits were as follows:

1. The free convertibility of money into gold was a force that prevented governments from printing too much money and banks from creating too much checkbook money. (How banks create checkbook money is one of the subjects of the next chapter.) Since a great increase in the amount of paper money would demand an increase in the amount of gold, governments and banks were somewhat inhibited from flooding the country with paper money—only "somewhat," because no ironclad ratio need be set between amount of gold and amount of paper money. Governments and bankers have learned much about economizing gold as support for paper money, so much so that small amounts of gold can support great monetary structures, although there are limits. One advantage of gold, then, was that it helped to prevent a vast cheapening of money (or vast increase in price level) by setting broad limits to the amount of money that would be manufactured out of pure paper.

2. The free and unqualified gold standard tied prices together all over the world. Under gold the values of the franc, dollar, pound, deviated from gold or from their established ratios only by negligible quantities—at least, negligible to all but specialized dealers. Because the gold content of all important currencies was stated in gold, because govern-

ments until the First World War considered this gold-
content a hallowed figure, and because paper could always
be changed into gold, the world had, in effect, an international currency, namely gold. There was, also, under the gold
standard (but not because of it) relative freedom of trade
between nations. For many basic commodities like cotton,
wheat, coal, steel, there was a free international market and
an international money. These two unifying forces helped
to keep all prices everywhere in line. This did not mean that
your Harris tweed overcoat cost as much gold in London
as in New York, or that your daughter could not live more
cheaply in a French pension than in an American boarding-
house, but it did mean that spreads were not too great. This
second advantage boils down to the fact that the entire
world was—never completely so, to be sure—a huge ho-
mogeneous market in which gold was the international currency.

But there were also disadvantages in this arrangement.
One disadvantage was that no nation could cushion itself
against economic shocks produced elsewhere. The gold
standard tied the world's prices together in a beautifully
unified structure, but the unified structure itself was on the
loose, like Frank Lloyd Wright's hotel in Tokyo, which
is said to slither about in the mud, all in one piece, during
an earthquake. Or, to use a different figure: we were in a
train of cars hitched together by automatic gold couplings,
but the train was on a roller coaster. Gold gave no stability
to our internal price level; it only insured that our price
level was reasonably in line with the price level of other
countries. About all this means to the underlying population
in practical terms was that if we were having a depression
in this country, then they were having one in England; when

high prices were wrecking the food budgets of American women, Austrian women were having a hard time, too. Very consoling, but scarcely anything to line one's nest with.

The First World War bore most of the belligerents and neutrals away from the gold standard. Great emergencies tend to do this, partly because crises shake people's faith in paper money and make them want to convert paper into metal. Since there is never enough gold for everybody, governments have to suspend gold payments. During the period of suspension—that is, during the war and the immediate postwar period—the world's prices got out of line. It took heroic measures to get them back into line. In a few nations, a depression was all but deliberately induced to bring down prices; in others, the former gold content of the currency was drastically cut down. Whichever way it went, many members of the community were badly hurt. Even so, the world never really got back on the old, free, unqualified gold standard. Just about the time most nations had got aboard the gold standard train again it dipped steeply on the international roller coaster, for this was in the year 1929. Suspension of gold convertibility again.

This time, nations were beginning to wonder whether the good old gold standard was worth fighting for. Indeed, the United States did not even fight. We went off the gold standard at a time when we were not forced off. Our government and its economists decided that you could not hope to have internal economic stability so long as you were on the roller coaster. And so did other countries. After temporary suspension, we got on a modified gold standard again, to be sure, but have never returned to the absolutely free gold standard of the Victorian era.

The Second World War, which began while we were still

in the depression, further weakened what was left of the gold standard and weakened the world's will ever to return to the unqualified gold standard. Nations are refusing to submit their price structure to the tyranny of gold. Some people say this proves that economic nationalism has triumphed; others that the desire of human beings to manage their currency instead of allowing it to be managed badly for them by gold is evidence of a groping toward true internationalism. The latter point to the regulating functions of the United Nations' social and economic agencies, particularly the International Bank and the Fund, as substitutes for the gold standard. Still others say that refusing to be kicked around by gold is socialism, and some say it is the primrose path to fascism. There is probably at least a grain of truth in all the above statements; and cautious men refuse to say too much about what managed currencies may lead to.

Serious economists tell us that the United States is now on the international gold bullion standard; lighthearted ones say it is the "hypothetical-psychological gold standard." Whichever way you look at it, gold still rules, but as a constitutional monarch rather than as a tyrant. And so long as our currency is linked to gold, so long will the nations whose economies depend on ours—which means much of the remainder of the non-Communist world—feel that link, too. And even the Communists will probably not be completely insulated. Yet we have, all of us, more freedom to manage our currency than we did under the strict gold standard. This gives us at least some leeway and some effective power to control economic forces that were formerly beyond control. Whether this power can be used as one of the great forces to sustain the most desirable price level, to prevent mass unemployment, to sustain a high level of production, to encourage imports and exports, is a question that cannot be answered yet. Money is after all only the handmaiden to economic activity. Theodore Roosevelt once said that it is difficult to make our material condition better by the best laws, but it is easy enough to ruin it by bad laws. Substitute "money" for "laws" in the above, and you have an equally great truth: you may not be able to improve economic conditions with soundly managed money but you can cause great hardship with badly managed money.

Thus far we have talked mainly about the concerns of standard economic theory in the study of money. What do the dissenters have to say? Here, as elsewhere, we find that dissenters do not speak with one voice, that they do not completely repudiate everything put forward by standard theory and that their work consists of a series of individual contributions rather than a cooperatively cultivated field of endeavor.

Perhaps one of the chief areas of dissident critique has been a critique of standard theory's implicit denial of the complete integration of money with its culture. What I mean is this: standard theory has often assumed that money—like safety matches—was a mere external convenience in economic life. It made life easier by eliminating barter, as matches make life simpler by sparing us the labor of rubbing two sticks together. Dissident theory, appealing oftener to anthropology, cultural history, and social philosophy than standard theory does, would be more inclined to assign to money a deeper cultural significance than to such real but superficial conveniences as matches. This attitude is reflected in Georg Simmel's view of money, in the early paragraphs of this chapter.

This difference may, in part, seem to be a purely academic difference of viewpoint as to origins. Or it may even seem to be a gratuitous criticism by dissenters, who here would have an opportunity to upbraid standard theory for the "conjectural history" it has so often invented. Veblen, particularly, loved to torment economists with taunts about their shallow scholarship in allied fields. If that were really all there was to it, the anthropological, or cultural, criticism would scarcely be worth mentioning. But this attitude does lead to other interests in the monetary field.

According to standard theory, money has certain normative "functions": measure of value, store of wealth, and the like. But money actually serves quite different functions and these the dissenters are quick to recognize. Actually, money can be made to do many perverse things and can be made to serve intergroup conflicts.

The Germans, by their confiscatory inflation of the 1920's, made money a means of pinning large parts of their war costs on the middle classes. In our country, silver-state Congressmen have used the monetary system to subsidize the silver producers they represented. The financing of the Civil War through greenbacks, we learn from Wesley Mitchell's writings, resulted in an increase in profits at the expense of wages, interest, and rent. It is to be doubted that the results noted by Mitchell were purely accidental, or the unexpected outcome of fiscal policies set in motion by Congressmen who had flunked economics in college. There is some reason to believe that the results achieved were consciously desired. Incidentally, it is worth noting that Mitchell undertook his study of the greenbacks at a time when most standard economists, approaching the same subject, would probably have been interested in how the greenback episode squared with the quantity theory of money. He, however, showed no particular interest in the quantity theory, though his conclusions shed some light on it. What he found was that, when the amount of currency was increased, prices did not automatically go up. What sent prices up was, rather, a temporarily declining confidence of the North in the victory of their arms. This does not mean that the quantity theory is all wrong. For the theory holds that prices rise when money is increased *only when other things are equal.* The most devastating thing Mitchell gives us here against the quantity theory is that, since nothing is ever equal in the great industrial democracies, the theory is almost empty of meaning; or that it only points vaguely in this general direction rather than that. Elsewhere Mitchell does deliver a few left hooks and an uppercut at the quantity theory, but makes no real bid for a knockout—probably because it cannot be knocked out. After all, the quantity theory can be interpreted as saying only that the amount of money in a society is equal to the number of things purchased in that society, times their average price. Stated thus as an equation, it is a truism. The real problem is, Which item in the equation is the trigger that sets off the chain reaction? The older standard economists seemed to think that increases or decreases of money were the activating force. Mitchell could not agree to this without making important exceptions. He felt that often the prospect of higher prices was the force that would increase the amount of money—just the reverse of what was generally believed. Keynes, though not treated as a dissenter in this book, probably comes closer to Mitchell than to the strict quantity theorists of another day, like Irving Fisher (1867–1947).

If one thinks of monetary theory as being, in part, a

theory of how wealth can be redistributed among groups in the population, of how it can be used by one class to secure advantages at the expense of another, many monetary phenomena of American history become clearer. Part of our history, like part of England's, has for its grand theme the rapid rise of industry at the expense of the agricultural classes. In this intergroup conflict, monetary policies—including proposed policies—played their part. Populism, Greenbackism, Cross of Gold, bimetallism, gold standard, all these words suggest monetary policies that if or when put into effect would work to the advantage of one economic pressure group at the expense of another. And it must not be believed that this pulling and hauling is of historical interest only and has stopped. All over the world the redistribution of income and redistribution of wealth is being effectuated by positive and negative, explicit, and implicit, monetary policies.

Another point (the dissenting theorist is completely fascinated by things like this): the Masai, an African tribe, use goats and cattle for money, but then let the animals dominate their lives. Paul Einzig describes the situation as follows:

> Goats and cattle were until comparatively recently the principal currency of a large part of Kenya. . . .
> It is among the Masai that the cattle cult has achieved the most advanced stage. This warlike pastoral race has practically no other store of value, and its primitive economy is based entirely on values expressed in cattle. Owing to the fact that cattle . . . is the sole currency of the Masai, they are greatly overstocked, far beyond economic requirements. Quality is neglected . . . for the sake of possessing the largest number of this token of wealth. Before British control . . . the difficulties of overstocking were overcome through raids on agricultural communities whose population was destroyed or enslaved, and

whose cultivated land was turned into pasturage. Now that this can no longer be done, overstocking tends to cause soil erosion. . . . Deficiency of water supplies is also aggravated by overstocking.[3]

What dissenters would conclude from the Masai is that the pursuit of goat-wealth leads to group impoverishment—provided that well-being is measured by some yardstick other than that of being thickly surrounded by starveling goats. If welfare means peace instead of war, good land instead of eroded land, enough water instead of drought, fat cattle rather than skeletons, then the Masai are made poor by their very success in getting their kind of wealth. It can, of course, be argued that dissenting American economists are presumtuous even to suggest that Masai should use criteria other than their own to determine what wealth and welfare are; maybe the Masai don't care so much for things Americans like: alarm clocks, comics, subways, breakfast foods that are alleged to talk. What right, then, have any outsiders to pass judgment on the standards of welfare of this tribe? If the Masai love skinny goats, let them have skinny goats. This argument is very sound up to a point, and nobody making it can justly be accused of ethnocentrism. On the other hand, peace, rich soil, fat herds and abundant water are not exactly mere matters of taste, prized in some cultures and despised in others. They are universally among the essential bases of animal life and cannot be compensated for by the largest herds of starveling goats.

A dissenter might end the story of the Masai by suggesting that perhaps our own economic life is characterized by the willing and doing of contradictory things and that modern man, even as the Masai, builds up with his right hand wealth that is torn down with the left. The money of the

[3] Paul Einzig, *Primitive Money*, pp. 126–127.

Masai is indeed a curious thing; and perhaps ours would bring a smile to African lips.

We have covered many pages of a long and difficult subject, but the end is not in sight. Bank money and checkbook money have not yet been crossed off the list. Those are the subjects of the next chapter.

14. THE BANKER'S JOB

BANKS CONDUCT A greater variety of transactions than almost any other form of business organization. They rent out space in vaults by the cubic inch, they sell insurance, they make loans, they hold your money in a sort of reservoir that facilitates your timing of the outflow, they help you budget for Christmas, they control great corporations, they lend to governments, they teach thrift to children through junior accounts, they sell you foreign money, they serve as middlemen between great borrowers and small lenders, they act as guardians of the estates of lunatics. The late Justice Brandeis bitterly described them—at least some of the big ones—as institutions that were in the somewhat dishonest but enviable position of being both sellers and buyers in the same market, with all the strategic advantages that this position confers. The prime function of banks is to earn money for those stockholders and officers who are entitled to its earnings. In this they resemble cheeseburger palaces and other business enterprises.

The economist's chief interest in banks is that they create certain forms of money. Bank money, which includes loans, credit, demand deposits, checking accounts, are as real as is money printed by the government. All these forms or means of payment are basically similar. When a bank "grants" a loan it performs much the same function that government does when it prints money, as we shall see. This is a most important fact, and important consequences flow from that fact.

The reader will recall that in the last chapter we spoke of the quantity theory: that increases in the amount (or velocity) of money tended to increase prices. Too much money created by banks will increase prices just as surely as if too much is printed by governments. Thus, to an economist, the study of banking is a necessary second chapter to his study of money.

The discussion below can be followed more easily if the reader will keep this little list of questions in mind:

1. How do banks go about creating money (or demand deposits, or loans, or the other forms of surrogate money)?

2. Do they ever create too much money? If so, why?

3. Do they ever create too little money? If so, why?

4. Since it cannot be concealed that the answers to 2 and 3 are "yes," the next question is: What are the wider economic implications of creating too much or too little money?

5. If the economic repercussions are bad, can anything be done to prevent the creation of too much or too little money?

6. And, finally, why do banks create money, anyway? Isn't the federal government supposed to do that according to the Constitution of the United States? Haven't we already got our money—like the Beacon Hill ladies in the old joke, who never shop for chic new hats because they already *have* their hats?

How do banks create credit? Perhaps the best way to answer this question is to go back to a simpler age, when banking practices were not so highly developed as they are today. Some of the functions of modern commercial banks were understood by the Romans, but we pass over them to see what the English goldsmiths of the seventeenth century, "the fathers of our banking system," were doing. The business of the goldsmith was such that he had to take special precautions against theft of his raw and finished materials, just as jewelers do today. If he seemed to be an honest fellow, merchants in his neighborhood would ask to leave their money in his care rather than in their own less well guarded tills or houses. Usually the goldsmith agreed, for a consideration, to take care of the money. As evidence of receiving valuables he issued a claim check, worded more or less as follows:

I promise to pay unto the Rt. Honble Ye Lord North & Grey or bearer ninety pounds at demand.

> For Mr. Francis Child & Myself
> Jno. Rogers [1]

Since gold and coins, unlike rugs and fur coats that we also store for safekeeping, bear no marks of personality, the goldsmith could spend or lend the actual ninety pounds left by Lord North and Grey, so long as he was prepared to give the holder of the claim check an equal amount of money "at" demand. As for Lord North and Grey, he could, in settlement of a ninety-pound debt (or partial settlement of a greater one) give the claim check to Lord South and Magenta, for the claim check would be honored regardless of who presented it. If Lord South and Magenta, in turn,

[1] Taken from L. D. Edie, *Money, Bank Credit and Prices* (New York, Harper, 1928), p. 103. See also R. D. Richards, "The Evolution of Paper Money in England," *Quarterly Journal of Economics*, XLI (1927), 380.

were in debt to Lord East and Shocking Pink, the claim check could be passed on again instead of being presented to the goldsmith. And this could continue indefinitely; the little claim check could, in theory, extinguish an infinite chain of debts. It might even fall into the hands of somebody who owed money to our original North and Grey. Lord North, the original owner, might thus get his busy little claim check back again and of course his gold, if he wanted it. This claim check is an ancestor of the bank note. If you have a five- or ten-dollar or larger bill in your pocketbook, the chances are that it is a Federal Reserve Note, a very urbane descendant of Lord North and Grey's crude, handwritten receipt.

But this receipt is also something like a check (or checkbook, or checking account). That is, A gives to B what has been deposited with C for safekeeping. To be sure, one of the major conveniences of the checkbook had not yet been developed: the ability to pay out in small amounts over a period of time through several small checks the large sum deposited. Here Lord North pays over all or nothing. But for all that, nobody will deny that Lord North and Grey's receipt is closely related to a checkbook. Thus we establish the fact that bank notes and checking accounts are members of the same species.

Until about 1650, goldsmiths merely held the gold that was deposited with them. They held exactly as much gold as there were claim checks outstanding—just as the hat-check girl at the club has an actual hat for each of her numbered pasteboards. But in the second half of the century they began to see that they could issue claim checks unbacked by gold. This action was made possible, as everyone knows, not only because owners of gold or coin left their valuables undisturbed with the goldsmith for long periods; but also because even when owners did want their money back they would not usually come flocking in together on the same day (unless, of course, confidence in the goldsmith's integrity or capacity to pay out had somehow been shaken).

Beginning about 1650 goldsmiths of good and wide reputation began to issue documents like the claim checks, but these were not covered by actual and earmarked quantities of gold or other hard money. If we now add a new character to our cast we can follow the implications of issuing claim checks unbacked by hard money. The new character, Wm. Green, a young member of the newly rising merchant class, drops in to see the goldsmith and confides:

"A ship from India, heavy-laden, has freshly come to port. The long journey was undertaken on behalf of more exalted and wealthier than I, yet am I by the merchant princes allowed two hundredweight of pungent peppercorns had I but ninety pounds wherewith to pay."

To which the goldsmith would reply, "And, prithee, sirrah, what wouldst thou do with peppercorns hadst thou thy ninety pounds in gold?"

Wm. Green would then whisper to the goldsmith that, within six weeks, the price of peppercorns in London must rise. Stocks are now low. There are reports—not yet confirmed, to be sure—that one convoy of homeward-bound ships from India has been caught in a gale, and another wrecked. In any event this is the season of foul weather in the South Atlantic and, besides, reports of increasing piracy have been confirmed. Green is sure that in a few weeks he can double his ninety pounds—if he had ninety pounds. Alas, his funds are all tied up in other ventures which, though prospering, cannot yet be made to bear their fruit.

The goldsmith is interested. He knows the young man to be honorable and of good judgment, and that his sources of information are highly placed and reliable. When Green offers him a share of the profits if a loan can be arranged, the goldsmith agrees to make a loan, but not in gold. He will give Green a receipt, a claim check, like the one originally given to Lord North and Grey, "pay to Wm. Green or bearer at demand, ninety pounds in gold." Jubilantly the borrower takes this piece of paper to the greater merchants who had offered to let him have "two hundredweight of pungent peppercorns." The merchants accept this piece of paper in payment and release the peppercorns. In due course of time, the young merchant sells his pepper for twice the cost, repays the ninety pounds and also gives the goldsmith five pounds as his share—or, as we might say, as interest.

In normal and quiet times the goldsmith could safely give Green a claim check exactly like the claim check given to Lord North and Grey, despite the fact that Green had not deposited a blessed grain of gold with the goldsmith. This completely hollow claim check could be passed along to the greater merchants who could pass it on to Ed. Miller or Jno. Stevens, who could in turn pass it on to others. This hollow claim check looked exactly like Lord North's, and, like it, had some of the properties of a bank note and some of the properties of a checking account.

This piece of paper, so far as we know, might very well have left the hands of both Wm. Green and the goldsmith for 6 months. It might have entered a long and glorious career of extinguishing debt after debt, as Lord North's full-bodied claim check did. It might have been mislaid by some flighty young matron and found only a year later. Whatever happened, it is quite possible that by the time the

claim check came back to the goldsmith to be honored, the
ninety pounds had been "repaid" with interest, and the transaction forgotten by all but the goldsmith. His ledgers told
him that someday somebody would turn up with Wm.
Green's hollow claim check and, for all its hollowness, would
demand solid gold in return.

The goldsmith did several paradoxical things in this transaction. He made what is in effect a loan, yet lent nothing.
He did not lend the actual money of Lord North or of any
other depositor. There was no embezzlement in the usual
sense of the word. What he did was this: for a consideration
(the cut, bonus or interest), he allowed Green to use his
name and reputation, which were better known in business
circles than Green's. Businessmen had come to know that
the goldsmith's promises to pay would be honored; they did
not know this quite so generally about William Green,
though he had a good enough reputation for honesty among
those who had heard of him.

For the sake of clarifying several points I shall ask the
reader to let me make a few fantastic assumptions, and to
pick up the same story again near the beginning, but give
it a different ending. Here are the assumptions:

1) That the ninety-pound loan made to Wm. Green is
   the first and only loan made by the goldsmith;
2) That the hollow claim check given to Wm. Green is
   immediately cashed by the great merchants to whom
   he turned it over; and that the goldsmith would thus
   be ninety pounds shy of being able to meet the claims
   of all depositors, should all be presented at once;
3) That the goldsmith's depositors hear of the transaction
   through rumors, magnified and expanded to say that
   the goldsmith had absconded;

4) That all the depositors rush to the goldsmith's shop to get the facts and, if possible, their money, and that our original Lord North arrives last and latest of all (it will be remembered that his deposit was ninety pounds, exactly the amount that was "lent" to Wm. Green);

5) That the goldsmith has no personal funds of his own with which to make up the deficit of ninety pounds.

Under these improbable conditions, as each depositor comes up (except the last), the goldsmith has no trouble meeting the claims made on him. But at the very moment that he is mopping his forehead and thinks he is safe, he sees Lord North approaching, presumably to cash *his* claim check, too. The goldsmith realizes that he is cleaned out and has nothing to make repayment with. What can a quick-thinking goldsmith do under these circumstances? The goldsmith has no money but he does have a valuable document in his safe: Green's promise to repay 90 pounds with interest, for obviously the goldsmith had demanded something from Green when the "loan" was made, if only a rag of an IOU. This promise has value because Green is an honest man of good business judgment, a property owner and smart pepper broker. When the goldsmith sees Lord North coming up last he may, if there is time, slip out the back way, leave the shop in charge of his wife, and ask her to stall his lordship for ten minutes. He goes to a fellow goldsmith in the next street, slaps down Wm. Green's IOU, and breathlessly asks whether he can get 90 pounds on the basis of the paper. If the neighboring goldsmith is friendly and willing to lend our goldsmith 90 pounds and in return take over Green's promise to pay principal and interest, all is well. Lord North will be paid in gold. This—to anticipate—is what in modern banks we name "rediscounting."

If the neighboring goldsmith cannot or will not make the loan, our goldsmith can still face it out directly with Lord North. After explaining that this has been a day in a million, he can say:

"I am unable to give your lordship ninety pounds in cash; but if your lordship would be willing to accept Wm. Green's note for 90 pounds plus my own promise to pay with interest if he defaults, your lordship need not feel that the sum deposited has been irrevocably lost."

We may assume that Lord North would be irritated; that he might threaten prosecution for embezzlement. But we may also assume that Lord North would be willing to settle on this basis. Why? He doesn't really need the cash. He came to get his money only because everybody else was doing it. He knows Green as one of London's up-and-coming pepper men; he knows the goldsmith to be fundamentally honest even if addicted to newfangled ideas; he likes the idea of getting interest for awhile on his 90 pounds. The goldsmith is saved. We have, of course, made things very easy for our goldsmith. He had only one loan to wriggle out of. We might have had a quite different story to tell if the goldsmith had built up a vast network of loans.

One of the important points of this improbable tale was that the *loan made to Wm. Green* was an *asset to the goldsmith*. More than that, it played the same role as a deposit of real gold money. In a final analysis, the goldsmith was able to use William Green's evidence of debt (IOU) as a substitute for the deposit of actual money originally made by Lord North.

Before closing this brief historical section—embellished by imagination—let us take a closer look at early bank notes. To go back to the beginning: the goldsmith originally gave Lord North and Grey a promise to pay to him or bearer 90 pounds at demand. We may presume that the piece of paper looked rather homemade and was handwritten for the occasion. Suppose now, that instead of a promise of this sort, the goldsmith had had a stock of uniform and ornately engraved promises to pay made up in several denominations —say one-pound, five-pound, and ten-pound promises—all printed and signed in advance. When Lord North first put down his 90 pounds in coin for safekeeping, the goldsmith might have said: "An it please your lordship, I've been trying to streamline this business a bit, and I pray your lordship will be pleased to accept these printed promises to pay." Then he would count out nine of the previously printed ten-pound promises to pay, and tender them to the depositor in return for his cash. Though Lord North might conceivably refuse at first to accept these newfangled, impersonal, uniform promises to pay, once other people had accepted them he would eventually fall in line. As goldsmiths became banks and certain banks became generally known and widely trusted, these printed promises to pay became as acceptable everywhere as real coin of the realm. Since it was generally acceptable, it was money. And now we really do have bank notes, though not quite yet the Federal Reserve note in your pocketbook.

Now notice something else of even more importance. When William Green was granted his loan, the goldsmith could have given him these uniformly engraved promises to pay just as well as the little claim check. In other words, a loan or debt can be converted into bank notes! And this *does* come very close to the Federal Reserve notes in your wallet.

The reader should by now have a good idea of the family resemblances among loans, bank notes, deposits, checkbook money, and "real" governmental money. I have made quite a point of the underlying similarities because this is a basic economic concept, and the reader will have difficulty understanding even the simplest banking news on the financial page if he does not grasp it.

The reader will also see how the goldsmiths—and also modern banks—can increase the amount of money as easily as governments can. Under the quantity theory, increases of money—any kind of money—increase prices. If banks lend very freely, they can add so much to the means of payment that prices will rise. They may also act to lower prices if excessive caution prevents them from making or renewing loans, or still greater caution impels them to call in outstanding and callable loans (not all loans can be called at will, but some can).

Although modern commercial banks, with their glass, polished metal, and impersonally smiling employees differ obviously from the informal little goldsmith's shop, they are, in many ways, surprisingly alike. The most visible differences are not of the essence.

Modern banks make commercial loans, like the one made to Green, and for similar reasons. The loans usually take the form of demand deposits (subject to check) in the name of the borrower. In some senses, modern banks really lend nothing; they sell the use of their name, which is what the goldsmith did. Sometimes they find it desirable to surrender the IOU of a Wm. Green to another bank in order to get cash for it or increase their own deposits in that bank. That is rediscounting. Certain types of banks issue bank notes—indeed, most of the paper money we carry around with us for ordinary shopping is in the form of bank notes: Federal Reserve notes. And behind the smoke screens of red tape and complex bank procedures, there are many similarities between the uniform, impersonal receipts, hollow or full-bodied, of our goldsmith and the folding money we Americans have used and are now using. Perhaps the essential differences between the two eras is the greater amount of self-discipline, comprehension of banking theory, and government regulation (or quasi-regulation) in the modern banking system. Every advanced country has some form of "central banking," of which more later—but which, for the moment we may think of as a cooperative system whereby privately owned banks follow similar policies at the same time in the public interest, often in consultation with government.

Among the questions asked at the beginning of the chapter was whether or not banks ever created too much or too little money and, if so, how harmful that was and, if harmful, whether there were any remedies. One difficulty with this question is that we have no criterion as to what "too much" or "too little" are. These are questions of how much money there "ought" to be, and "ought" belongs to the field of human values primarily and either not at all or only peripherally to economics. Still, economists do have their "oughts," and most would agree that we should have, at certain normal and stable levels of prices, a quantity of money sufficient to maintain that desirable stability. In a growing country like ours where there are both an increasing population and an increasing standard of life, there should be comparable increases in the amount of money to take care of the new people and the new products. This does not mean that parents should be given new money for every child produced, or that every new television set should somehow have its price in crisp, new bills attached somewhere or other, but it does mean that some sort of balance should be maintained between increased population and production on the one hand, and amount of money on the other.

It may at this point be asked why government doesn't attend to that. Why doesn't it print new money as population and production growth show up in the census figures? A partial answer is that government does increase the amount of its kind of money over the years but not precisely to meet the day-to-day needs of business. More on this later, and the present reply is only half the story.

For historical reasons and otherwise, banks in the short run, at least, bear the brunt of the job of expanding or, when occasion demands, of contracting, the amount of money through loans. But unfortunately banks are not always able to expand or contract the money supply in accordance with the broader public interest. A striking American example of failure, now remedied, was the annual American shortage of money half a century ago at crop-moving time. Our great crops then as now began to be sold in August. The New York banks had to ship to the agricultural areas nearly twice as much money in August as in July; and in October three times as much. As those great crops of ours—in those days an even more important item relatively in our total annual production—went Eastward and Northward, real money and bank money went in the opposite direction from New York. The Wall Street reservoir of money fell to a low level. A low level of funds, alone, caused no special problems; but combined with a jittery business outlook, the dearth of money in New York sometimes precipitated panics and excessively wide swings in the stock market. Many honest and well-run business establishments and banks went to the wall in those days because banks could not create enough extra new money to move the newly grown crops. The money had to be taken from somewhere else—from Wall Street primarily—where the resulting stringency of funds sometimes contributed toward a debacle. Then in December, money would rush back to New York again and in January there was a flood of it. But for some people, it came too late.

Why did this happen then and why does it no longer happen today? That is a long and intricate story which I shall try to oversimplify. One trouble then was that banks could, by law, issue bank notes only if these were backed by government bonds in the possession of the issuing bank. Thus, unless the government offered new bonds for sale in the crop-moving season, there was no profitable way in which banks could legally increase the amount of their bank notes. And the government did not normally offer new bonds for sale at crop-moving time (in a few crises it did do something of the sort). The law was a little silly from the viewpoint of banking theory. We have already seen how the goldsmith could issue a perfectly sound—though hollow—claim check on the basis of an honest business transaction; and we have seen that a claim check is akin to a bank note. Sound bank notes can be based on sound business transactions as well as on government bonds. Indeed, this is the basic principle of commercial banking. But in the era of the national banking law (1864-1913) a harsh view was taken of this principle (there were some good reasons for this—previous abuses, mainly).

But the bank note-government bond problem was not really the only or even the basic difficulty. The basic difficulty was that in the management of their reserves, banks found it more profitable to allow the monetary stringency to develop than to take steps to prevent it. This was dangerous, of course; but if the bank survived the stringency, profits were greater. If they did not, *tant pis*.

Private banks, then as now, were impelled through competition and otherwise, to operate as profitably as possible. To operate profitably, a bank must lend or invest or issue bank notes up to the limit of its capacity. Its capacity, in normal and quiet times, is some multiple of its reserves, maybe five or six times, depending on the community's banking habits. Reserves are sums of money (or near money) put aside by a bank to enable it to meet instantly the requests of depositors for cash. "Near money" includes deposits that one bank has with another bank. Because reserves, to be reserves, must be kept in highly liquid form, it is obvious that they earn little or nothing at all in the way of interest. Thus we see that a banker can be pretty schizophrenic about his reserves: if large, he has safety when emergencies arise and depositors clamor for their money, but he makes relatively little profit; if small, he has only a slender margin of safety but a large margin of profit. Each dollar in his reserves is barren; only sums lent out to borrowers—illiquid, partially frozen, unavailable if demands are made—can bring income.

Now this dilemma of the banker (size of reserves versus

size of earning assets) was normally resolved by keeping
reserves as low as possible and (or) legally permissible, while
loans were kept as high as possible. When new crops came
from the West and demanded new money or credit, banks
had no reserves left on the basis of which to pyramid new
loans. Since it was important that the farmer get his money,
and profitable that the crops should change hands and move,
the banks called in all callable loans, loans made during the
spring and summer to various kinds of merchants, dealers in
stocks and bonds, and so on. This sometimes caught the
springtime borrowers short of money with which to pay,
and when it did, a chain reaction started up that spread
widely and often dangerously. But for the banker who was
not himself squeezed, this process released his reserves (gave
him more cash). On the basis of his released reserves, he
could supply the new credit or money needed in the farm
belt.

From this we can see that banks, when properly operated
from the viewpoint of their stockholders are not always
operated in the best public interest. They are given the
responsibility of creating enough money to meet certain
types of situations, but unless they are given inducement,
guidance, or leadership to act in the public interest, they are
compelled by understandable pressures to ignore it, at least
partly.

How to combine the banker's quest for profit with the
broader public interest is, of course, a difficult problem. It
is partly met by the institution of central banking. There
are forty ways of defining and describing a central bank,
but perhaps it is enough for the moment to say that a central
bank is a bank powerful enough, and sufficiently above the
cat-and-dog fight for profits, to function in the public inter-

est and thereby induce other banks to behave in the same
way.

These difficulties and many others have been corrected
by the creation of a central bank in the United States: the
Federal Reserve System. This may be described as a vast
banking cooperative, or league, to which at least half the
banks of the country belong, the larger half from the viewpoint of assets. This vast cooperative, or federation, main-
tains a dozen bankers' banks, one in each of the twelve
important financial centers of the United States (for example, New York, Chicago, Dallas, San Francisco). At the
top of the structure is the Board of Governors, selected by
the President of the United States and the Senate.

In this banking system it is possible to issue bank notes on
the basis of a sound loan, as the goldsmith did, and as banks
of fifty years ago could not do. Thus, whenever a salable
washing machine has been newly produced, it is possible to
create new money with which it can be bought—something
like the arrangement by which the goldsmith gave Wm.
Green a new claim check to cover the newly imported
peppercorns. The bank notes are the Federal Reserve notes
we constantly use. Though they bear an official stamp, they
are really the notes of private banks and may arise out of
transactions conducted entirely and exclusively by private
business.

Another thing is possible in the Federal Reserve System.
You will remember that, at one stage, the goldsmith asked
his wife to stall off Lord North and Grey while he rushed
to the goldsmith in the next street to see if he could raise
money on Green's IOU. In this deal, the first goldsmith was
entirely dependent on the goodwill of the second. But under

the Federal Reserve System, any banker in the system with a good IOU arising out of a reasonably sound business transaction—any such banker may demand that his regional reserve bank give him money or its equivalent for the IOU. There is a small charge (the rediscount rate, to be technical about it), but the charge seems small when the need is great. It is normally less, considerably less, than the rate charged by the member bank to businessmen for loans.

The top brass of the Federal Reserve System can slow up the creation of bank money in its various forms, or speed it up, by raising or lowering the rediscount rate. Lowering the rediscount rate induces member banks of the System to bring their IOU's to be rediscounted, and to lower their interest rate to businessmen who may wish to borrow. Cheap loans encourage businessmen to borrow. Thus, in a depression the rediscount rate should be very low, so that businessmen, through easy credit, may be emboldened to take advantage of any money-making opportunity. And if prosperity threatens to turn into a dangerously speculative inflation, the rediscount rate can be increased; this will damp down frenzied activity. The rediscount policy of central banks may be reinforced by so-called open-market operations. In this type of operation the central bank, to increase the money supply, buys government bonds and other "paper" in the open market; or, if it wishes to reduce the amount of money in the community, it can sell bonds in the open market. The way this works is the obvious way: when the bank acquires bonds persistently, it sprays the community with the money that must be paid to previous owners of bonds; when it sells, it absorbs some of the community's money, and in return gives bonds to the community.

A banking system dominated by a central bank has long

been looked upon by many economists as a superb instrument for maintaining economic stability. On this view the business cycle could be flattened out by a strong, prompt, contracyclical rediscount policy—a high rediscount rate to head off a feverish boom and a low rate to forestall depression. The rediscount policy may be made even more effective when it is accompanied by the appropriate type of open-market activity. Control through the central bank has the advantage, it is argued, of supplying guidance to private enterprise without violating the institutional framework of capitalism, that is, without leading to government ownership of basic industries, to rationing and price control, or to other detailed or invasive forms of control.

On the whole, the possibilities of this admirable instrument have been but modestly exploited in the United States. Federal Reserve officials have shown neither the vigor nor the capacity for prompt action that economists would have liked to see. The reasons for this state of affairs are found partly in practical politics and partly in the changing character of the banking system and of the economy it serves.

The responsible, in-the-flesh, all-too-human formulators of monetary policy are at the mercy of all kinds of pressure groups, and cannot listen exclusively to the voice of the expert economist. One would hardly expect the political party in power to feel happy about the lowering of the rediscount rate just before an important November election. The clear suggestion that a period of prosperity was drawing to a close would doom its chances of reelection. It should, incidentally, be observed here that until 1946, when the Employment Act was passed, the American people had never given its monetary officials a genuine mandate to control boom-and-bust. Neither the original Federal Reserve

Act nor its later amendments make full employment a goal
of national policy.

When economists, about thirty years ago, first began to
advocate use of the central bank as an instrument of stabilization, they did not foresee the great changes that would
soon come about in commercial banking and in the economy
at large. A "true" commercial bank to them was one that
made short-term loans to facilitate trade, like the goldsmith's
loan to Green. But the commercial bank, itself a mirror of
the whole economy, has taken on new functions and partly
sloughed off others. Many businessmen no longer go regu-
larly to banks for loans; they finance themselves—an unexpected development. At the beginning of the Second World
War the government was borrowing as much from commercial banks as private businessmen were; and at the end
of the War, twice as much. Thus the banks have become
large holders of government obligations, not mere lenders
of short-term notes to facilitate trade. The government,
though a great borrower from banks, has also become a great
lender to businessmen and to farmers. This further muddies
up "pure" commercial banking.

Under such circumstances, in a system of mixed banking
in a mixed economy, there are often sound objections to
using the rediscount rate as an instrument of business-cycle
control. For example, the low rediscount rate of recent
years, in a period of inflation, was maintained in order to
keep the prices of government bonds stable. This, presumably, was a more desirable objective than that of damping
down exuberant business activity. Moreover, economists are
looking to other methods of control. Many of the Keynesians, as was intimated in Chapter 12, would use taxation
instead of central-bank policies as the chief instrument to

get rid of depressions. War has also made us attempt to achieve more than mere stabilization, and to tolerate direct and detailed controls over wages, prices, use of metals, and the like. Federal Reserve officials have been empowered to use other methods of control, and some of these have been extremely effective in recent years. The Federal Reserve Board may require member banks to increase or decrease their reserves, that is, increase or decrease the ratio of idle money to loans. They may cut down stock-market loans by raising margin requirements—or vice versa; and they may cut down installment buying by requiring that buyers pay larger deposits and monthly payments on cars, deep-freezers, and the like—or vice versa.

The rediscount rate is still a powerful instrument of control, but other and equally important instruments have robbed it of the primacy that it had in the economist's mind a short generation ago.

We have come to a point in our study of banking where it would perhaps be more useful to stand back and appraise the picture as a whole than to elaborate the detail. I have given a description of basic banking practices. No great issues of economic theory have arisen. Standard and dissenting theorists both would describe the banking system approximately as I have described it. But there are issues here, and they will be raised in these last few pages of this chapter.

Here is an extremely complicated set of establishments, rules, laws, and traditions fastened upon our economic system. What real advantages have been conferred on us by these institutions? In a narrow and perhaps meaningless sense this great complex that we call banking is partly nonproductive, on the face of it. It creates credit, which is neither tangible, like bubble gum, nor in the same realm of service as a shoe shine. Credit performs many of the functions of money itself; but we already *have* our government's money. Why do we need surrogate money? If all bank credit, and all bank notes were destroyed, there would still be silver certificates and various other kinds of government-made money; moreover, the Treasury could print a few hundred bales quickly and cheaply if we needed more. After all, why banks? credit? loans? bank notes? deposit accounts?

Certainly the banking system yields us many valuable services. Checking accounts are conveniences and facilitate the work of household payments. Most of us, unlike the French peasant of tradition, feel safer if our money is in the bank than if it is hidden under the mattress. It is safer to mail a check than to mail money, and, in the case of odd amounts like $18.73, it is also easier. Tremendous sums are exchanged without the cost of insurance or the need of transportation (always dangerous because of the possibility of loss through theft or other casualty) by the clearing-house system, whereby banks cancel interbank debts down to residual sums, as is sometimes done in scoring at bridge and other games.

All these things make life easier for us, diminish effort, give us peace of mind, or are in other ways thoroughly justifiable by economic criteria. But they are only the by-products of banking. Bankers are not in business so that you can conveniently and safely send $9.67 by check to your stranded brother-in-law in Albuquerque. Bankers are lenders; if they stop making loans either to government or business or both, they stop being banks.

The key to banking is loans. What good are *loans* economically? Do they, like checking-account convenience, make life easier for us, diminish effort, give us peace of mind, or, are they in other ways justifiable by economic criteria? Do they cause two blades of grass to grow where only one grew before? Opinion on this question seems to be divided.

On one point there is general agreement, namely, that loans are a device to put industrial equipment under the control of those who are willing to exercise control—hence, presumably under the control of reasonably capable persons. In other words, more venturesome men borrow funds from less venturesome men and "put the money to work." Moreover these venturesome men are not entirely self-appointed; their appointments are confirmed by lenders (usually bankers) who look over the would-be enterprisers before they make loans. Thus, businessmen, if they do not pass state examinations like doctors or lawyers—and perhaps they should—are at least scrutinized by their fellows; and it is their need for credit that automatically subjects them to this minimum scrutiny, at least.

What else does credit, or credit seeking do? One of the best contemporary manuals on economics says that credit is "a sort of solvent factor—enabling us in a sense to make use of future goods at the present time." [2] This metaphorical and tentative language describes very well what we feel about credit, but it really says little about the productive usefulness of credit. "Solvent" is here used figuratively with a natural-science flavor, and since economics is not a natural science the word conveys small meaning. How can we make use of "future goods" now? Does this mean that credit ripens green apples overnight? Why should we make use of future goods now, even if we could? If we do, what happens in the

[2] F. R. Fairchild, E. S. Furniss, and N. S. Buck, *Elementary Economics* (5th ed., New York, Macmillan, 1948), I, 447.

future, when we shall need them? It does enable an individual to buy now what he would otherwise spend two years
saving for. He can, through credit, save up backwards—
that is to say, consume now and pay later. The possibility of
doing this may mean the difference between life and death
for anybody needing expensive medical services and long
hospitalization. Timely loans to individuals under less dramatic circumstances, for a college education, let us say, may
enrich our society in various ways. But after all, banks make
few loans to sick men and college students. This ability to
save after the fact is the basis of installment buying and selling—and that is a dubious blessing.

Both Marx and Veblen have wondered a good deal about
the benefits of the larger uses of credit. That it enables the
individual businessman who can get it freely to make more
money (get more income or, loosely, profits) than he would
otherwise make, was clear to Veblen, but he saw no great
benefit in this to the society as a whole. Anyone who has
bought a house, or land, or stocks on a rising market with a
small down payment and been able to sell quickly at a profit,
understands how one may agreeably realize a thousand
dollars within a year on the base of a few hundred. This is
fine for the lucky or enterprising individuals, Veblen conceded. But economics is not much concerned with what
makes individuals richer. The economist wants to know
whether such deals increase the material wealth of the community at large. Are more goods produced for consumption?
Are more machines produced for the purpose of producing
more goods? Is eroded land reclaimed? After all, Green's
pungent peppercorns were already produced and ready to
consume when the goldsmith made the loan. The loan

merely enabled Green to buy them cheap and sell them dear. It created nothing new.

Out of his questioning attitude toward the larger uses of credit, Veblen develops a theory of the business cycle which, even after the more elaborate work of Keynes and Mitchell, still stands up pretty well. And from this he goes on to show that credit plays a large role in great concentrations of wealth. In economic crises, creditors have the upper hand, are able to take over the ownership of properties held by debtors and thereby increase their holdings. If creditors would press their advantage whenever possible, they would presumably soon own the whole economic system. Some day a truly ruthless creditor may arise to exploit every advantage to the full. When that time comes, says Veblen, "It will be worth going out of one's way to see the phenomenal gains and the picturesque accompaniments of such a man's work." [3]

I do not mean to suggest that standard theory is *for* credit and dissenting theory *against* credit. It is impossible to conceive any kind of human life in organized communities without some lending or borrowing. There is, however, a great deal of difference between borrowing your neighbor's garden tools to spade up a corn patch, and borrowing purchasing power from your broker to buy some pieces of paper, named "stocks," that represent nothing physical or tangible, but only the anticipated earning-power of a new holding company. Perhaps all the dissenters are trying to say is that the latter type of borrowing, insecurely based on expectations of future worth, may contribute more to economic disorganization and to the development of the arts

[3] *The Theory of Business Enterprise* (New York, Scribner, 1904), p. 208.

of financial wizardry than to the industrial arts, or to a harmonious ordering of economic life.

Whatever may be thought of the dissenters' findings on the larger uses of credit, it seems fairly clear that human beings have created an exceedingly complex mechanism for the exchange of goods; a mightier instrument than is required just to convert the extra kohlrabies you harvested into the extra doilies I crocheted.

15. AS SURE AS TAXES

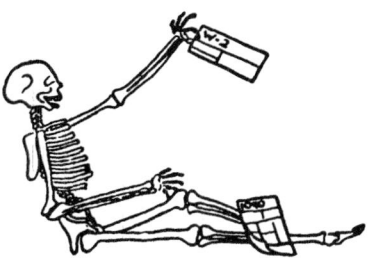

NINE HUNDRED YEARS ago Lady Godiva, clad only in her tresses and mounted on a horse, rode through the streets of Coventry, a lovely expostulation against high taxes. Though perhaps more effective than most, this was neither the first nor the last protest from a tithe-ridden populace to its sovereign. People have never ceased to complain about taxes. Especially is this true in the United States today, when peacetime rates are higher than ever before, and the sums collected are being used for purposes that violate the deepest instincts of the "virtuous" middle classes (as John Stuart Mill described us).

It is probably through our system of taxation, budgeting, and public finance that the most sensitive economic nerves of the lower-upper, middle-upper, and upper-upper classes are touched, and the most exquisite pains produced. What fur coats we might buy our ladies with the sums we give bureaucrats to fling away for us! What cars! What extensions of our business establishments! What cushions of safety when embarking on new ventures! Not only are large sums taken away from us but also, it is widely thought, these

staggering amounts are being used to undermine the pillars
of American society, the moral fiber of its citizens, and to
drain the very springs that made the large sums possible in
the first place. The seed corn is being destroyed. The hard-
working and thrifty are being penalized while a devitalized
population seeks soft security. Meanwhile, heresies are
spreading: impractical idealists are saying that government
might as well print the money as collect it by taxation; that
budget-balancing is old-fashioned; that a good budget is an
unbalanced budget; that a public debt is only a debt we owe
ourselves, so what does it matter how large it is, and why not
cancel it, anyhow?

Are things really like that? Are our fiscal policies really as
unsound as they appear to be and do modern economists
ridicule such axioms as are contained in the notion that expenditures of government must equal income of government? Well, our taxation and budgetary situation is not
perfect. One could wish things were otherwise, but let us
suspend judgment on the state of our fiscal system until after
we have taken a look at it and at some of the theories that
underlie and inform it.

The simplest way to proceed is to take a recent federal
budget as a basis of discussion. As we go through it, ample
opportunity will arise to throw at least a little light on the
issues suggested above and on other relevant issues as well.
If we are to keep within reasonable bounds, we will be able
to discuss federal fiscal policies only. State taxation and
finance is an enormous topic in itself. Moreover, from the
viewpoint of the average citizen, what the federal government does about taxes and expenditures is vastly more important than what his state government does.

The budget selected for study is the last one of peacetime

—the "fifty-one" budget, for the fiscal year extending from July 1, 1950, to June 30, 1951. It was transmitted to Congress by the President in January, 1950, several months before Korea. Just now as I write—or, rather, rewrite and revise this chapter—estimates for the "fifty-two" budget are being published. The two budgets are very much alike in most important respects except one: the "fifty-two" budget allots about 25 billion dollars more than the earlier one for expenses relating to defense and war. The deficit is, therefore, greater; it is three times as much. Despite these differences the discussion below will, in broad outline, be as appropriate to one year as to the other. In any event, we are concerned with basic issues rather than with particular budgets, and for these, the 1951 budget will do as well as the 1952 estimates.

There are certain important extrabudgetary revenues and expenses that will have to be omitted from this chapter: the social security income and outgo. Federal pensions for the aged and compensation for the unemployed are activities conducted outside the regular budgetary scheme. Although these activities are of considerable economic importance and raise problems that cannot be ignored, they do not cry out for attention as certain other fiscal problems do. Just now, the pay-roll deductions contributed toward these activities more than cover the amounts paid out. Some years hence this agreeable current of monetary flow may be reversed. But for the present one may safely forget the social-security system in an introductory chapter on taxes and public debt.

The 1950–1951 budget calls for an expenditure of 42.4 billion dollars. Reduced to manageable terms, this means about one fifth of the total income of the United States, or about $280 for every man, woman, and child; for a standard

family of four, more than a thousand dollars. This is, of
course, shocking when compared with the 1920's, when the
government spent only about $25 per person, or $100 per
family. The federal government then spent only about four
cents out of every dollar of national income; the comparable
figure in recent years is twenty cents. And, as we have seen,
these figures take no account of the social-security expenditures.

Could not this 42.4 billion dollars be reduced somehow?
It probably could, but never to anything remotely comparable to the figures of the 1920's, even when allowances
are made for increased population and various other growth
changes that have steadily increased annual budgets since
1790.

Why does the budget successfully resist large cuts? First,
it can be argued that a general, over-all slash could be made
by a "streamlining" of the Executive Departments in accordance with the Hoover Commission on governmental
reorganization. Through the Commission we have been informed of seemingly intolerable waste: that to buy a $1.25
box of paper clips requires eleven dollars worth of paper-
work: that discharging a visibly inefficient stenographer
costs more time and money than is lost by letting her stay
around with nothing to do until she gets married, has a baby,
or expires of boredom. One cannot deny the truth of such
statements but there is danger that the isolated instance is
mistaken for the general case. Some ardent advocates of the
Hoover Commission proposals argue that four billions could
be saved by putting them into effect. This appears to be
extreme. The feasible rather than possible figure is more
likely to be in the neighborhood of one billion. Let us put
down a billion saved by what is known as streamlining. This

is the first visible saving as we go through the budget. Maybe more could be saved here, but the aim is to get rough figures of what might really be done rather than a precise figure of what could ideally be done if politicians were more competent and high-minded than other men.

Nearly three-quarters of the 42.4 billion dollars budgeted goes for expenditures concerned with foreign relations, past wars, the servicing of the public debt (largely a war-and-defense debt) the present cold war, European recovery and rearmament, and miscellaneous items primarily for defense like merchant-marine and air subsidies and atomic research. It is true that "national defense" appears on the officially printed budget as only a 32 percent expenditure, and I have said the figure was 75 percent. The discrepancy arises from the fact that the "national defense" item of the Budget Bureau includes only strictly military items, like paying soldiers, buying aircraft and submarines. I have defined "defense" much more broadly, including such things as atomic research and the unpaid bills of past wars.

It is doubtful whether any appreciable savings could be made on this item in the present state of world affairs—except, of course, such economies as would result from general streamlining of government, already spoken of and allowed for above. In any event it is not here that public opinion demands heavy budgetary slashing, particularly now that the Korean experience suggests even heavier armaments.

It is interesting to recall that sixty years ago, Lord Bryce commented on how painless American taxation was by comparison with European, but he also pointed out that we had virtually no military establishment. Now we have a great defense structure and a unique position in world affairs. This position we could perhaps relinquish if we wanted to.

No doubt our taxes could then go down appreciably. But we, as the world's greatest power, would go down with our taxes. We can, therefore, do little more than make whatever small additional economies are possible, here and there.

After war-and-defense items have been subtracted from the total, 11½ billion budgetary dollars remain for the other functions of government. It is within this relatively small sum that the large economies must be found. This is the area —the now circumscribed area—left for heavy blue-penciling, if it is conceded that the defense parts of the budget must be left virtually undisturbed. Through executive reorganization, economies could be made here as elsewhere, no doubt. But again we do not count them here, since they were subtracted initially in a billion-dollar lump sum.

Part of the 11½ billion goes for unchallenged expenditures. Out of it we support the FBI, take the census, maintain public parks, provide highways, enforce the Taft-Hartley Act, improve rivers and harbors, forecast weather, print money and stamps, pay Congressmen and civil servants, and so on. Savings could admittedly be made on some of these items, however. Some of the river and harbor expenditures are admittedly pure pork barrel, but nevertheless, river and harbor improvements are useful and necessary. Several subsidies are imbedded in the sections here considered: silver subsidies; business loans; low mail rates that result in a heavy operating deficit for the Post Office. If third and fourth class mail were self-supporting, a half billion dollars could probably be saved. But an increase in mail rates would not be very different from an increase in taxes. Our problem just now is not to find new and justifiable sources of revenue, but pure economies. Better put down total savings of only half a billion for all the items mentioned in this paragraph. By now we have saved a total of a 1½ billion dollars.

Another part of the 11½ billions is allocated to the controversial field of welfare and agriculture. For social welfare, health, housing, education, agriculture, water power, labor placement, labor standards, and the like, the 1951 budget calls for about 6 billion dollars. We should notice that this is a smallish fraction of the total budget; even deep slashes here would subtract little from the large whole. Nobody dreams of taking the government completely out of the welfare business. All responsible persons would concede that part of the job of government is to maintain certain health, welfare, and educational services; and nobody would be willing to abandon the farmer completely. The present farm program may be fantastic, but even a much better-devised scheme would cost plenty of money. There will have to be a subsidized farm program of some kind, for aid to the farmer cannot be suddenly lopped off.

How much could be cut without disastrous effect upon the various groups and without throwing domestic tranquility into disequilibrium can here, too, only be guessed at. We may call the possible saving 1½ billion dollars, though many would think this too much, by far. With an equal sum carried over from the foregoing, this makes a total of 3 billions and completes our survey of feasible budgetary economies. Three billions saved is a good deal, of course; it means about $80 a year per family—more for some and less for most. But it does not bring us back to the 1920's by a long shot.

The figures I have given are obviously not precise. They suggest an order of magnitude, rather than the magnitude itself. A fine-toothed comb might pick up a good deal more.

Perhaps a total of 4 billion dollars might have been saved (before Korea). If so, the extra billion would have permitted our saving another $7 per person. But we are still miles and miles away from the 1920's, or even 1930's, when government expenditures averaged around $50. Remember, in 1950, the figure was $280.

The tremendous discrepancy between $280 per person and the much lower figures of past decades is almost entirely a war-engendered discrepancy: veterans' payments, European aid, intensive preparations against new wars. If our military establishment and costs of past wars were down to what they were in the period between wars, we could probably reduce our expenditures to around $100 per person—which would be a very modest sum. Though it would still be higher than in the 1920's and 1930's, it would not weigh us down, since money incomes as well as prices generally, are now nearly twice what they were in the 1930's.

Where will all this money come from? It is expected to come from the following sources:

Source	Amount (in billion dollars)
Income taxes	17.3
Corporation taxes	10.1
Excise taxes	7.6
Tariff and other taxes	2.3
Deficit (this sum will be borrowed)	5.1
Total	42.4

Each one of these taxes has a personality of its own. We shall study them as individuals.

The tax in our fiscal structure that is principally alleged to soak the rich is the first in the list, the direct tax on individual incomes. If the issue were merely one of cutting a few lush million dollar incomes back to the sparser hundreds of thousands, the economist would have little to say about this tax. The principal issue then would be for the moralist: has a government the moral right to demand *proportionally* more from the rich than from the middle-income class and the poor? In itself, this is not economics, but ethics.

The economist gets into the debate through another issue: does the moderately firm progressiveness of American income taxes destroy the seed corn of American economic growth? The argument concealed in the question is that the rich save most; by saving they have made possible the laying of Atlantic cables, the building of railroads and, today, the mass production of television sets. If the government takes away all their extra money it reduces the amount that might be invested in new, magnificent enterprises, and, perhaps even worse, it reduces generally the incentives to create, earn, improve.

We take the latter point first: incentives to create and earn. This argument is certainly plausible, but it is not easy to verify. John Ise, an economist, suggests for example, that we might have had more films from the incomparable Garbo if her most productive years had come in the period of very high taxation. She presumably made too much untaxed money in too short a time to permit a full exploitation of her glamor and genius. And, of course, Garbo is used only as an example of a whole category of producers. On the other hand, Ise also intimates that many physicians, lecturers, and musicians have, in recent years, taken excessively long vacations because steadier work would have meant turning over most of their additional earnings to Uncle Sam. So far, the score is nothing to nothing. Heavy taxation may increase production; heavy taxation may decrease production.

As to savings (which are the basis of new investment),

the picture is not very clear either. During the period of American participation in the Second World War the American people saved a larger percentage of their income than ever before—or, rather, than since 1869, when the records begin. And during the war period, taxation was higher than ever before. This may be dismissed as meaningless, since the war restricted our movements and purchases. With the return of gasoline, garbage choppers, new cars, diaper services, civilian air transportation, horse racing, and the other amenities of American culture, our savings (as percentage of income) plummeted. Only the worst years of the prewar depression show less saving. But this, of course, also proves little. Economic generalizations cannot be based on a few short years of postwar readjustment when people were hungry for goods. Canadian income taxes are, if anything, slightly higher than ours, yet Canada is surging ahead industrially faster than any other nation in the world. On the other hand her corporation tax is lower. Again the score is nothing to nothing.

Other evidence is inconclusive and economists do not, with one voice, protest that our high income taxes destroy the seed corn. Theoretical and deductive arguments not based on fact also tend both ways. On the whole, many Keynesians believe that the public interest would be served by a continuance of moderately high and progressive income taxes. Ludwig von Mises is perhaps the leader of the other camp. More evidence is needed. Economists would agree, however, that we are approaching a danger point. Neither capitalist society as a whole nor any special group stands to benefit much from a renewed wave of heavy taxation in the higher brackets. This does not mean that the limit has been reached, quite, or that a desperate national emergency might

not demand an even greater equalization of incomes—a step
that might do much to maintain morale. But it does mean
that the lower-income groups will in the long run benefit
more by increased production of goods and services than by
a further sharing of income.

Before leaving the personal income tax we should note
that the law contains admitted inequities and contradictions
of purpose which, though perhaps unimportant to most people, may work considerable hardship on individuals. It also
has loopholes—contrary, we must suppose, to the intent of
Congress or to the general spirit of the remainder of the
law—which permit tax avoidance by those who find it worth
while to retain counsel. One example of hardship is the man
whose income is irregular, a songwriter, say, who reaches
the hit parade and makes a killing every three years or so, but
gets nowhere in other years. He probably pays a much
higher tax than if he could pay on the basis of an annual
average over several years. An example of loopholes is that
some types of income can be made to appear as capital gains,
which are often taxed at a lower rate than income.

The second important tax which is also perhaps popularly
thought of as a soaking of the rich is the corporation income
tax. In some ways this federal corporation tax—there are
several taxes on corporations but a tax on their incomes is
the most important—seems to be the product of confused
thinking. It treats a corporation as if it were an individual.
If Joseph Doakes has a net income of a million a year, we
can safely say he has a high income and we may with justice
argue that he should be heavily taxed. But if a corporation
has a net income of a million, we cannot, on the basis of that
fact alone, determine whether its income is high or low. We
would have to know more about the amount of capital com-

mitted. A taxable net income of a million would be very
little for a steel company that owned a few blast furnaces,
a coal mine, a rolling mill, and a couple of ore-carrying
vessels. But a million-dollar income suggests unreasonably
high profits for, say, a small contracting firm. The corporation tax does not take all this into account. It just taxes the
million. Oddly, the British socialist government is more
lenient on corporations than we are.

But the corporations are probably not hurt too badly.
Actually, a part of the corporation tax is quite probably
passed along through higher prices to the consumer—or
even to employees through lower wages—though the owners of the corporation must also meet part of it. What really
happens has not been clearly determined by the economist.
Some of the burden could also fall heavily on a widow and
her children, if her legacy consisted of a small portfolio of
stocks in the great American companies. Such a little family
might pay an insignificant tax on total income if there were
no corporation income tax. But with the corporation income
tax, 50 per cent of the total is taken away at the source—
that is, from corporation earnings before they are distributed
to the widow as dividends. Among other alleged inequities
of the tax is that it seems to have a stifling effect on small,
new, growing enterprises. Many corporations are young and
struggling concerns.

The outbreak of hostilities in Korea has stimulated public
discussion of an excess-profits tax. The economist, in principle, sees many points in favor of such a tax as a war measure. There are many technical problems in administering it,
however. To prevent grave inequities or abuses, an extremely
complex law must be enacted, and procedures to consider
hardship cases should be established. The nipping of excess

profits in the bud by renegotiation of government contracts, as was often successfully done during the Second World War, also has its very great virtues—but also its miles of red tape.

The remaining important federal taxes are often named consumption taxes. They are *regressive* in that they demand a larger share of income from low-income persons than from high-income receivers. If each of the two men smokes a pack of cigarettes a day, the $2,500-a-year man pays 1 per cent of his income in cigarette taxes while the $10,000 man pays a quarter of 1 per cent. When such taxes are laid on the poor man's daily needs and small luxuries, like beer, movies, sugar (tax laid through the tariff), they have the effect of soaking the poor.

These taxes are not always levied directly on the consumer. They are like freight charges. Sometimes the shipper and seller pays the railroad company. Sometimes, as when one buys from mail-order houses, the final consumer pays the express charges. But he pays in the first case just as surely as in the second. And so with many taxes. The manufacturer pays cigarette and liquor taxes initially, but we consumers pay them in the end. To be sure, the manufacturer feels the tax, too, for he could sell more of his goods if the tax did not increase the price. No manufacturer likes to see his product taxed, even if he knows he can shift the burden, for sales always go down when cost to consumer goes up.

It should be remarked, incidentally, that the question of who finally bears the tax burden is one of the larger issues of tax theory. The usual approach to the question is made through the little diagrams described in Chapter 4. But diagrams are not really needed. The basic rule is that if a tax decreases the supply (for example, by increasing the cost

of production), then it can be shifted to the consumer, at
least in part. If it does not decrease the supply, it cannot be
so shifted.

The most important theoretical issues of taxation today,
however, are not questions of who bears what burden. They
follow a rather different pattern of treatment than that suggested by the descriptive matter above. The pattern thus far
suggested has been about as follows: 42 billion dollars are
needed; we ought to be able to get it (or most of it) through
taxes; what kind of taxes are there? what are their virtues and
faults? and on what economic class do they fall hardest?
The most recent questions of theoretical importance revolve
around economic control through taxation: control in wartime, for example, to prevent inflation, and in depression,
to stimulate recovery.

In recent years a few economists have so heavily stressed
the role of taxation as a prime weapon in the arsenal of economic control, that they have minimized its revenue-raising
function. They have gone so far as to hint that taxation is
completely unnecessary for revenue, since governments can
print (or borrow) for their needs. Thus, the only justification is economic control. All this is argued of course only
as applied to a fairly synthetic state; it is not meant to be
taken too literally for the world as it really is. And yet this
theory at once influences and is influenced by actual developments in the real world. Taxation is in fact being used
increasingly as an instrument of control. Gone are the days
when taxation resembled the modest collections taken up
at sandlot baseball games to pay the umpire's expenses. Now
the umpire has flowered into one of the big-league financial
magnates and his business dealings reverberate throughout
the "major circuits," as the sports casters phrase it.

The trend of control theory through taxation seems to

be directed toward a reduction of the violent upswings and downswings of business by leveling purchasing power. Policy seems to be crystallizing as follows: In high prosperity or in wartime, reduce either the consumption of goods by the public (or the vigorous bidding up of the price of a limited supply) through the device of heavy taxation; but when times are slack, encourage consumers to spend by reducing taxes. This, and a variety of other measures, will insure a constant flow of purchasing power. Theory has been haltingly reflected in practice. President Truman and his Council of Economic Advisers have in recent years called for maintenance of high taxes as a method of holding down the lid on a bubbling inflationary brew. In part, that policy was followed just after the Second World War. Later, the theory was again implemented by a reduction of taxes as we slid gently downhill economically during the spring of 1949 and had a touch of unemployment. When we snapped back, early in 1950, to a lively period of prosperity, taxes were not immediately laid on heavily as this theory of control demands. But the Korean police action and the inflationary fears engendered thereby have brought on new taxes. The heavy flow of new revenue will serve at least two important anti-inflationary purposes. It will reduce the governmental borrowing that would otherwise be made necessary, and will cut down the amount of money that John Doe can use to bid for things against Richard Roe. It will further prevent both John and Richard from bidding too actively against Uncle Sam for the steel, wool, and food required to equip our fighting men.

We now take up the third great source of governmental revenue: borrowing, our resort when we live beyond our means. When governments need money but cannot or will

not raise it by heavier taxation, they print it, as we printed
greenbacks during the Civil War, or they borrow it. Borrowing money is not very different from printing it. When
our federal government borrows, it prints *bonds* instead of
greenbacks or other currency. Bankers accept the bonds
and, in return, create bank deposits against which the government may write checks. Or the bankers may give the
government Federal Reserve notes, which they are now at
liberty to print because the newly printed bonds can be
used as collateral! This is all very fancy, and requires the
payment of a lot of interest on the bonds, but apparently
that is how we like to do business. Ever since the Civil War,
borrowing instead of printing has become the standard
American way of filling the gap between low income and
high outgo. In the 1950–1951 budget, 12 percent is to be
raised that way. This is a rather shocking figure, when one
considers that we were not actively at war when the budget
was made up, or in the grip of depression—on the contrary.
Whether this is the result of a premature reduction of taxes
by the 80th Congress, or careless rapture on the part of
President Truman and his budget makers need not concern
us here.[1]

An examination of government borrowing leads directly
into the larger question of the public debt as a community
problem. How big may it be? Whom does it hurt and how?
Who benefits and how? The net amount of unrepaid bor-
rowings over the centuries—or decades in the case of new
governments—is the public debt. By "unrepaid" I do not

[1] As fiscal year 1951 comes to a close, it appears that there may be a
7 billion dollar cash *surplus* instead of the 5.1 billion dollar deficit esti-
mated in January, 1950. This complete reversal is accounted for in part
by the economic stimulus of the Korean War. When business is good and
confidence great, tax money piles up surprisingly fast.

mean repudiated, of course. Simply unpaid as yet. The American public debt is now above $250 billion, or more than a quarter of a trillion. This is a way of saying that, since this Republic broke away from England and went into business for itself, we have spent about $250 billion more than we have taken in through taxation or otherwise. The public debt is like the fabled soup of a French peasant family, the *pot-au-feu*, begun generations ago, and left on the back of the stove to simmer through wars, revolutions, births, and deaths. The successive women of the house nourish it daily with a few carrots or onions or pieces of meat, add water, and subtract from it daily—day in and day out, through the centuries. Ever changing, ever the same, full-bodied when crops are good, thin when bad, it has roots in the past and tendrils into the future as few other inanimate objects have. Some of our Civil War debt still flavors the *pot-au-feu* that is our current national debt.

Like having a healthy vermiform appendix, there is nothing very serious or very dangerous financially about having a public debt, though we could get along comfortably without either. What *is* dangerous is too large a debt or a demagogic reliance on borrowing as a temporary solution to economic problems. How can we determine the size of a dangerously large public debt? To this there is no easy answer. If we should engage in a final war for survival against the Communist nations, the American people would probably accept the creation of a debt of whatever magnitude was required to finance the war effort. The military danger would outweigh the danger of overindebtedness. Under conditions of peace, relative security, and ordinary prosperity, a much smaller public debt would be demanded. Some students of this question say the public debt should not exceed twice the annual national income. Currently, the two amounts are approximately equal in size.

The immediate and tangible burden of the public debt arises not from size, but from the annual interest charge. This sum is now about 5 billion dollars, or about 2½ percent of the national income. Thus, out of every dollar each one of us earns we spend 2½ cents to support our debt in the style to which it is accustomed. This assessment of around 2½ cents on the dollar may be looked upon, primarily, as a legacy of the depression of the 1930's and of the Second World War, for those were the events that expanded the debt to its present huge size—particularly the war. Without saying that a smaller interest charge would be undesirable, one may safely assert that the present sum devoted to debt service is not too onerous under present conditions. It should also be recalled that some of the income out of which we pay 2½ cents comes from the interest we get on our bonds. There is, of course, a measure of absurdity in our receiving income from Uncle Sam which we pay back to him in order that he can pay us interest on our bonds. More about this merry-go-round later. The point to notice is that for some of us the burden of the 2½ cent interest charge is lightened by the fact that we derive income from owning the bonds that make up the debt and pay us interest.

What could make the debt a truly onerous burden would be a great decline in national income. If our income should be cut in half, our per capita contribution to the debt would be doubled—doubled for every dollar of income. Instead of paying, as we now do, 2½ cents out of our salaries and wages, we would have to pay 5 cents. And a halving of the national income is not an unheard of thing. Between 1929 and 1933, the national income dropped from about 87 bil-

lions to about 40 billions. In 4 years it was more than cut
in two! And, of course, the amount taken out of each dollar
of income for the public debt of those days was approximately doubled. But the debt, by any criterion, was small
then; the interest charge doubled from approximately .8¢
to 1.6¢ (the debt itself went up a little in this period, but
that is not germane). A serious depression would find us
paying a nickel out of each dollar of income on the debt
alone. That would probably be hard to bear. Nickels become more valuable in depression.

The government, to counteract this threat, might intervene to sustain the national income by lowering taxes and by
deficit spending—that is, by increasing the very debt whose
burden it was seeking to reduce. For a while this might work,
paradoxically, according to the Keynesian formula. But perhaps not for long, or not long enough. It is not safe to predict
what would happen over a fifty-year period of reliance on
this system. A slow, irregular, but persistent rise in prices
would be one conceivable outcome. This would benefit industry and farmers primarily. It would not be harsh on wage
earners, particularly if one third of the working class were,
as at present, organized into unions with strong leadership.
It would hurt holders of mortgages and insurance policies,
salaried persons like teachers and librarians, holders of bonds,
and old persons living on pensions. In these victimized classes,
the only group with real political power is the old-age
group, which is yearly increasing in number and in proportion to the whole population. Many old people would be
receiving government pensions. To win their support or
seal off their possible discontent in a creeping inflation,
politicians could periodically grant them "temporary" cost-
of-living bonuses to add to the monthly paychecks. In due

course of time, these could be made permanent; later, new
temporary bonuses could be paid again, made permanent,
and so on.

What would happen after an appreciable amount of this
sort of thing had been going on a reasonably long time is
anybody's guess. By that time, the world might be locked
in a war of unbelievable severity and duration. In it such
vexing losses of property as are here suggested would be
buried along with things we hold even more precious. But
enough of this dreary crystal gazing! Let us go back smil-
ingly to our debt of a quarter of a trillion.

It is being alleged that many economists have become
completely contemptuous of the public debt. "Why," they
are quoted as saying, "do we bother our balding heads with
the public debt anyhow? We only owe it to ourselves,
don't we? After all, isn't it silly to pay two or three cents
out of every dollar of income to the government, just to
have it pay the money back to us as interest on our bonds,
and then to pay income tax on that interest, which is then
partly used to pay us interest again?" If, in a family, a wife
should put down a credit of twenty-five cents every time
she darned a pair of socks, or a half dollar every time she
baked a cake, if the husband charged hourly rates for var-
nishing a floor or cleaning little brother's shoes, could not
a tremendous structure of family debt be created—tremendous but meaningless? And is not the public debt equally
meaningless? Is not the American nation simply a vast family? And is not the public debt a mere figment of a zealous
bookkeeper's mind?

It is true that the writings of a few responsible and able
economists seem to say this; but they do not really say it.
Some economists have intimated that if the bonds of the

public debt were all held domestically, and if there were an almost equal distribution of income, and if the harmony among economic groups were greater, and if the government had no special will of its own apart from the united will of its united citizens, and if in a variety of other ways government were virtuous, omniscient and omnipotent, then the size of the public debt would have considerably less significance than it has today. Since all these "ifs" take the argument completely out of this real world, we can dismiss it, even if true.

On the other hand it cannot be denied that out of this purely suppositious argument we have hatched a race of economists and government officials who are willing to expand the public debt generously when depression seems only possibly to lurk around the corner. Yet even these do not say that the size of the public debt should be ignored because, after all, we owe it only to ourselves. They also honestly believe that the debt can be reduced in good years and that, over a long period, there should be no expansion of the debt, except, perhaps, the very slow kind of unobjectionable expansion that keeps up with but does not outpace growth of population and growth of productive power.

Yet there is something elusive about the concept of a public debt. Exactly what is it and who owes what to whom, and why? There really is some truth in the statement that we owe the money only to ourselves (if bondholders are mostly of the same nationality as the debt). And it *is* a little like the fictitious—or at least bootless—debt that a married couple could create by bookkeeping the value of every household task performed. A brief study of the burden of debt as increased by the last war may help us to clarify some aspects of public indebtedness.

The Second World War increased our public debt by about 220 billion dollars, which accounts for the lion's share of the current debt. Is this not a mere paper debt? It cannot be real debt. What is it a debt of? Were not the costs met as we went along? The greatest real costs, the expenditure of human lives and direct injury to combatants were met then and were not postponable. But neither were the lesser costs. The great discomforts of soldiers and the smaller ones of civilians; the longer hours of monotonous labor; cold houses; no Sunday rides in the family car; no silk stockings; crowded quarters and busses and denial of ample supplies of sugar, butter, steaks, favored cigarettes—all these were among the real costs of the war, paid in full at the time. The laborers who made munitions were paid; the manufacturers who directed the work got their profits; landlords were compensated. The fighting has been done; the work has been done; the ores and coal and oil used have long since been brought to the surface. All this was necessarily done on the pay-as-you-go principle. So what is the public debt all about, at least the war-debt part of it, the 220 of the 250 billions?

Everything has been paid for. This generation really paid the major costs of the war. It is true that future generations are also somewhat involved in real costs: some children lost their fathers prematurely; a vast amount of irreplaceable oil, coal, copper, tin, and the like was used up forever. But this cannot be made up for by reducing the debt and is not exactly what we mean when we speak of saddling war costs on future generations. We do have the idea that each little boy or girl that's born alive comes into this world with a two-thousand-dollar burden on his or her poor little

back. There is a residual bill of 220 billion dollars that still
has to be paid, we say.[2]

If everybody above forty years of age were suddenly to
die, we oldsters would leave the youngsters a war debt of
220 billion dollars; but we would also leave them compensating assets in the form of government bonds—bonds that
have no reason to exist except for the war and which most
of us would have been unable to buy had there not been
the free and easy money of wartime prosperity. When you
think of it that way, you begin to wonder why we do not,
at one stroke, abolish both the debt and the bonds. But we
can't do that. Why not? A quick answer is that a large
portion of the debt is held in the banking system and is
therefore part of the basis of our money supply. Canceling
the debt would touch off all kinds of fires on this score alone.
But even if we could ignore this, there would still be obstacles.

The paradoxes involved are, in fact, not too easy to re-
solve. They are part of that make-believe world of money,
credit, banking, and finance which reflects the depth and
mystery of human nature. Two things we must clear up
first before we can see the issues clearly. Thus far I have
perhaps led the reader to believe that the public debt and
the debt of the war are one and the same thing. This is not
strictly true, but is so nearly true that it may be allowed to
stand. The federal debt has always zoomed upward after a
hard war. Our present debt would be more than completely
wiped out if the total cost of the last war could be subtracted

[2] I speak of a "residual" bill because the actual monetary cost of the war
was 380 billion dollars. Of this amount, enough was raised from current
revenues to increase our debt during the war years by only about 220 billions. It is this 220 billions that we are talking about.

from it. It is true that Roosevelt added $20 billion to the debt in times of peace; even so, about half the total debt at the end of 1939 may, if one wishes, be regarded as the unsettled expenses of the Civil War and the First World War. It seems quite proper to think of the American public debt, up to the present, as a debt composed mostly of unresolved war expenditures.

Second, we must clearly understand that there is a considerable difference between a domestic public debt and a foreign-held debt. If bonds and other evidences of American public indebtedness are owed primarily to Americans, then the public debt is largely a domestic debt. Our government does not, unlike many others, borrow much from abroad. A domestic public debt and a foreign public debt are quite different, and theories about the one do not necessarily apply to the other. In some senses it is quite correct to say that the public debt is one we owe to ourselves; obviously this statement contains no truth whatever if the public debt, or any significant part of it, is also a foreign debt.

From this it follows that no nation can go bankrupt if its public debt is mainly a domestic one. It can always print new money to pay its domestic obligations, for citizens must use their own government's money. The money may decline in value; citizens may lose confidence in it; they may, in black markets and otherwise, prefer to acquire gold or the money of some other nation, or convert their money into durable goods today against a further decline in value tomorrow. Despite all this, their government's money is their money, and no government needs to go bankrupt vis-à-vis its own citizens. Only a vast foreign public debt leads to a situation like that of the bankruptcy of an individual. Even so, the analogy must not be carried too far. Bankruptcy is a legal concept rather than an economic one; its laws, and subsequent procedures, differ in different countries. A creditor nation might decide to move into a "bankrupt" nation and take over; in such circumstances a "bankrupt" nation, unlike an individual, could fight and, if its arms were successful, could beat off its creditors. All this merely points up the fact that to speak of the public debt's leading us into bankruptcy is to use highly figurative language—language that raises false issues.

We now return to our paradoxes. When a war begins— and it usually begins suddenly—there is not much time for lengthy debate as to how it should be paid for. Governments make various compromises. They slap a tax on excess war profits and on certain luxuries; they slap on a few taxes that can easily be defended politically. Beyond this the government has neither time nor inclination to go, and therefore it is short of money. But it needs money—lots of it. It therefore prints bonds to sell to whoever will buy, or prints greenbacks to pass on to whoever will or must take them. That is how the war is provisionally paid for in a pecuniary sense. But only provisionally, because after many years have passed there will still be pulling and hauling between those who provisionally paid for the war and those who did not, or, rather, between those who provisionally paid more and those who paid less. And this tug of war is what is inherited by our children and our children's children.

Let us see how this would work out in a specific case. Mr. Smith and Mr. Brown are neighbors, have about the same economic status and make approximately the same contributions to the war effort in taxes, long hours of work, amenities foregone. The only difference is that Mr. Smith has a thousand dollars with which he buys government bonds. Brown also has an extra thousand, but with it he completes payment on the house he is buying. Both have "invested" their money, as they think, in safe investments. Neither has yet contributed any part of his thousand to the war effort though Smith feels rather virtuous about having bought war bonds. Smith holds his bonds until 1952 when they are called in by the Treasury. By 1952, let us assume, the purchasing power of the money Smith gets back is only one third that of the money he puts in. In other words, wartime finance, postwar economic dislocations, inflation, and mismanagement generally, result in Mr. Smith's losing much of the former value of his bond. He can buy only one third as much with the thousand dollars as he would have been able to buy in 1942. Brown, on the other hand, has done much better. His house can be sold for many more dollars in 1952 than it would have brought in 1942, when he made his last payment on it. Thus, in the end, Smith did make a contribution toward the costs of war, while Brown did not. But neither could know at the time which one was going to make the greater contribution (or sacrifice). Had there been a progressive price decline from wartime highs, had Smith's redeemed bond bought more things in 1952 than in 1942, and had Brown's house gone down in value as it probably would have under these circumstances, then Smith instead of Brown would have profited from the disturbance of war, and the dislocations of the postwar period. And then Brown would have lost through war.

A public debt incurred in an emergency is not exactly a cooperative sharing of aggregate costs with posterity. It is, rather, a postponement of the decision as to who pays what residual costs. If, in our example, the government had, during wartime, decided arbitrarily to take $1,000 away from all the Smith's and nothing away from any of the Brown's, the injustice would have been too flagrant to perpetrate. But after ten years, old issues are forgotten, new ones arise, luck enters the picture, and the relationship between current problems and a redistribution of the original costs of war is lost sight of. The real costs of war are paid for on a pay-as-you-go basis; they have to be. There is no way of postponing death on the battlefield or the much smaller sacrifice of civilians. But one decision can be postponed; which class or group or individuals pay the most money. If ten, fifteen, or twenty years later, it so turns out that those who hold greenbacks or bonds are fully reimbursed at a time when the price level is low, then we conclude that this group paid less and that nonbondholders or nongreenback holders paid more. If, on the other hand, greenbacks are repudiated, or if bonds become worthless, or if prices have risen inordinately, then the greenback and bondholders pay more and others pay less.

Suppose four couples decide to go out for dinner and dancing. One man acts as treasurer. Each couple pays him ten dollars in advance. (This is something like wartime taxation.) As the evening wears on they go from one night spot to another; the cost is higher than was expected. The treasurer, instead of collecting from each one again, advances his own money (wartime borrowing). The next day the treasurer tries to figure out who owes him what. He decides that the youngest couple, which has just had large hospital bills, has let itself in for much more then it could afford to spend, and quietly asks the better-to-do couples to share the extra expense. For the group as a whole it was pay-as-you-go. Within the group, however, there were post-party adjustments based on various considerations.

Something like this happens with public debts arising out of great emergencies, except, of course, that the generous motive of excusing those who have less money and more hard luck does not necessarily play a role in the final settlement. Also, it may be presumed that, in the example, final intercouple adjustments are made in full within a few days; in the case of a public debt, adjustments are rarely completed or finally cleared up. Nations go on to new deficit spending before the costs of the last deficit are fully adjusted. The larger the public debt, the greater the amount of money over which there is subsequent skirmishing. The larger, therefore, the injustices and disturbances that may result.

Who eventually pays the residual costs of a war depends, then, on how the public debt and the economy at large are "managed" afterwards. If the debt is "managed" by repudiation, or if prices are allowed to run away, then those who accept and hold government paper are losers. If, however, people acquire paper (as some did during the Civil War) for 60 cents per unit and are able, later, to get a dollar for it, then those people gain most who are willing to buy or hold their paper through the long period of doubt. Just before the Korean War broke out, in 1950, it seemed likely that the price level would stabilize itself at the point where a dollar would buy approximately what 65 cents had bought before Pearl Harbor. Thus, the man who bought a bond in 1941 and later got back four dollars for every three he put in, still lost something in terms of purchasing power. A realization of this sad fact, plus a further increase in the price level (autumn, 1950), has caused a massive sale of bonds by many investors and a flight to the stock market. To prevent a continuation and recurrence of this, Sumner Slichter, the well-known Harvard economist, proposes that the government issue bonds of constant purchasing power. That is, the bondholder would be guaranteed as much bread, pork, coal, clothing, and so on, when he redeems his bond, as he was able to buy when he purchased it. Such an arrangement would be most attractive. The government would now promise not to return four dollars for every three put in, but, instead, whatever number of dollars is required to buy the same quantity of goods—plus interest, of course. The number of dollars to be returned would be determined by the official cost-of-living index. Slichter's proposal is fair and meritorious. It does come into conflict, however, with the practical politics of inflationary finance and economic drift. We are apparently more willing to toss around the financial burden of war until it wears out than to distribute the load fairly and squarely in the first instance. Statesmen are aware of this—perhaps only subconsciously, to be sure —and act upon it.

Our children—as a total group—will never exactly have to pay the costs of the Second World War. But, like squabbling heirs, they may for generations toss back and forth the question as to which subgroup gains or loses most by unscrambling the financial wartime tangle that is our legacy to them. Indeed, fifty years hence, people will scarcely realize that the question of who paid what part of the costs is still unsettled. Besides, the ever-simmering *pot-au-feu* of the public debt will have been reinvigorated or diluted by new carrots, onions, or water, in the form of booms, depressions, war, and the other incidents that make history fascinating to read.

We are now better able to answer some of the questions that were asked earlier. Can we not cancel the public debt, since we owe it only to ourselves? Certainly we can, but

those who hold bonds will object violently, for they will feel
that war costs have been fastened on them retroactively and
arbitrarily. Actual repudiation of the bonds would violate
our belief in the sanctity of contract. A gradual inflation
does not immediately affront our sense of justice, is easier to
tolerate at first, but may be extremely painful in the long
run. It weakens the economic power of our middle class,
where many fixed incomes are to be found, and may leave
them vulnerable to opportunistic and un-American political
philosophies. Inflation scales down every form of debt, of
course, whether contracted by the government or by the
private citizen for housebuilding. Mortgage owners, savings-
bank depositors, pensioners, life-insurance beneficiaries—all
suffer together under inflation. Does it matter how big the
domestic debt is since we owe it only to ourselves? In a kind
or reckless, theoretical sense, no. More practically, yes; for
interest charges may be too high to bear, particularly in
depression. Another disadvantage about a too-large public
debt is that the larger the debt the larger the uncertainty as
to who, eventually, is to pay how much for past emergencies
and the more frenzied the finance connected with this
process.

Thus, the size of the public debt for a rich and productive
country like ours is a partial index of the degree to which we
are willing to postpone final decisions and be content with
stopgap solutions to economic problems. It is also, of course,
partly an index of the magnitude of past emergencies. If an
enemy can be cheaply and promptly polished off, the resulting war debt will obviously be smaller. But all in all,
even in the blackest emergency, the greater the willingness
to trust to a policy of drift and to the good or bad luck of
the future in apportioning costs, the greater the debt is likely

to be. The blame for this tendency to let a doubtful future decide the ultimate allocation of costs should not be placed entirely on the shoulders of politicians. Often the private and substantial citizen is the one most willing in emergencies to have solutions postponed; but he also turns out to be the same individual who, later, most deplores the size of the debt and most bitterly assails the opportunism of the politician. When a debt is overlarge and invites "management" by inflation, the thing to fear is not national bankruptcy, but an ill-planned—perhaps even wanton—redistribution of wealth among the several groups of the community.

The above discussion of government finance is not precisely identifiable as that of standard or dissident theory. It only suggests what every economist knows about fiscal policy, and the theories and proposals relating thereto. There are differences of opinion about taxation and debt management, but the greatest cleavages are not along the standard-dissident axis. Take the issue of steeply progressive income taxes. Some economists believe that these inhibit continued prosperity by cutting down new investment; others disagree; many frankly say they don't know. These differences of view have nothing to do with the standard-dissenting categories.

The only great doctrinal difference is the Marxian interpretation of a burdensome public debt. I have, at least in large part, made the massive proportions of the debt seem to be primarily a result of the costs of warfare thrust upon us. To the Marxian, ever in search of evidence for his thesis of disintegration, an oversized debt is but another symptom of declining economic institutions.

16. AMERICAN DOLLARS AND WORLD GOODS

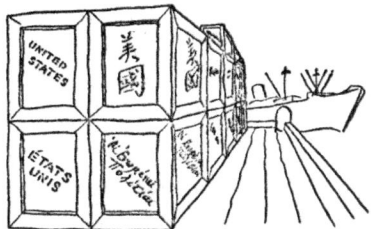

Foreign trade is important to some nations and relatively unimportant to others. In the large, poor, overpopulated nations of the East there is but a small surplus to export—if one thinks of the hundreds of millions of people concerned—and they are too poor to import. It is doubtful whether one dollar's worth annually, per person, has ever come from abroad into these areas. The comparable American figure is about twelve dollars a year (before the Second World War). Even this relatively large American figure is low compared with the figures of nations that depend greatly on food from abroad, like the British. We are so nearly self-sufficient, our resources and skills are so versatile, that we rely to a comparatively slight degree on imports. Nevertheless, the things we do import, like chrome and rubber and some drugs, are crucial items in our economy. Certain other countries, though their per capita trade figure is low, are cruelly dependent on exports to the foreign market, and on the export of only one commodity. Brazil relies painfully on a good coffee market and her welfare depends perhaps rather too exclusively on

her one big crop. Other nations, though not enslaved to one
commodity, still depend heavily and precariously on foreign trade. The compact, prosperous nations like the United
Kingdom, Switzerland, and Denmark, have had an import
figure of about fifty dollars per year per person. The British
have for many decades now, relied on a frail bridge of ships
for their daily bread, and any interruption with this flow
of imports causes immediate alarm.

Time and technology tend to disrupt the pattern of foreign trade even in crucial goods. Chile was once the chief
source of the vital nitrates. Now nitrates can be made
cheaply wherever there is cheap electricity. We emancipate
ourselves with rayon and nylon from the Japanese silkworm,
but gradually become dependent on Soviet chrome and
uranium from the Belgian Congo. Some informed people
say that the number of new and critical imports of today is
smaller than the number on which we were sorely dependent twenty years ago, with the result that international trade
will eventually dry up like an August brook. Thus the au-
tarchy dreamed of by Hitler may dominate the world, not
as the result of political strategy, but because there is no
stopping our scientists and technicians. The argument is not,
however, entirely convincing. But here is something to
watch. If food and fibers can be produced synthetically and
cheaply everywhere, the bottom of international trade will
drop out.

This kind of world would be a far cry from the interdependent world, with an international harmony of interest,
so glowingly described as the ideal by many nineteenth century economists. It was even thought at one time that when
all nations were economically dependent on all other nations, when the world was tied together in a tangled net of

foreign trade made desirable and necessary by a high degree of specialization in each region, that then war would be impossible, for each nation would have much too much to lose. But it has not worked out that way.

Americans are great tourists, and our dollars are so eagerly accepted abroad that one of the fundamental principles of foreign trade is rarely brought home sharply to us. This principle is that our money is completely worthless abroad, *in itself*. It possesses value only because a complex mechanism exists to convert it into American goods or services. What makes foreign trade so different from domestic trade is that payment cannot, in final analysis, be made in the currency of the buying (or importing) nation. It is true that any small shopkeeper in Aiguebellette will gladly take your dollars, but only because there is an offsetting mechanism of exchange. The dollars you leave with the French shopkeeper get a good workout before the transaction is completed. It is as impossible, in the literal sense, to change dollars into francs as to change apples into pears. But it is possible to barter pears and apples; and it is also possible to barter francs and dollars. How does this offsetting or bartering mechanism work?

We pay for the things we buy abroad by an elaborate system of clearance or of transferring debts. International trade is carried on without actual dollars, francs, pounds, or pesos—at least, without the transportation of much actual money across the borders. If we lend the British 4 billion dollars, the "money" all stays here. For this reason: in international trade, the importers of any given country pay the exporters of the same country in their own national currency. No money passes to or from another country, for there the same system prevails.

Let us follow the process in a simplified transaction. If you buy a few cases of champagne in France for $150, you owe some Frenchman that amount or its French equivalent (let us call it 30,000 francs). If I sell some Frenchman an adding machine for $150, some Frenchman owes me 30,000 francs. Accounts are squared in this fashion:

1. You pay me the champagne money (thus, I get my $150).

2. I tell the French adding-machine buyer not to try to pay me, but instead to give the 30,000 francs to the seller of champagne.

3. The adding-machine buyer follows instructions and pays 30,000 francs to the champagne seller (thus, the champagne man gets his money).

4. The French champagne seller informs you that he has been paid, that everything is in order.

By such a transaction everybody has what he wants: you have your champagne, one Frenchman has an adding machine, the other his 30,000 francs, and I have my $150. The only question left to consider is how to get four people so neatly together every time a foreign sale is made.

The agency that gets people together is a broker of some sort with a correspondent abroad, often a bank. We shall now, with simplifications, trace the same transaction through two such brokers: a broker in the United States, who will be named BUS; and his partner in France, BF. If I do not know you and therefore that you are buying champagne I can go direct to BUS for my money. I present to him documents as evidence that I have made a bona fide sale, that an adding machine is being shipped, that it is insured and so on. BUS takes my papers and gives me $150 minus a commission for his service. Of course, I authorize BUS to collect, through his partner in France, the 30,000 francs that the French buyer of the adding machine has agreed to pay me. Not only collect but keep. I have no further interest in the transaction, for I have been given my money. The deal is over for me. Now, BUS has paid me out of a kitty which would soon be exhausted if he dealt only with exporters like me. But he also deals with importers and knows that somebody like you will come along presently and that you will want to pay money *into* the kitty. That is, you will want to give BUS $150 for your champagne on the understanding that his partner stationed in France, BF, will pay 30,000 francs to the French seller of champagne.

So long as total transactions among all importing and exporting Frenchmen and all importing and exporting Americans approximately balance each other, our brokers will get along all right. But this does not always happen. Americans may sell much more to Frenchmen than the latter sell to us. Let us see what happens now.

If Americans, by excessive sales in France are constantly taking dollars away from BUS and rarely paying dollars into his kitty, then there is trouble. When this happens, our transatlantic BF is being uncomfortably deluged with francs. Frenchmen are buying a lot of things in the United States and not selling much. BF's kitty of francs is becoming huge. Unless something happens to change the trend, our partners will soon have to give up their brokerage firm. When BUS has run out of dollars to give to American exporters he is unable to perform the very service for which he is paid commissions. There is no point in his staying in business; he has nothing to offer. BF will go out of business, too. They are not bankrupt. They simply have nothing to offer potential customers. There is stalemate. BF has all the money—that is, he has both kitties—not only the fund BUS started out with, but his own as well. But all the money is now in francs! In the absence of any other mechanism or firm that can "convert" francs into dollars—and we have been tacitly assuming that ours is the only one—BUS will, if he wants his money back, have to move to France, claim his share of francs out of the firm's combined funds, and live there until he has consumed his share of the partnership's assets. The firm has run into the same problem that has long plagued most of Europe: it has a "dollar shortage." Indeed, we can go a step farther. In this case not only our brokers but also the whole of *France* has a dollar shortage! We have assumed that all Franco-American trade funnels through the BF-BUS firm. If this firm has a dollar shortage, then all of France has a dollar shortage, too. In its simplest terms, a French dollar shortage only means that Frenchmen would like to buy more from us than we are prepared to buy from them (or, that Frenchmen are not able to tempt us with the quality and price of their wares in sufficient amount); they are therefore unable to build up credits in this country to pay for the things they would like to buy here.

There are, of course, ways of preventing so untoward an outcome under favoring conditions; in wartime, deep depression, or in postwar periods, nothing may avail. Ordinarily, when too many francs begin coming in and too many dollars going out, BF could fix BUS up with gold. BF might buy gold for his excess francs and ship it across the ocean to BUS. The American partner can then convert the gold into ordinary dollars, which he can use to build up his faltering kitty. Since this operation may place heavier costs on the firm, they can increase their commission or use some other equalizing method. It costs money to transport and insure gold; if the sum is large, interest foregone amounts to a tidy sum. Loss by abrasion is a cost. But these are details.

Why gold? Why cannot BF buy up and send French gloves or perfume or some other French product instead? On the surface it may appear that BF can as well convert his excess francs into chypre, and that BUS can convert that famous odor into dollars by selling it in the United States. One answer is that gold is less speculative. Normally the selling price and buying price of gold in different currencies are figures you can rely on, while the prices of merchandise normally waver, particularly if large lots are dumped onto the market. But the more basic reason is that we Americans have shown—and the clear evidence is the unbalanced kitties of BF and BUS—that we simply do not want or cannot afford the things that France has to offer. In short, the reason that BF has all the francs is that Americans cannot absorb any more champagne, cognac, gloves, perfume, gowns, or anything else that the French are prepared to sell us. Gold, because of its special position in the economic system, we are always ready—God save the mark!—to take. Goods are poison to us.

Another way to prevent stalemate is to alter the rate of exchange. This can be done without using gold. When the kitties begin to reveal imbalance, BF can tell his French customers that, hereafter, they will have to give him 220 francs for every dollar of debt they want to settle in the United States. (The rate first used in this example was 200 francs to the dollar.) This new rate will make Frenchmen pause before buying here, for to them it is equivalent to an increase in the price of American goods. BUS, at the same moment, will inform his American clients that they can now settle 220 francs' worth of French debt for every dollar they pay in. This encourages American importers to buy in France. In terms of dollars they can buy French goods more cheaply. Soon American importers will be paying dollars into BUS' kitty again, while French exporters will be withdrawing francs from the futile and excessive hoard of BF.

The reader will already have recognized the action of our two brokers as merely another manifestation of the ubiquitous law of supply and demand. The desire of French importers to pay debts in the United States became so great in our example, that, to prevent stalemate, the brokers had to charge them more for dollars. Or, as businessmen and economists prefer to put it; the demand for "dollar exchange" was great enough to send up its price in terms of francs. The other side of the picture was that the American desire to pay debts in francs was so small that the price of that currency went down. If the new rate of 220 to the dollar undercorrects or overcorrects, the rate of exchange can be changed again, and again, until an acceptable figure is reached.

The above is the basic mechanism. In real life it is much more complex. There are countless brokers and scores of countries whose accounts must be balanced simultaneously. Before the last war Europe derived much of its power to "convert" its currencies into dollars through its Oriental colonies. From the Far East we bought rubber, tin, tea, cocoa, copra, and other colonial products. The colonies bought relatively little from us. They had, to use the figurative language of business and economics, more dollars than they needed. But the European mother countries, which bought less in their colonies than they sold to them, were able to get hold of the excess dollars, and to use them in their trade with us. This is only one example of the type of serial transfer that characterizes international trade.

A multiplicity of documents—sight bills of exchange and 30-day bills and letters of credit, each of several varieties— adds further complexity to the picture. One type of document is used when spot payment is desired (usually because the buyer's credit is not established); another when credit is good. Sometimes the broker not only pays for the buyer but at the same time makes him an ordinary commercial loan. Some brokers speculate in the currencies, without themselves effectuating an underlying exchange of goods. These double-header and other kinds of transactions obscure the basic fact that importers pay exporters. Currencies never leave home, if we except a little hoarding of favored currencies and small pocket-expense amounts carried by travelers. Gold, however, does leave home.

Exports—and therefore imports, for an export from A is an import for B—are not always tangible and material. Services can be exported. If you buy a ticket for passage on a Cunarder, you import a boatride; that is to say, you cancel some British debt in this country in exactly the same way that you would if you bought a British bicycle. If you go to England, eat their food, sleep in their beds, ride in their trains, you again help to cancel their debts in this country and you are as surely an importer as if you had offices in New York and were bringing in English tweeds and worsted. The making of loans abroad, buying of stocks and bonds, receipt of dividends, purchase of insurance—all such transactions in foreign countries take their proper place either under the categories of exports or imports. Such transactions are referred to as invisible imports.

This concept of invisible imports requires that I amend somewhat the things I said above about the world's "dollar shortage." The implication left a page or two ago was that the dollar shortage came about only because we Americans want fewer *goods* from the remainder of the world than the remainder wants from us. It should now be observed that we could (and do) relieve the dollar shortage by buying *services* abroad; by taking passage on British planes, buying Swedish insurance, gaping our way as tourists through galleries and palaces, sending our freight across the sea in Norwegian hulls. We further relieve the shortage by investing abroad, acquiring pounds, marks, or pesos to pay for the branch factories we build on foreign soil, or by bona fide lending to foreign governments and individuals. All this we do now. Even so it is not enough. The goods, services, and investment opportunities offered us abroad are simply less attractive to us than those we ourselves offer to the outside world. That is partly why, ever since the First World War, we have had to make gifts abroad. To prevent sharp declines in levels of living and the consequent political unrest, we have had to send goods without demanding dollars, and to forgive loans. Even this is not enough; the dollar shortage persists. It gives you some idea of the awesome economic strength of these United States.

Consideration of these facts should, incidentally, allay general fears of low-wage competition from abroad. Foreign labor costs may be lower than ours, but we *give* much of our product away, regardless of cost! And when we do make bona fide sales we often tend to undersell. American workers, though paid high wages, are inordinately efficient;

and that efficiency is magnified by the imagination and capacity of our industrialists. No automobile combines good-
ness and cheapness as does the American car—and this is
true of an imposing list of fine but cheap American products. We are, in a sense, and long have been, because of our
vast physical and human resources, the great sellers of cheap
goods abroad.

There are, of course, certain industries—perhaps textiles
is one—in which we are at a genuine disadvantage because
of low labor costs abroad. Even so, that is what international
trade is all about, supposedly—the cheapest producing nations should be able to make things for those who would have
to spend more in their manufacture. Every region, presumably, should sell abroad what it can make most easily, and
get in return what other regions make cheapest. At least,
that is what the old-time economics said in its good, old
books.

One of the issues that has been of great interest to standard economic theory relates to the reasons for international
exchanges. The easiest approach to this question is to take
an extreme case: bananas, for example. It is obviously cheaper
for North Americans to buy Latin American bananas than
to grow them in Vermont hothouses. The advantage of hot
countries in producing bananas is absolute. Therefore we
import Nicaraguan bananas, and one need not go into the
economic blue to understand such a transaction. Many imports offer less extreme examples, but conform to a similar
principle: the great wines, perfumes, dresses of France; Russian caviar; Scotch whiskey; Hungarian Tokay. These
things simply would not be what they are if they came from

Gambia or even Texas; therefore, they are imported by all but originating countries.

When we consider something like plain muslin the issue deepens. Two or three dozen countries can make muslin quite cheaply. Should all make muslin for export? Should all make at least enough to meet their own needs, or should some cheap-muslin countries import from other cheap-muslin countries? One answer to this question is that, in quiet and normal times, importers never ask such questions. If they find bargains in muslins across the border, such that they could with importing expenses be put more cheaply on the domestic market than muslins made at home, then the importer buys the muslins abroad without bothering his head as to who should, could, or would produce what quantity of muslin for which market. No doubt many international transactions are just like that: a bargain is picked up here, there, or elsewhere, with scant regard to economic laws. Still, there are certain economic principles that probably help to determine the larger drift of foreign trade.

Ricardo was the first economist to discuss this matter fully and to give an answer that was satisfactory—at least for half a century. His answer has a historical background. During the Napoleonic wars, wheat growing in England had been a most profitable occupation, since there had been little competition from foreign grain. After the wars, landowners took steps to win, through a wheat tariff, the monopolistic position thrust upon them in wartime.[1] They argued that it was absurd to import wheat when England could grow it quite as advantageously as any other competing country.

[1] Much of the material in this section follows the position taken in Charles Gide and Charles Rist, *A History of Economic Doctrines* (2d English ed., New York, Heath, 1948), Book VI (by Rist).

Ricardo was interested in the progress of manufacture and the decline of landlordism. He found an answer to the landlord's argument of equal advantage in the doctrine of comparative advantage. "Granted," he said, in effect, "that we can grow wheat as cheaply as Russia or Poland; but what really matters is that we can produce textiles *more* cheaply than they. Let us make textiles for them and let them grow wheat for us. The final result will be that they will benefit by getting more textiles than they would otherwise get, and the English will have more wheat." He clinched the argument with the following:

Two men can both make shoes and hats, and one is superior to the other in both employments; but in making hats he can only exceed his competitor by one-fifth, or 20 per cent, and in making shoes he can excel him by one-third or 33⅓ per cent. Will it not be for the interest of both that the superior man should employ himself exclusively in making shoes, and the inferior man in making hats? [2]

This theory of comparative advantage, in all its ramifications was developed by Anglo-American economists, notably and perhaps most urbanely by Frank W. Taussig, formerly at Harvard, whose elementary textbook is well-known to contemporary American college graduates in middle age or better. But the theory was never wholeheartedly accepted on the Continent, and has been questioned by Vilfredo Pareto, Gustav Cassel, and Bertil Ohlin (the last of whom is still alive).

What are the objections of Ohlin's followers and precursors to the Ricardian thesis? For one thing, Ricardo assumes that labor cost determines exchange—that is to say, his theory of international trade is based on the labor theory

[2] David Ricardo, *Political Economy* (Everyman's Library edition, London, 1911), p. 83, footnote.

of value which, as we saw, has been abandoned (p. 55). Secondly, the force of demand is not given place in Ricardo's analysis. The state of demand may cause things to sell above or below their cost of production, and therefore to determine in part the direction of the flow of goods. The attackers of Ricardo also lay stress on the fact that trade arises out of the different relationships among the prices of goods in trading nations. Ohlin's most telling argument is that varying relationships among national price structures, the basis of international trade, arise out of the basic economic pattern of trading nations. Each country has its own pattern: some have much labor, some relatively little; in some, special arts have been handed down under a tradition of high craftsmanship; some have much virgin soil, others a highly developed industrial plant. Out of these differences of pattern, some historical and some natural, arise the price differences that make foreign trade profitable.

If, according to standard theory, the governments of the world would foster international freedom of trade, each nation and region would soon specialize in the things in which it had the highest degree of advantage. The international division of labor would be most fully realized. The entire globe would presently be organized to produce most economically; the standard of living everywhere would be the highest possible under our institutions and technology. It has even been argued that such a world, a world without tariffs, import quotas, export bonuses, exchange control, blocked currencies, and all the other fancy devices used to balk freedom of trade, would have such a strong community of economic interest that wars would be unthinkable.

If all this is true, or only partly true, or even plausible, why do nations build artificial barriers in the form of tariffs and other impediments to trade?

Two great advocates of tariffs have been Alexander Hamilton and the German Friedrich List (1789–1846). Their arguments against free trade varied somewhat, but both agreed that nations which had within themselves the qualities needed to become great, but were behind the British—then the pace setters—in economic development, needed tariffs to protect infant industries. List particularly felt that here, as in so many other cases, British economic theory was a purely local theory, one which, if followed by others would merely redound to the benefit of the British. Since England was ahead of all other nations in industrial development at that time (about 1820), and since the British geographical situation and certain other natural advantages made her an ideal importer and processor of raw materials, and exporter of finished materials, free trade was the ideal policy for England. Indeed, it was a kind of protection or tariff in reverse. The most enriching policy for the British would be to build up a giant workshop, then to buy crude materials from all the underdeveloped nations and to sell back the same materials after processing. Since England was a generation ahead of everybody else industrially, she would, through free trade, be able to keep the rest of the world in a state of something like agricultural peonage, while securing for herself a great and profitable manufacturing monopoly.

Thus List saw the world as a congeries of states aspiring to become great powers and to overcome the handicap imposed on them economically by the advanced industrial position of the British. He repudiated the idea that the regional specialization allegedly fostered by free trade would result in a great harmony of interest. What he saw, instead, was the subjection of the rest of the world to the British. On the whole the arguments of List prevailed in the real world. Politicians who had never heard of him were independently sizing up the situation in Listian terms. Anglo-American economists have not seen it that way and continue to argue for freedom of trade.

There are, of course, other arguments for tariffs. Tariffs, particularly low tariffs that do not too much discourage importation, do raise revenue, and may be a fairly sound method of taxation, depending, of course, on what is taxed, how much, and the relation of the commodity to national needs. But let it be made clear that under such a tariff, it is ultimately the American who pays the tax, not the foreigner, as has often been popularly argued. There may be a few exceptions to the general rule, but the broad principle is that American tariff revenues are paid by Americans in the end, and sometimes doubly paid, regardless of who actually turns the money over to the customs agent.

Tariffs are also justified on the ground of national defense. It may, for example, be desirable to protect and therefore encourage manufacturers of synthetic rubber in order to establish a mature industry when war breaks out and imports are cut off. Our merchant marine is a subsidized industry, frankly supported in part by taxpayers' money, to serve us in time of war. The subsidy operates like a tariff when our shippers compete with foreign shippers.

Tariffs are often justified by the man on the street, especially during depression, on the ground that they make possible the employment of domestic labor. Why, it was asked in 1934, should we be buying Japanese electric-light bulbs when our own bulb-makers were on relief? The usual replies of economists in those days to that question were: if we do not buy Japanese bulbs we will throw Japanese bulb-makers out of their jobs, and their diminished purchasing-power will make it impossible for them to buy American products, thereby throwing out of work American producers for the Japanese trade; the Japanese, too, can retaliate, and will erect as high barriers against our goods as we erect against theirs; prosperity is indivisible—we beggar ourselves if we beggar our neighbors. If, however, the Japanese light bulbs have been ruthlessly dumped on the American market, then the arguments against keeping them out lose their force.

The Keynesians have questioned this simon-pure argument of the older standard theorists. When there is under-employment, they say, exports should be stimulated at the sacrifice of some of the lesser benefits promised by the older theories. Here, as in various other ways, Keynes realizes that one course of action is acceptable under the assumption of full employment, but quite a different one under the assumption of underemployment.

The dissenters have supplied a most provocative theory of international trade. It is the theory of imperialism. Perhaps the least painful way of opening up this subject is to follow George Bernard Shaw's development of it in his *Intelligent Woman's Guide to Socialism and Capitalism*. Since Shaw was an unique combination of wealthy bourgeois, Marxian, and Shavian, his approach will be interesting and, in its characteristic way, illuminating.

His chapter on foreign trade immediately follows that on the industrial revolution in England. This is no accident of organization. On the contrary, foreign trade is, to him, something more than a special topic under the subject of exchange; it is the spread of the industrial revolution to the remainder of the world. The argument continues as follows:

1. Capitalism, in its productive efforts, has normally begun at the wrong end, first producing luxuries and only later going in for the production of the more basic necessities.

2. One of the luxuries first produced by early capitalism was cheap gin, so cheap that a woman (the book is addressed to women) could get drunk for a penny and dead drunk for twopence. This was more or less true in the United States as well. Both governments stepped in to restrict liquor consumption either by taxation, as in England, or by prohibition (as in the United States).

3. When British capitalists (who have begun at the wrong end) find their sales efforts thwarted by taxation, prohibition, saturation of the domestic market, or other casualty, they invest their money abroad or seek overseas markets.

4. Thus, British capital has sold its cheap gin abroad, poisoning multitudes. During American prohibition, it produced liquor to be smuggled into the United States. If the United States had been as weak as China was in 1840, the British would have smashed American prohibition and forced liquor down our throats and made us pay for it, too. ("The Anglo-Chinese war of 1840-42 is frequently called the *Opium War* because the forcing of China to accept the drug traffic was one of the issues at stake"—*The Columbia Encyclopedia.*)

5. Profitable as the liquor trade has been to the British, the slave trade was even richer.

6. The sad thing about all this is that, if British capital had not started at the wrong end—had not, so to speak, merely skimmed the cream at home and abroad—if British capital had stayed at home to build cheap houses, harness

water power, and so forth, England would be a much better place to live in today.

These points introduce the idea only. While it is true that capital invested abroad deprives the nation of what it might have in the way of slum clearance and abundant electric power, it must not be overlooked, Shaw continues, that the great profit of the overseas trade comes back to the homeland. This makes possible a higher, or different, standard of living for the United Kingdom. Unchecked, such a tendency could result in making all of England and Scotland a vast Miami or Biarritz. The sons and daughters of the present British working class would not become factory hands; instead they would become waiters, chambermaids, chefs, racehorse trainers, and the like. In short, the service and recreational industries would become highly developed, while the basic ones would languish. Would languish because they would be carried on elsewhere: in Asia, Latin America, Africa, and other as yet backward countries.

This would seem fine—to some, at least. Everybody would either be engaged in a genteel, white-collar occupation, or be receiving directly the large incomes from foreign investment. But the change-over from industrial England to Biarritz-England would be accompanied by large transitional unemployment. Or, rather, is now being accompanied by unemployment for the tendency is clearly present; the process is in full swing even though it has not reached its absurd culmination. Unemployment means demoralizing doles and assisted emigration, and what a paradox it is, Shaw observes, that a great country wishes to get rid of its citizenry. When such a country at last becomes almost entirely dependent on the outside world for the products of basic industry it becomes easy prey for any ambitious and warlike nation. In this Shaw sees shades of decadent Rome and other magnificent but rotting empires.

Thus far, Shaw goes on, we have been talking only about the British and the extension of their trading empire; but other nations have the same imperial aims: investing abroad or buying cheap and selling dear everywhere. Conflicts between nations over markets and investment opportunities snowball into armament races; armament races—what with one thing and another—flower into global wars. For this outcome neither human nature nor individuals are to blame, but the "capitalist system" which so completely dominates our lives; indeed, ruinous wars are as much dreaded by capitalists as by anybody else. The real cause of the First World War was the first vessel that carried for sale to African natives things that could not be sold at home, like gin.

Now all this, Shaw says, does not mean that there should be no foreign trade, though it would perhaps be just as well not to import such unwholesome stimulants as tea. "Honest" foreign trade is all right. But capitalism is not satisfied with "honest" profits. It must have more; must dominate foreign markets; forestall traders of other nations. It takes poverty with it overseas and neglects the full economic development of the homeland because it can make a little more money elsewhere. To say that this vicious process is motivated by greed alone is not to see that we are all involuntarily caught up in a senseless and even suicidal rhythm.

Shaw's theory of foreign trade leaves some things to be desired. There are anachronisms, and the British sell abroad many less poisonous wares than gin, or even Scotch. To assume, as he does, that basic industries (like coal-mining and steel-making) can be moved at will from their present sites to the backward areas of the earth, is to display ignorance of the location of natural resources, technology, and the facts of economic geography at large. Steel, to take one basic industry, is produced only where competent labor, coal, limestone and ore can be brought together cheaply, as in the Pittsburgh or Birmingham areas. To move the steel industry to an undeveloped country, where labor is not trained to modern methods of production, and where coal, limestone, and ore are not cheaply available, is unthinkable. Yet one cannot entirely laugh off certain ideas in this dissident view of foreign trade. That the great powers have taken advantage of some backward nations and races is a matter of general knowledge, and that some wars have an economic background is undeniable.

Shaw's analysis of foreign trade does not differ greatly from Lenin's. In 1916, in Zurich, about 18 months before the October revolution, Lenin was writing his booklet on imperialism; this has become a Marxian classic. He says many things that were later said by Shaw in the *Intelligent Woman's Guide*. There are, however, a few differences of emphasis. Lenin introduces his topic by calling attention to the large increase in recent years of monopolies both in banking and industry and the growing dependency of industry on a small group of powerful bankers. This he underlines as a basic condition under which imperialism flourishes. In the early competitive regime, *goods* were most frequently exported; in the present system of enormous financial concentration, *capital* is exported, and the investment of latter-day capitalism abroad is the characteristic feature of world trade. For the rest, the differences between Shaw and Lenin —except for emphasis on gin—are not very great.

Here we have two ways of looking upon international trade: the standard school thinks of it as a special case under the exchange of goods and develops laws of comparative advantage or successor theories to account for exchange; some dissenters look upon international trade as an outcome of economic development and the latter-day manifestations of what, in their view is a life-and-death search for markets or investment opportunities.

War and its aftermath in this troubled twentieth century have made almost any economic theory of foreign trade look a little silly. Since 1917 we have been helping our Allies, sometimes through gifts, sometimes through defaulted loans. The government has for years been buying up things with our tax money and giving it away. Sometimes food, sometimes arms, sometimes machines that could be used to produce things needed to increase the production of food or arms. Movements of this sort have bulked large in our "foreign trade." But they are not foreign trade at all and are explained by political theory, not economic theory.

When, in the nineteenth century, England called the world's economic tunes, she was a great sucker-in of raw materials and a great puffer out of manufactured goods. To economists there was and still is a sort of axiomatic soundness about this kind of activity. The United Kingdom is now a second-rate nation and her empire is disintegrating. Today the United States calls the economic tunes. We are very great puffers out, but very poor suckers in. There appears to be a basic economic unsoundness in this position. But soundness didn't save the British. Will unsoundness save us?

Part Five

CONCLUSION

17. WHAT NEXT?

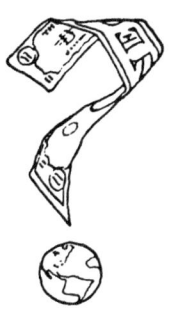

WHAT SHOULD A WRITER put into the last chapter of his book on economics in this year of grace, 1951? I have recently been rereading the last chapters of several books of economics, and find that no pattern for a close imposes itself. A few textbooks end abruptly with the part on foreign trade, for no obviously good reason. Neither Adam Smith nor Ricardo felt it necessary to speak a graceful exit line, and their great books also end somewhere close to the middle of nowhere. Among books that do round themselves out through a last chapter, the dominant theme is one of a better economic world and how to get it. This better world is conceived in a variety of ways and on a variety of levels.

Several last chapters handle the improvement theme in reverse, and brighten our lives with dismal prediction. Veblen's final chapters sometimes strongly suggest the results of collaboration by Isaiah, Jeremiah and Cassandra. Reflection on all this leads one to conclude that discussion of our economic future is perhaps the proper way for the well-bred economist to take leave of his gentle readers.

But this book is, in conception, not quite like any other

book I have consulted. It is, of course, partly like an introductory text, but it is also, in a sense, a book on comparative
economic theory. Books of that general kind—they are
usually organized as histories of economic doctrines rather
than like this one—choose another type of exit. Their normal
ending is to suggest unexplored areas of theory that lie ahead,
to indicate which schools and which theoretical issues show
promise and will most likely hold the center of the stage in
the calculable future.

This means, that to be doubly correct, two final questions
must be tackled:

1. The future of the economic world
2. The future of economic theory

The economic world we have been studying in these
pages, whether we looked at it through the lens of standard
or dissident theory, has been mostly a world of drift: a world
of no imposed objectives. No government or moral law or
external or authoritarian compulsion of any kind has set
specific, major, and public objectives for our economy to
meet (except transiently as in time of war). Nothing compels us to produce 3,000 calories per person per day or to
provide full employment, or to construct 1,000 cubic feet
of housing per person, or to neglect grossly (as in the
U.S.S.R.) the consumers' goods industries for heavy industry. We have, to be sure, attained many laudable objectives
as certainly as if they had been publicly and compulsorily
set, but they have nonetheless been achieved mainly through
drift and rarely through plan. This was even more true of
the nineteenth century than of the twentieth.

We seem now to be entering an economy of increasingly
imposed goals. They are being imposed by a variety of

forces. The great successes of capitalism in fostering literacy and science are beginning to impose certain biological goals: we now know, for example, that men must have about 3,000 calories daily to lay the basis for good health. What is still only a biological principle is by way of becoming a moral law and may eventually become statute law. We may reasonably expect that all governments will in the calculable future, intervene in rich countries to assure each citizen his 3,000 calories, or to approach that standard most nearly and equitably if the nation is poor. And the reason is that a norm scientifically arrived at sometimes becomes, through the peculiarities of our culture, an ethical norm. Or, as we put it perhaps more simply, our standard of living increases as our technology develops and that standard soon becomes a minimum.

Unhappily, many of the goals of the immediate and perhaps calculable future will not be set by the benignity of science. For a long time it has been clear that some sort of massive struggle between the Western community of nations and Communist nations impends. Already this impending struggle has set goals for our economy: armaments and economic goods to our allies, a staggering weight of heavy armaments for ourselves. Such goals are being imposed by law. Other goals are in the offing. One such is reasonably full employment. A great depression like that of the 1930's is unthinkable if the Western democracies are to keep strong their defenses against Communism.

In some ways the imposition of major, indeed overriding, goals will make the task of the economist easier. His problem will then be the devising of controls to achieve ends that have been explicitly, publicly and clearly stated: 50,000 planes, 35,000 tanks, 1,000 ships, 50 million cans of emer-

gency rations, half the national product for civilians and
half for the armed forces. It is easier to figure out how
to achieve such aims (granting that resources are available) than to study how mankind, when free of collectively
established goals, gets his living, and to figure out why he
adopts this course rather than that. Economics has been
made difficult by the fact that it has always studied means
to achieve goals that are not clearly defined; part of its job
has been to clarify and even evaluate the goals themselves,
despite the fact that Lionel Robbins, the distinguished British economist, does not want his colleagues to think about
goals, ever; just means.

In other ways the economist's task will be harder. History
seems to point to the conclusion that economic drift (meaning again no imposition of clearly defined, major economic
goals by legal, theological, or similar compulsion) has been
compatible with the extension of human freedom, but that
the imposing of economic goals by authority has hindered
the development of freedom—or, at best, has not stimulated
its development. Economists will be among the guardians
of freedom as we move toward an economy of increasingly
rigid goals. To be sure, this is not the problem of the economist alone, for the problem is not one of mere economic
freedom. It is the freedom of human beings to develop what
is nobly human in them that is at stake. This is the problem
of every man, woman, and child. It is not a mere Irish bull
to say that the great economic problem of the twentieth
century is political: how to extend human freedom, yet
fulfill economic goals set by the public authority and attain
certain norms established by science. The relationship between freedom and economic productivity has always been
a central economic problem. It was what most interested

Adam Smith. Today it concerns such leading authors as F. A. Hayek, who wrote *The Road to Serfdom*, and J. M. Clark, who countered with *Alternative to Serfdom*.

There is evidence that economists are better prepared to meet their problems today than they would have been a few decades ago. They have, first of all, an armory of statistical weapons that were not possessed even only a few years ago. In 1932–1933, at the depth of the depression, we had no reliable figures on the number of unemployed. Useful figures on this are now made available in regular flow. The social-security files, in existence only fifteen years, give us a basis for important studies of all kinds. The scope of the decennial census has become very broad. And these are only a few instances of many that flock to mind.

Economists have also shifted the center of their interest into new fields. Keynes's greatest contribution has probably been to teach his fellows that what may be good or bad under a condition of full employment may have precisely the opposite effect in depression. This is tantamount to a doubling of the weapons in the arsenal of standard theory. Other standard theorists have focused attention on monopoly and various kinds of imperfect markets. Although they have perhaps wrought only "knives of bone," they have completely dissolved an almost neurotic fixation on the perfect market. And that must be put down as a great gain.

Economists have the sense of prestige and community support that comes to those who have received recognition for serving their fellows well. This cannot but give them courage in their tasks—hence help them to throw their entire strength even more wholeheartedly into their difficult labors. In the First World War, in the depression, in the next war, and in the present state of tension, the economist has

been consulted and heeded, and each new emergency has
put greater responsibility in his hands than the last. He is
an important figure in the civil service and in the secretariats
of the international organizations. An economist has become
an influential figure in the Senate, partly because he is a
very good economist, and the possibility of his being elected
to an even higher office is being seriously discussed. The
day does not seem remote when the American people will
want more than just one or two distinguished economists
in their legislatures.

We might put down greater unity among economists as
a strengthening of their science—if we could be sure that
unity was indeed greater today than in the past. The question as to whether cleavages between schools of economic
thought have remained as great as ever or closed up is a hard
one to answer. I would be disposed to say they had not nar-
rowed, but this is a very personal view; and, in any case, I
should want to add hastily that on many day-to-day problems, from a sound rationing program for meat to the ad-
visability of stiffer taxes as inflation stoppers, economists of
all breeds are better able to work together than they would
have been some twenty years ago. And this, too, is a great
gain. The reason is that few economists hold on to the ikon
of an automatically regulating economy under the govern-
ance of a lively competitive process and under an inner
compulsion to seek equilibrium only at the level of full
employment.

The breaking of this ikon is indeed a milestone for standard theory and gives it new points of contact with dissident
theory. But this lost ikon must ultimately be replaced by a
new one. Standard theory appears to have no ikon today.
It has, indeed, what it names "models" such as the "perfectly

competitive model" and the "imperfectly competitive model." But the sum of a series of models does not make an organic whole.

If I am right in believing that standard theory has no ikon and should be searching for one, the next question is where to look. Certainly the Marxian ikon is not prescribed. The Veblenian ikon has something to recommend it, but is far from perfect; and Mitchell's ikon is a shadow of Veblen's. Perhaps what all economists need to do—along with their routine tasks—is to combine in search of a useful ikon of social and economic life.

If this task seems to be a worthy one, there is one pitfall to avoid, and one promising source to exploit. The pitfall has already claimed many. A thoughtful person can, I hope not too wrongly, read the history of economic doctrines in such a way as to conclude that policy or commitment came first and theory too often second. Men like Smith, Ricardo, and Keynes seemed to have a sort of sixth sense for some of the important economic changes that were going on about them. On the whole, they approved these changes; and their theory was a rationalization or a bringing into consciousness of these changes. The changes became the policy of what ought to be; and the resulting "ought" determined economic theory. This was even true of Marx—with a special twist of his own, naturally—and this may help to explain why Marx admired the great classical economists, within limits, and used their methods.

What this means is that the economic world has not been surveyed as a whole, that theory is the rationalizing of what is going to happen or ought to happen at some time and place (usually England) and that very little "pure" economic thought goes on in the minds of men. By "pure" I

mean uncommitted to the economic drift, or to an Utopia
(Marx), or to a widely acceptable policy. Something like
what Veblen meant when he spoke of "idle curiosity."
There is, to be sure, considerable idle curiosity expended on
the smaller issues within an established framework of theory.
This finds embodiment in a host of special and detailed books
and articles on everything from the rate of interest in 1066
to the economics of antimony and molybdenum. My statement refers primarily to the great lines of theory laid down
by the great economists. Out of this kind of committed
theory, it is unlikely that an ikon of our economic world
will be derived.

That was the pitfall. The promising source to exploit is
the nature of man. Man determines his institutions—which
then turn around and determine him. But there cannot be a
real gap between the two. The picture we have in our minds
of human society, or of any of its vast subdivisions, such as
government or the economic system, reflects in part the
picture we have in our minds of individual human beings.
Neither can be good if the other is defective. And study of
the one teaches us about the other; indeed, neither can be
known if the other is ignored. Economics is one of the sciences of man, and man will probably have to be made the
central figure in an ikon of economic organization—man,
who moved Pascal to exclaim:

What a chimera, then, is man! What a novelty, what a monster,
what a chaos, what a subject of contradiction, what a prodigy!
A judge of all things, feeble worm of the earth, depositary of
the truth, cloaca of uncertainty and error, the glory and the
shame of the universe.

This is the kind of creature we rely on to get us our daily
bread, and on two thirds of the earth's land surface he is

unable to get enough bread. Elsewhere this featherless biped of Aristotle's has to combine inflation, depression and sometimes warfare or worse with his search for worldly goods. Perhaps we need to find out more about *him*, if economics is to progress.

BIBLIOGRAPHY

THE READER who wants to go forward in the study of economics may move along many different paths, but two seem to stand out. One path leads to a deeper knowledge of theory; the other, to the study of currently important problems. Group A, below, is a theory list; Group B is a list of books that discuss certain important contemporary problems. Group C is a miscellany of good books in general.

GROUP A

BOOKS ON ECONOMIC THEORY

Probably the best way to tighten one's grasp on economic theory is to read a history of economic doctrines, or a somewhat similar book on comparative economics. Among books of this class that combine readability with excellence are:

Dillard, Dudley. The Economics of John Maynard Keynes. New York, Prentice-Hall, 1948. This is an almost perfect book on Keynes for the student who already knows something about economics.

Gide, Charles, and Charles Rist. A History of Economic Doctrines. Boston, Heath, 1948. This book, first published in France in 1909 and brought up to date as recently as 1947, is well known among economists and has been widely used by students in at least three countries: France, England, and the United States. The French have the reputation of not inventing any new economic theories but of doing a superior job of explaining, evaluating, and clarifying the theories of others. This book is a fine example of that gift. It is, of course, a translation.

Gruchy, Allan G. Modern Economic Thought; the American
    Contribution. New York, Prentice-Hall, 1947. A book about
    six more or less contemporary American economists, all be-
    longing to the non-Marxian but dissenting category. Here the
    reader will find material on Veblen and Mitchell.
Homan, Paul T. Contemporary Economic Thought. New
    York, Harper, 1928. This book ably discusses the five Anglo-
    American economists who seemed tops at the time of writing.
    The selection is a very good one.
Mitchell, Wesley C. Lecture Notes on Types of Economic
    Theory. New York, A. M. Kelley, Inc., 1949. These are the
    lectures, taken down stenographically by a student and mim-
    eographed, of Mitchell's famous theory course at Columbia,
    given over a long period of years. Mitchell apparently was
    never quite satisfied to have them published, and it was only
    after his death that these "lecture notes" were placed publicly
    on sale. They are still in the tentative, mimeographed form.
    Mitchell's thesis is that economic theory arose out of the
    great problems of the time—a thesis which I find better
    worked out for the period 1750–1850 than for the last hun-
    dred years. Despite all this it is a great work.
Soule, George. Introduction to Economic Science. New York,
    Viking, 1948. An interesting little volume which, taking
    boom-and-bust as a central theme, discusses that and a variety
    of related topics. Written for the general reader.

Standard American college textbooks are, of course, excellent
books to use and to have on hand for reference. There are a
great many of these. I have before me a list of seventy. Even
this is incomplete. To choose among these would be invidious.
Many in the list I have never seen. Among writers whose books
I have found particularly helpful are K. E. Boulding, M. J.
Bowman and G. L. Bach, John Ise, A. L. Meyers, Broadus
Mitchell and others, H. R. Mussey and E. Donnan, Paul Samuel-
son.

GROUP B

An excellent single-volume description of the American
economy as a whole is H. Taylor and H. Barger, *The American
Economy in Operation* (New York, Harcourt Brace, 1949). For

the general reader it has the usual disadvantages of a textbook; but its merits are considerable. The remaining books in this group are broken down under some of the great special problems of the day.

1. BOOKS ON HOW BIG SHOULD BIG BUSINESS BE?

Berle, A. A., and G. C. Means. The Modern Corporation and Private Property. New York, Macmillan, 1933. A great book on ownership vs. control in the large firm and on other important topics.

Edwards, Corwin D. Maintaining Competition; Requisites of a Governmental Policy. New York, McGraw-Hill, 1949. An anti-trust policy for the United States, by a man who knows the subject.

Brady, Robert A. Business as a System of Power. New York, Columbia University Press, 1943. Fascism and big business.

Hamilton, Walton H. The Pattern of Competition. New York, Columbia University Press, 1940. Although now a little dated, partly because it does not describe the relatively vigorous anti-trust activity of the government during the 1940's, the brevity and charm of style of this book recommend it to the reader.

Temporary National Economic Committee. Hearings and Monographs. Hearings conducted over a period of 15 months or so, principally during 1939. A many-volumed investigation of how our economic system works. Available in libraries and for sale by the Superintendent of Documents, Washington, D.C.

Twentieth Century Fund. Several volumes have been published by the fund on the problem of cartels and monopoly. The final volume, written by George W. Stocking and Myron W. Watkins, is Monopoly; a Problem for Democracy (New York, 1951).

2. BOOKS ON UNEMPLOYMENT AND DEPRESSION

The famous books by Mitchell and Keynes, mentioned in the text, pp. 182, 203, are hard sledding. Dillard's book on Keynes (in Group A of this bibliography) treats its subject satisfactorily.

Mitchell is well handled in the books by Gruchy and by Homan, also in Group A.

Achinstein, Asher. Introduction to Business Cycles. New York, Crowell, 1950. A general survey by a follower of the Mitchell approach.

Hansen, Alvin H. Business Cycles and National Income. New York, Norton, 1951. A survey by a distinguished American economist whose theories resemble those of Keynes.

Soule, George. Introduction to Economic Science. This was also listed in Group A.

Wright, David McCord. The Economics of Disturbance, New York, Macmillan, 1951. An interesting book by a lively and original author.

3. WORLD TRADE

Buchanan, N. S. and Lutz, F. A. Rebuilding the World Economy. New York, Twentieth Century Fund, 1947. A book that combines history, theory, and a statement of policy in a lucid and scholarly presentation.

Condliffe, J. B. The Commerce of Nations. New York, Norton, 1950. A recent book that has won high praise. The author has had a wide experience in international affairs.

Soule, George. America's Stake in Britain's Future. New York, Viking, 1945. Easy to read and competent.

Ward, Barbara. The West at Bay. New York, Norton, 1948. For the general reader. Very well done.

4. DISTRIBUTION OF INCOME

Clark, Colin. The Conditions of Economic Progress. New York, Macmillan, 1940. A statistical study of the world's poverty.

National Bureau of Economic Research, Inc. Various current studies on income. Though incomes of all kinds vary from year to year, the fundamental relationships are less volatile, and are nowhere better analyzed than in the National Bureau's very first publication, 1921, *Income in the United States—Its Amount and Distribution*. This is a brief publication, 152 pages, the summary of a longer study. It was published 30 years ago by Harcourt, Brace and Company, and is probably available in libraries rather than through ordinary bookstores.

U.S. Government. Current figures on income may be found in *The Survey of Current Business*, a Department of Commerce monthly. The U.S. Bureau of Labor Statistics published an interesting study in 1945, *Family Spending and Saving in Wartime*, Bulletin 822.

GROUP C

This group contains books that do not seem to fit into our major classifications but which may be of considerable interest to the general reader.

Chandler, Lester V. The Economics of Money and Banking, New York, Harper, 1948. Perhaps one of the best in this field.

Chase, Stuart. A popular writer, author of several excellent books on economic problems.

Clark, J. M. Alternative to Serfdom. New York, Knopf, 1948. A search for controls without totalitarianism, written on a lofty plane by a distinguished American economist.

—— Guideposts in Time of Change. New York, Harper, 1949. Essentials for a sound American economy.

Groves, Harold M. Financing Government. Third edition. New York, Holt, 1950. A standard work on taxation, debt management and allied topics.

McDonald, John. Strategy in Poker, Business and War. New York, Norton, 1950. Not exactly a treatise on economics, but Part 3 of the book tells more about the Von Neumann-Morgenstern theory mentioned in the text (p. 119) as promising.

Marx, Karl. Readers wishing to learn more about Karl Marx should begin with the *Communist Manifesto*, a very short publication, available in many forms. His monumental, multivolumed, *Capital*, is read only by the most serious scholars, for it makes great demands on the reader. G. B. Shaw's *The Intelligent Woman's Guide to Socialism and Capitalism* (New York, Brentano, 1928), a Marxian approach, is much more amusing than Marx, but cannot be recommended as a consistently faithful popularization of Marxian ideas—or of any other school of economic thought. The test of responsible popularization is much better met by John Strachey's *The Nature of Capitalist Crisis*, New York, Covici-Friede, 1935.

Mitchell, Wesley C. Backward Art of Spending Money. New York, McGraw-Hill, 1937. A series of random essays, some delightful, all thoughtful.

Robbins, Lionel. An Essay on the Nature and Significance of Economic Science. Second edition. London, Macmillan, 1935. A well-known work, which holds that economists should confine themselves to a study of means, not ends. A little unconvincing to those who believe that means sometimes become ends, and that ends are often in conflict and hard to discover. See p. 320, above.

Tawney, R. H. The Acquisitive Society, New York, Harcourt Brace, 1920. Tawney is a guild socialist who here analyzes modern society from that standpoint.

Veblen, Thorstein. Veblen is well treated in Allan Gruchy's book, mentioned above. A portable Veblen is published by the Viking Press. Veblenian beginners usually cut their teeth on his *Theory of the Leisure Class* (various reprints). His *The Theory of Business Enterprise* (New York, Scribner, 1904), is his nearest approach to a "principles of economics." A few recent books have noted an interesting and possibly fruitful relation between the theories of Veblen and Freud. Among them are Louis Schneider's *The Freudian Psychology and Veblen's Social Theory* (New York, King's Crown Press, 1948), and my *Beyond Supply and Demand* (New York, Columbia University Press, 1946).

INDEX